Creole Cultures, Vol. 1

Violet Cuffy • Jane Carr
Editors

Creole Cultures, Vol. 1

Safeguarding Creole Intangible Cultural Heritage

palgrave
macmillan

Editors
Violet Cuffy
Intl. Business, Marketing and Tourism
University of Bedfordshire
Luton, UK

Jane Carr
Research Institute for Media
Arts and Performance
University of Bedfordshire
Luton, UK

ISBN 978-3-031-24274-8 ISBN 978-3-031-24275-5 (eBook)
https://doi.org/10.1007/978-3-031-24275-5

Cover illustration: Maram_shutterstock.com

This Palgrave Macmillan imprint is published by the registered company Springer Nature Switzerland AG.
The registered company address is: Gewerbestrasse 11, 6330 Cham, Switzerland

Paper in this product is recyclable.

In memory of Violet Cuffy and with thanks to all her family, friends, colleagues, authors, and industry collaborators who supported us along this journey to see our Creole research project to the end.

Preface

This volume considers the significance of Creole cultures within the current, changing global contexts. It explores the particular importance of Creole cultures in post-colonial Small Island Developing States. It also examines issues that arise in relation to safeguarding the cultural practices that sustain Creole identities.

The concepts of 'creolization' and 'creole societies' are pillars of cultural changes in the Caribbean and the Asian Pacific which emerged during the colonial period (Brathwaite, 1974; Nettleford, 1988; Patterson, cited in Williams, 1995). Further, Afro-Creole culture, which has its roots in African, East Indian, Indigenous American, and European heritage elements, has now become a pivotal part of the process of nation-building (Cuffy, 2018; Rabess, 2018), with many Creole-speaking countries advancing this aspect of their culture to the level of national significance in contemporary societies.

National identities are made increasingly complex in the post-colonial period and with the increasing diversity of populations. Further it is suggested that within post-colonial contexts, perceived ethnic identities are necessarily 'positional, conditional and conjunctural' (Hall, 1996). Moreover, for small island economies with developing tourist (or other service) industries, external perceptions of indigenous populations have economic repercussions that may affect internal social and political dynamics (Hudepohl, 2007). In the specific context of this volume, the perspectives of the indigenous populations are central to developing understanding of the complexities of Creole identities. Such complexities are further emphasised by the viewpoints of those contemplating their identities as situated within other Small Island Developing States as explored in this volume on matters of safeguarding the rich Creole cultural heritage.

The contributors include academics, researchers, policymakers, and practitioners from Small Island Developing States including Dominica, St Lucia, Seychelles, and Mauritius and from their diasporic communities. In part the volume is developed from papers presented at conferences in the UK (Creole Fest: Building Bridges Across Borders, University of Bedfordshire, November 9–10, 2018) and Dominica (Creole as Cultural Heritage: Framing, Strengthening and Advocating, University of the West Indies at Dominica, August 15–16, 2019). These conferences were central to the AHRC-funded project 'Dominica as a Centre of Excellence for the Preservation & Celebration of the Creole Culture Through Language, the Arts and Its Indigenous Kalinago', creating a research network with this focus. In addition, the first event, also part of the National Social Science Festival in the UK, employed a multidisciplinary approach to Creole language, arts and tourism and issues arising from aligning their preservation with the UNESCO (2003) adoption of the Convention for the Safeguarding of Intangible Cultural Heritage. The second brought together academics, researchers, policymakers, practitioners, indigenous leaders and students exploring Creole and indigenous issues to collaborate in the building of resiliency in Creole-speaking countries and indigenous communities.

In the series Creole Cultures in Changing Global Contexts, Volume 1: Safeguarding Creole Intangible Cultural Heritage, clusters mainly on issues and challenges on policy and planning, arts & performance, and future directions.

Luton, UK Violet Cuffy
Luton, UK Jane Carr

References

Brathwaite, E. (1974). *Contradictory Omens Cultural Diversity and Integration in the Caribbean*. MONA.

Cuffy, V. (2018). Carnival Tourism. In S. Agarwal, G. Busby, & K. R. Huang (Eds.), *Special Interest Tourism: Concepts, Contexts and Cases* (pp. 97–111). CABI. https://www.cabidigitallibrary.org/doi/book/10.1079/9781780645667.0000

Hall, S. (1996). New Ethnicities. In D. Morley & K. Chen (Eds.), *Stuart Hall Critical Dialogues in Cultural Studies* (pp. 442–451, 448). Routledge.

Hudepohl, K. (2007). Consuming Culture: Extralocal Exchanges and Kalinago Identity on Dominica. *Tipití: Journal of the Society for the Anthropology of Lowland South America, 5*(2), 224–230.

Nettleford, R. M. (1988). *The Caribbean: Crisis and Challenges* (Concerning Women & Development). Publication Unknown.

Rabess, G. (2018). Promoting vs Preserving: Dilemmas of Indigenous Cultures: The Kalinago Story. Dominica, Creole Fest: Building Bridges Across Borders, University of Bedfordshire, November 9–10.

UNESCO. (2003). Text of the Convention for the Safeguarding of the Intangible Cultural Heritage. Internet Page. https://ich.unesco.org/en/convention

Williams, R. (1995). Orlando Patterson. Interview. *Sociological Forum, 10*(4), 653–671.

Acknowledgement

We wish to make special mention of the Arts and Humanities Research Council, University of Bedfordshire, and our authors.

The least we can do is to say thank you to those who have
Listened without judgment; spoken without prejudice;
Helped without entitlement; understood without pretension;
And continue to serve in the name of safeguarding the Creole cultural heritage.
Adapted: Unknown

Contents

1 **Intangible Cultural Heritage: Safeguarding Embodied Creole Cultures** 1
Violet Cuffy and Jane Carr

2 **Towards Safeguarding Creole Intangible Cultural Heritage: The 2003 UNESCO Convention** 19
Alexis Weedon

3 **The Rejuvenation of Arts and Culture Through Folklore** 41
Penda Thérésia Choppy

4 **Valorisation of the Intangible Creole Heritage in Mauritius: A Case Study** 61
Didier Michel and Daniella Police-Michel

5 **The Spirit of Koudmen: The Genesis of Identity, Community and Cooperation in Saint Lucian Society** 83
Rhyesa Joseph

6 **Embodying Creole Heritage: The Dominican Bélé** 103
Jane Carr, Delia Cuffy-Weeks, Aristedes Narh Hargoe, Terry Ofosu, and Nii Tete Yartey

7 **Entangled Threads: Creolization of Plants and Landscape** 123
Carol Sorhaindo and Violet Cuffy

8 **Tourism Development in Creole Spaces: A Saint Lucia Island Perspective** 145
Chrisentia Combie and Violet Cuffy

9 **Advancing a Creole Centre of Excellence Framework** 169
Violet Cuffy

10 **Conclusions: Looking Ahead to the *After Acts*** 193
Violet Cuffy and Jane Carr

Index 199

Notes on Contributors

Jane Carr, Phd is Head of Academic Studies at Bird College and a Research Fellow at the University of Bedfordshire. She trained and worked as a dancer before being awarded her PhD from the University of Surrey. Previously working at Morley College, London, she developed accessible learning opportunities in dance and theatre for adults and young people. Her work is focused on an interdisciplinary approach to exploring embodiment in relation to dance, identity, and culture in changing post-colonial contexts. Further to her performance work, Jane has contributed to a range of dance books and leading journals.

Penda Thérésia Choppy is the director of the Creole Language and Culture Research Institute at the University of Seychelles. She was the director of the Creole Institute of Seychelles from 1999 to 2014, when she became its CEO. She moved to the University of Seychelles in 2016. Penda studied English at Leeds University and has completed a research degree at Master's level from the University of Birmingham, UK, in 2018. She is currently working towards a doctoral research degree with the Islands and Small States Institute, University of Malta. Her main research interests are the oral and written Creole traditions of the Western Indian Ocean in the post-colonial context.

Chrisentia Combie is the acting Principal of the Soufriere Comprehensive. A graduate from the University of the West Indies Open Campus with a Bachelor's Degree in Language Education—Literatures in English (Hons)—in 2014 and Master of Arts in English Language (with distinction) in 2020, Chrisentia is now a doctoral student at the same university.

The study of language and literature are embedded in culture. Therefore, examining the culture of a people has always been of paramount interest. She is an active participant in community life, particularly community sports, cultural activities, Credit Union and Trade Union Movements.

Violet Cuffy, Phd was a Dominican and strong advocate of safeguarding the Creole cultural heritage. Before her untimely death while working on this volume, Violet was developing a body of work on safeguarding indigenous populations and cultures, with particular focus on the Kalinago and Creole heritage of the Commonwealth of Dominica. Her works are published in a range of books and leading journals.

Delia Cuffy-Weeks is a cultural enthusiast from the cultural village of Grand Bay in the Commonwealth of Dominica. She is a practitioner in traditional dance, Creole head-tying and Creole wear, folk tales, storytelling, and the Kwéyòl language. She is an active member of Konmité pou Étide Kwéyòl KÈK (Committee for Creole Studies) and teaches a Conversational Kwéyòl course at the University of the West Indies Open Campus, Dominica. Delia is an agriculturist with a Bachelor's Degree in Social Work from University of the West Indies Open Campus and volunteers with several NGOs.

Aristedes Narh Hargoe, Phd is currently a lecturer at the Department of Dance Studies, School of Performing Arts, University of Ghana, Legon. He is a University of Michigan African Presidential Scholar (UMAPS-Fall 2022) and doubles as the Artistic Director of the Ghana Dance Ensemble of the Institute of African Studies, University of Ghana, Legon. He holds a PhD in Ethnomusicology from the University of Cape Coast, a Master of Fine Arts (MFA) and a Bachelor of Fine Arts (BFA) degrees from the University of Ghana. His research interest lies within the domain of dance aesthetics, performance studies, and semiotics. He is also interested in Dance Therapy and Dance Ethnography.

Rhyesa Joseph is the Executive Director of Monsignor Anthony Folk Research Centre. She is a former educator in Communication Studies and Caribbean Studies. Joseph holds a Bachelor of Science Degree in Political Science with International Relations, a Master of Philosophy in Political Science from the University of the West Indies (UWI), and an MPhil based on the political ideology of Saint Lucian Koudmen. Since 2019, she has been a Saint Lucia National Reparations Committee member. Joseph founded a political science consultancy, 'From Classroom to Community'.

Didier Michel, Phd is a Doctor in Law with specialisation in slavery and historical wrongs. He is a senior lecturer at the University of Mauritius, Mauritius. His research is based on the issue of slavery in the Mauritian context. He lectures criminal law, criminal procedure, and the law of evidence at the Faculty of Law and Management, University of Mauritius.

Terry Ofosu, Phd is an assistant lecturer in the Department of Dance Studies at the University of Ghana. Terry has a Diploma in Theatre Arts (Dance, 1993) and a Master of Fine Arts (M.F.A. 2009). He currently holds a PhD in African Studies from the Institute of African Studies in the same University.

Daniella Police-Michel, Phd is the Vice-President of the Green Reparations Foundation and member of the editorial committee of its monthly journal, Lekolozis. She holds a Doctorate in African Studies option Languages and has worked on multilingualism and Creole culture and language in the Mauritian context. Until 2019, she was a senior lecturer at the University of Mauritius where, before her retirement, Daniella previously lectured in general linguistics, discourse analysis, text linguistics, Creole, and French languages.

Carol Sorhaindo is a freelance visual artist/designer/tutor, with an MA in Creative Practice. She has recently relocated to Dominica after living in the UK for many years. Her art practice and research explore the entangled culture, history, and heritage with a focus on plants and landscape. She has a keen interest in mental wellbeing and uses art as a therapeutic medium to explore and encourage discourse on culture, identity, and roots. Carol's multidisciplinary practice includes botanical art, natural plant dyes and textiles, painting, sculpture, installation, and carnival costume design.

Alexis Weedon, Phd is Professor Emerita at the University of Bedfordshire. She has researched and published 12 books in the fields of the history of publishing, the cultural impact of new communication technologies, and storytelling across media.

Nii Tete Yartey is a former director of the Ghana Dance Ensemble (National Theatre), and current director of the Noyam African Dance Institute. Nii-Tete envisions his works as a re-contextualisation of traditions, focusing on dance-theatre and contemporary Africa dance. Nii-Tete has choreographed, lectured, and directed at both national and international levels.

Abbreviations

AHRC	Arts Humanities Research Council
CAMDU	Curriculum and Materials Development Unit
CCEF	Creole Centres of Excellence Framework
CCTS	Creole Cultural Tourism Space
CDF	Cultural Development Foundation
CIRCE	Canada-India Research Centre of Excellence
CLCRI	Culture Research Institute
CoE	Centres of Excellence
CTDP	Creole Tourism Development Product
CTO	Caribbean Tourism Organization
DMOs	Destination Management Organisations
ESRC	Economic and Social Research Council
FRC	Folk Research Centre
GDP	Gross Domestic Product
ICH	Intangible Cultural Heritage
JTB	Jamaican Tourism Board
MOT	Ministry of Tourism
MSM	Mouvement Socialiste Mauricien
NCE	Networks of Centres of Excellence
NCE-KM	NCE-Knowledge Mobilization
NRCD	National Resource Centre for Dance
SIDS	Small Island Developing States
TICERN	The Creole Research Network
TJC	Truth and Justice Commission
TQM	Total Quality Management
UNESCO	United Nations Educational, Scientific and Cultural Organization

UNFCCC	United Nations Framework Convention on Climate Change
UNWTO	United Nations World Tourism Organization
VF	Verts Fraternels
WHEC	World Higher Education Conference
WTTC	World Travel and Tourism Council

List of Figures

Fig. 1.1	Front of 'Wob Dwiyet', national dress of the Commonwealth of Dominica	13
Fig. 1.2	Back of 'Wob Dwiyet', national dress of the Commonwealth of Dominica	14
Fig. 1.3	The Honourable Prime Minister Roosevelt Skerrit of the Commonwealth of Dominica and Honourable Melissa Poponne-Skerrit, parliamentary representation of Roseau November 3, 2021, official national day parade celebrations	15
Fig. 3.1	Soungoula's capture by Brer' Tortoise and his judgement at the King's palace, followed by his escape (Source: Colbert Nourrice)	54
Fig. 3.2	Soungoula's temptation of the guardian at the King's pool (Source: Colbert Nourrice)	55
Fig. 6.1	Bélé dancers, Dominica. (Photo courtesy of Delia Cuffy-Weeks and Lennox Honychurch)	110
Fig. 7.1	Madras and white cotton	133
Fig. 7.2	Sugar cane artwork	138
Fig. 8.1	Map of St. Lucia (Google, n.d.)	153
Fig. 8.2	Map of Soufriere	156
Fig. 8.3	The four Cs framework for Creole Cultural Tourism Space (CCTS) development	162
Fig. 9.1	The three interactive processes of excellence. (Adapted from Fekadu et al. 2021)	173
Fig. 9.2	The four interactive processes of Creole Cultural Centres of Excellence	188

List of Tables

Table 1.1	Ethical principles of intangible cultural heritage	6
Table 1.2	List of digital Creole archives	7
Table 8.1	Cultural tourism development in Creole spaces	159
Table 9.1	Definitions of Centre of Excellence (CoE)	171
Table 9.2	Creole-speaking countries	178

CHAPTER 1

Intangible Cultural Heritage: Safeguarding Embodied Creole Cultures

Violet Cuffy and Jane Carr

1 Introduction

The UNESCO 2003 Convention for the Safeguarding of the Intangible Cultural Heritage (ICH) situates culture within a sustainable paradigm. Adopted in 2006, the Convention signals international recognition of the importance of the non-material heritage assets of a people for their continuance and advancement. It has been argued that UNESCO's previous initiatives, notably, the Convention Concerning the Protection of the World Cultural and Natural Heritage (1972), remained heavily Eurocentric (Labadi, 2005). While the 2003 convention emphasised the importance of cultural diversity, subscription to the principles of safeguarding of heritage as then outlined within the documentation nevertheless raises

V. Cuffy (Deceased)
University of Bedfordshire, Luton, UK

J. Carr (✉)
University of Bedfordshire, Luton, UK

Bird College, Sidcup, UK

V. Cuffy, J. Carr (eds.), *Creole Cultures, Vol. 1*,
https://doi.org/10.1007/978-3-031-24275-5_1

questions regarding the determination of 'value' in terms of what is recognised and representative of culture. Regardless, this framework offers a base from which the intangible culture of a society can be celebrated, upheld throughout generations and serve as a sense of pride and dignity of a shared heritage.

The universally recognised practice of archiving is renowned for creating records of the past that are regarded as being of intrinsic and international value. It enables a permanent record of knowledge for future use by scholars, researchers, academics and practitioners. The question which arises is, what benefit are archives to the knowledge bearers in a lived cultural context? Who has access to archives? How are they utilised? Moreover, what potential do they serve in influencing day-to-day evolving cultural practices on the ground?

The concept of safeguarding, as an alternative to the concept of preserving so closely associated with archival practices, accords with many researchers who argue that culture is alive and ever evolving. However, such concerns should be balanced by awareness of how several cultural activists advocate for adherence, sustenance and promotion to certain dimensions of expression of a social grouping for the values they embody in establishing social identity and communal safety nets within and across similar geographic boundaries and cultural heritage spaces.

Debatably, a focus on the embodied practices that sustain culture could be more significant for its safeguarding than the focus on identifying examples of ICH that raise problems of definition. Such a focus would ensure that a space is created for embracing and actively engaging in traditional practices, learning from elders and cultural icons and living out that which is ideally representative of ICH. Debates regarding the extent to which the practices that comprise ICH may change would then be understood to be founded in concerns regarding the vulnerability of cultural identities.

By way of an example, in this chapter, we turn our focus to the Creole cultural space rooted in a mixed history of Africanism, the slave trade and European colonisation. We seek to explore the currency of the UNESCO convention from the vantage point of the Creole space, predominantly in Small Island Developing States (SIDS) and less developed countries which are often challenged by several global crises and which may have few resources for investing in cultural heritage documentation and other criteria essential to meet the demands of inscription on UNESCO listings.

2 The UNESCO Convention

Implementation of the Convention for the Safeguarding of the Intangible Cultural Heritage (2003) provides recognition of the role of the non-artefactual aspects of heritage in providing people 'with a sense of identity and continuity' and in 'promoting respect for cultural diversity and human creativity' (UNESCO, 2003). In so doing, the Convention serves to emphasise that it is not just places and things that are important to a culture. The ways people speak, sing, dance, eat and perform traditional ceremonies, along with other significant aspects of their daily lives, are also important aspects of cultural heritage that may warrant protection. Since its adoption in 2006, UNESCO's concern to safeguard ICH has gathered momentum globally. In order that its potential is fully realised it is important to consider the relationships between embodied practices through which such heritage is manifested and the physical world in which they take place.

In this context, UNESCO's (2003) emphasis on 'safeguarding' rather than solely 'preserving' is valuable. Arguably, where preservation is conceptualised within the discourses of archival practices it becomes rooted in a Eurocentric epistemology. As Jacques Derrida (1995) argued, the process of consigning items to an archive is not simply a process of storing them. In reminding us that the term 'archives' is derived from the Greek 'archons'—the senior figures who not only stored but had the power to interpret documents—Derrida emphasises the role of archives in the formation of historical knowledge as a 'gathering together' of signs with the aim 'to coordinate a single corpus, in a system or a synchrony in which all the elements articulate the unity of an ideal configuration' (Derrida, 1995, p. 10). Building on this perspective Rebecca Schneider argues that '"archive culture" is appropriate to those who align historical knowledge with European traditions' (Schneider, 2012, p. 138). With regard to archival practices, a western orientated episteme possibly limits the capacity of institutions to recognise cultural values from the prism of those people and society, whose cultural practices are their focus. When considering Creole and Indigenous cultures within post-colonial contexts, the setting of our research, it is important to be mindful of the relationship between global power, culture and knowledge that affect what culture is protected, and what processes are deemed suitable to ensure its continuation.

In contrast, the notion of safeguarding may promote initiatives that open up new approaches to supporting the continuation of cultural practices. However, conceptualising cultural practices as 'intangible' could open up the risk that they are understood in ways that tend towards abstraction. Such an approach may not always best support embodied, in-the-world realisation in specific cultural locations.

In this chapter we outline some issues regarding questions of value, identity and embodiment in order to emphasise how safeguarding of ICH requires consideration of the relationships between cultural values, practices, places and material objects in relation to Creole cultural heritage.

3 A Question of Value: Safeguarding as Undoing Eurocentric Cultural Values

The history of the 2003 Convention traces back to the 1982 World Conference on Cultural Policies in Mexico City or 'Mondiacult'. It was at this conference that the term 'intangible heritage' became part of an official lexicon alongside, or sometimes supplanting, 'traditional culture and folklore' (UNESCO n.d.-a). This same conference also 'rejected any hierarchy between cultures' (UNESCO n.d.-a)—an important statement that has implications for the fraught questions of what counts as heritage worthy of protection, how to identify it and how to protect it. To continue this shift in focus, in 1997 UNESCO proposed a programme of the Proclamation of Masterpieces of the Oral and Intangible Heritage of Humanity. The criteria for selection included that they:

- Demonstrate their outstanding value as masterpiece of human creative genius.
- Provide proof of excellence in the application of skill and technical qualities displayed.
  UNESCO (n.d.-a)

Apart from its gender bias, in the context of UNESCO's aim not to privilege some cultures over others, the use of the term 'masterworks' is perhaps also inappropriate in that it is often associated with western aesthetic ideals. While an international selection panel aimed to guard against any cultural bias, there remains a question of whether excellence in the application of skills and creativity are ***universal*** indicators of value, begging the further query of: How and why are cultural practices valued by the people that practice them?

Importantly, by the time of the Convention of 2003, UNESCO recognised that the concept of 'outstanding universal value' that had previously informed the approach to the protection of world cultural and natural heritage (UNESCO, n.d.-b) does not apply to the safeguarding of intangible cultural heritage. Rather they state, 'International recognition is based on the importance of this living heritage for the sense of identity and continuity of the communities in which it is created, transmitted and re-created' (UNESCO, 2003).

In principle, the Convention for the Safeguarding of the Intangible Cultural Heritage aims to 'ensure the visibility of the intangible cultural heritage and awareness of its significance, and to encourage dialogue which respects cultural diversity' (UNESCO, 2003). But given the underlying ethnocentricity of their previous 'proclamation' (UNESCO. n.d.-a) there is a need to ensure the 12 ethical principles further developed in 2015 are adhered to (see Table 1.1 which follows).

As an example of how Creole heritage is vulnerable, it is perhaps ironic that it was during the period when UNESCO had started emphasising the importance of ICH, that changes in arts funding had a negative impact on support for African diasporic derived dance practices in the UK (Carr & Baddoo, 2020). With limited resources, Arts Council England often faces and navigates a wide range of competing priorities. Nevertheless, this instance serves to highlight how the values that inform funding decisions have implications for the protection of cultural heritage. This is significant for marginalised communities such as British people seeking a sense of identification that recognises the influence of diasporic 'Creole' heritage. In this instance, as a response, the dance producer Deborah Baddoo sought to develop the Black Dance Archives project, led by State of Emergency Productions (n.d.), a national arts organisation, in collaboration with archives partners including the National Resource Centre for Dance (NRCD), held at the University of Surrey. Her experiences of developing archival resources reveal that what people fear is not so much the loss of 'masterworks', but lack of continuity from one generation to the next, particularly when key figures within a particular community are ageing and do not necessarily have the resources to pass on or record their practice.

Table 1.1 Ethical principles of intangible cultural heritage

(1)	Communities, groups and, where applicable, individuals should have the **primary role** in safeguarding their own intangible cultural heritage.
(2)	The **right of communities, groups and, where applicable, individuals** to continue the practices, representations, expressions, knowledge and skills necessary to ensure the viability of the intangible cultural heritage should be recognised and respected.
(3)	**Mutual respect** as well as a respect for and mutual appreciation of intangible cultural heritage, should prevail in interactions between States and between communities, groups and, where applicable, individuals.
(4)	All interactions with the communities, groups and, where applicable, individuals who create, safeguard, maintain and transmit intangible cultural heritage should be characterised by **transparent** collaboration, dialogue, negotiation and consultation, and contingent upon their **free, prior, sustained and informed consent**.
(5)	**Access** of communities, groups and individuals to the instruments, objects, artefacts, cultural and natural spaces and places of memory whose existence is necessary for expressing the intangible cultural heritage should be ensured, including in situations of armed conflict. Customary practices governing access to intangible cultural heritage should be fully respected, even where these may limit broader public access.
(6)	Each community, group or individual should assess the value of its own intangible cultural heritage and this intangible cultural heritage should **not be subject to external judgements of value or worth**.
(7)	The communities, groups and individuals who create intangible cultural heritage should **benefit from the protection** of the moral and material interests resulting from such heritage, and particularly from its use, research, documentation, promotion or adaptation by members of the communities or others.
(8)	The **dynamic and living nature of intangible cultural heritage** should be continuously respected. Authenticity and exclusivity should not constitute concerns and obstacles in the safeguarding of intangible cultural heritage.
(9)	Communities, groups, local, national and transnational organisations and individuals should carefully assess the direct and indirect, short-term and long-term, potential and definitive **impact** of any action that may affect the viability of intangible cultural heritage or the communities who practise it.
(10)	Communities, groups and, where applicable, individuals should play a significant role in determining what constitutes **threats to their intangible cultural heritage** including the decontextualisation, commodification and misrepresentation of it and in deciding how to prevent and mitigate such threats.
(11)	**Cultural diversity** and the identities of communities, groups and individuals should be fully respected. In the respect of values recognised by communities, groups and individuals and sensitivity to cultural norms, specific attention to **gender** equality, **youth** involvement and **respect for ethnic identities** should be included in the design and implementation of safeguarding measures.
(12)	The safeguarding of intangible cultural heritage is of **general interest to humanity** and should therefore be undertaken through cooperation among bilateral, sub regional, regional and international parties; nevertheless, communities, groups and, where applicable, individuals should never be alienated from their own intangible cultural heritage.
	UNESCO (2015)

Table 1.2 List of digital Creole archives

Creole space	*Content type*	*Location*	*Access*
Cajun and Creole Folklore	Folklore interview series	University of Louisiana Lafayette	https://louisianadigitallibrary.org/islandora/object/ull-acc:collection
The Cajun and Creole Music Collection (CCMC)	9000 Commercial recordings, selected non-commercial recordings, and other music-related research materials	University of Louisiana Lafayette	https://library.louisiana.edu/collections/ccmc
New Orleans Creole Fiesta Assoc. Collection	4 photograph albums relating directly to the Creole Fiesta Association Events and Parades held from the 1950s to 1970s in New Orleans, Louisiana	Xavier University of Louisiana's Digital Archives	https://xula.contentdm.oclc.org/digital/collection/p16948coll2

Within the specifically Creole context, our investigations identified only one source of digital creole archives. These are held within the Louisiana University and are listed in Table 1.2.

At the time of writing, no other established archives of digital recordings of Creole cultural practices were identified by the researchers.

The abovementioned examples reveal the vulnerability of Creole ICH and emphasise the importance of safeguarding the core aspects of the Creole cultural heritage, which currently lies almost solely with elders, artists and expert practitioners. Their work gains new significance in ensuring the continuation of practices from one generation to the next that sustain the values important to the particular culture. While in order to develop a body of knowledge accessible beyond the life of its bearers there is a potential relationship of their work to archival recordings—even if archival practices remain contested in relation to their colonial roots.

For Creole and indigenous cultures, UNESCO recognition of ICH may deliver advantages of financial or other support. Hence, it is important to consider: On one hand, what options are available for representations of ICH that do not get on a list? On the other hand, what concerns arise, in relation to those that are identified as a representative example of heritage? In relation to the latter question, Barbara Kirshenblatt-Gimblett argues that 'heritage is a mode of production that gives the endangered or outmoded a second life as an exhibition of itself' (Kirshenblatt–Gimblett, 2004, p. 168). Is there a risk that by becoming identified as heritage, practices become removed from their very entanglement in daily life that sustains them? Importantly, if practices are to be safeguarded, as far as possible the process should ensure they remain important to people's lives and not become separate activities distanced from the people whose culture they are supposed to sustain.

4 A Question of Identity

A question closely related to that of value is that of identity. This is not identity as in the identity politics that may haunt questions of what or whose ICH is to be represented—which is part of the issue of values—but how to identify a named example of ICH so that different instances are recognised as such.

This question is similar to the concerns of many dance theorists who have long argued about how to distinguish the identity of a named dance work. For example, Barbara Kirshenblatt-Gimblett (2004) returns to the distinction made in the mid-twentieth century by the philosopher Nelson Goodman (1968) (often cited in dance theory) between autographic arts works—for example, a painting or sculpture that can be recognised as *the* work—and allographic works such as performances, that are not consistent with the identity of the work in the same way. But this still leaves many questions that have often been debated by dance scholars as to the identity of the work and how different instances of the same work are recognised as such (McFee, 2011). UNESCO in attending to ICH is concerned with cultural practices arising from communities and not works of arts with an identified creator or creators. Nevertheless, the underlying question regarding the ontological status of ICH has implications. Not least—how much can something change and still retain its identity?

The UNESCO convention allows for change and different cultural manifestations of ICH. Nevertheless, it is possible that there may be instances where the elements comprising a recognised example of ICH stay more or less the same, but its significance to those involved changes or even becomes irrelevant. For example, perhaps the practice of a style of music might be safeguarded. What if in performance it starts to seem so old fashioned no one listens to it? In this case, does it still need safeguarding? Or, in relation to Creole language, what if new words are not allowed as part of an authentic Creole—will young people be able to speak it, to discuss issues important to their lives? Alternatively, what if, in order to maintain its significance for a new generation, language or music changes to the extent an older generation no longer recognises the result as having the same identity as what was established in the past. For example, in music, perhaps they disapprove of the use of new instruments, or how advances in technologies change the sound or perhaps how newer up-to-date rhythmic elements change the music.

It may help if rather than thinking about some forms of heritage as 'intangible', a focus is directed towards the embodied interactions between people through which some forms of culture are constantly being re-created. What, for instance, might best be put in place to keep a practice of Kónte (Creole story telling) alive? Practices are dependent on a number of contributing elements most of which if not tangible are experienced physically: Story telling relies on the physicality of the story teller's voice, their presence and 'the response' to them of other people brought together to listen. This is best illustrated by the example of the passing of a leading almost sole Kóntecultural elder, Lawrence Brumant (deceased) from the island of the Commonwealth of Dominica as represented in the news article below.

Lawrence Brumant, one of Dominica's cultural icons, and the man whose name became synonymous with Kónte, (story telling in creole), has died.

Dominica News Online has learned that Brumant, who had been ailing for some time, died at the Portsmouth Hospital on Friday, September 23, 2016.

According to former Chief Cultural Officer, Raymond Lawrence, Brumant has left his mark on the cultural landscape of Dominica.

"He has left us a rich legacy of outstanding performance, especially in the area of Kónte. He was so skilful at it, and he won so many Independence Kónte competitions and also National Day competitions which was before the Independence, that he became known as the 'King of Kónte' in Dominica. So, he certainly can be considered a cultural icon in terms of the major contribution he made to Dominica's cultural development," Lawrence told Dominica News Online in an interview on Saturday.

Brumant's contribution to the art of Kónte telling in Dominica spanned more than forty years. He first competed in 1967 and his consistent success at the National Kónte Competition would see him emerge as the dominant Kónte teller on the island. He also represented Dominica at various story telling festivals in Jamaica, St. Croix, Martinique and Guadeloupe, among other places.

Brumant received the Golden Drum Award from the Cultural Division in 1987 and the LIME Creole Lifetime Award in 2013.

This is how Cultural Officer, Pearle Christian, described the Kónte maestro while reading his citation at the LIME awards ceremony: "Mr. Brumant has an unflagging resolve [and has] committed himself to perpetuating the tradition of Kónte, creole story creation and performance."

Brumant was born in the village of Vieille Case and according to Christian, was inspired by a brilliant storyteller Patrice Eloi. He relocated to Paix Bouche, and it was there that he developed his chosen art form.

"The King of Kónte" also made an active contribution to community development in the northern part of the island which extended way beyond his involvement in the Northern District Cultural Improvement Committee.

"He was involved in local government for many, many years, with hurricane disaster committees and in the Church, also with the

(*continued*)

(continued)

Banana Growers Association and several community groups. So, he was a community person as well," former Chief Cultural Officer Lawrence stated.

He said Brumant's passing is a sad loss to culture in Dominica.

"He was really a master of the Kónte, a very outstanding Konteur...I would like to extend condolences to the family and friends of Lawrence Brumant," Lawrence said.

He called on Dominicans to pay tribute to Brumant and to "salute and honour his memory for the contribution he made to keep Dominica's culture and heritage alive..."

The late Kónte teller's documented works include a book entitled "Ki Manye Domnik Twouve Nony" (How Dominica got its Name) and an album of his Kóntes.

—Dominica News Online—Saturday, September 24, 2016, at 2:54 PM

Brumant's Kóntes (stories) may be written down and preserved and their structures analysed, or recordings may be hosted on a YouTube channel, but such attempts to capture the stories do not constitute the practice of storytelling. Recognising this emphasises how the identity and significance of cultural events are bound up in the lived experience of engaging with them.

The above reinforces the importance of events that support the continuation of Creole cultural practices. Creole month is celebrated in October worldwide and is one of the most festive periods in Dominica. In this island state, during that period, several activities are held including traditional dance, song, Konte and heritage competitions. There is also a major international tourism-focused World Creole Music festival attracting international artists from the Creole space and beyond. The season culminates with Independence celebrations and Independence Day on November 3 in recognition of the anniversary of 1978's independence from Great Britain, becoming an independent republic within the Commonwealth (avirtualdominica.com, 2018). Among the festivities are Creole in the Park (traditionally led and sponsored by FLOW one of the major telephone companies on the island), Heritage Day, Creole Day, the Miss Wob Dwiyet Pageant, the Ti Matador Competition and Market Day with a Difference and smaller celebrations around the island.

The question then is how does this vibrant living heritage become safeguarded for future generations? This is particular concern as much of the events are isolated to Creole month in October and 'performed' mostly at this time of the year.

There might be no better time to immerse yourselfin true Dominican culture than during the

Independence season. Created to recognize Dominica's independence from Great Britain on November 3, 1978, Independence festivities celebrate music, dance, dress and cuisine. Every year, the country commemorates its Independence with a season of cultural activities which can last as long as four weeks.

These celebrations portray vivid examples of the island's cultural influences. The traditional dances display European traces in Hill & Toe, Waltz, and Quadrille; and borrow from African native dances in Bele.

Here are some of the aspects you shouldn't miss!

National Dress—The Wob Dwiyet is the centrepiece of this stunning costume and is widely worn. The last Friday before Independence is Creole Day, and all Dominicans will wear at least some variation of the national dress.

Jing Ping—Our traditional music, it is formally known as the Accordian Band and features the Bamboo Flute, the Boom (a long bamboo wind instrument), the Gwaj (an idiophone) and of course the Accordian.

National Dance—Our Quadrille and Bele dances evoke a time of elegance but with a distinct Caribbean flavour.

Market Day with A Difference—Our markets are generally a riot of colour, but at Independence they embrace the mood. Each week at one market around the island vendors will dress in national costume, and Jing Ping will be playing!

National Food—Independence would not be complete without enjoying our unique dishes. Crab—backs, Callaloo, Titiwi accras are just some of the many delicious foods you'll be able to try at this time of year.

—Discover Dominica (2021)

Fig. 1.1 Front of 'Wob Dwiyet', national dress of the Commonwealth of Dominica

Also, of particular interest and relevance to this discourse is evolution of the traditional national dress of Dominica, the Wob Dwiyet, its beauty, elegance and representation of the rich Creole heritage of the island (Figs. 1.1 and 1.2).

Today several variations to the national wear can be seen worn by the current generation of women, particularly adorned during national independence celebrations a time which marks the highlight of the island history and culture. Significantly, the island's political representative of the capital city, and wife of the Prime Minister, Honourable Melissa Poponne-Skerrit, can be deemed as setting new trends in cultural Creole fashion and creating

Fig. 1.2 Back of 'Wob Dwiyet', national dress of the Commonwealth of Dominica

a fabulous spectacle of colours and intricate design every year at the official national independence celebrations, a time when all that epitomises the island's Creole cultural and intangible heritage is on display (Fig. 1.3).

The perspective that focuses on the embodied practices that sustain culture provides for those inevitable heated debates that often occur *about* a practice as people participate in it, to become understood as *part* of that cultural activity. Arguments about what is allowable—be they the fabric of traditional costumes, the details within folktales, the instruments used in

Fig. 1.3 The Honourable Prime Minister Roosevelt Skerrit of the Commonwealth of Dominica and Honourable Melissa Poponne-Skerrit, parliamentary representation of Roseau November 3, 2021, official national day parade celebrations

music, the position of a hand in a dance—are part of a living cultural tradition. The identity of a cultural practice is thus understood through the ways in which it is brought into life, which may include moments of debate, rather than as an abstract intangible essence that no one can get hold of.

5 Embodiment

Consideration of the questions of identity and value raised above leads to an emphasis on the embodied and physically situated dimension of culture. The ways people move, speak, sing, dance and other expressions, are all part of culture and carry values in ways which are shared while not always explicitly stated. Embodied culture is also intrinsically related to the physical environments that people engage with. The weather, the terrain people walk on, the food available to eat and the shape and size of rooms and furniture all have a bearing on how people act, as do the activities they engage in.

UNESCO recognises that it is important to focus attention on more than just recording and preserving a way of speaking, dancing, singing or making to ensure the conditions that encourage activities to thrive as vital elements of cultural life. In that regard, the convention acknowledges:

> ...the deep-seated interdependence between the intangible cultural heritage and the tangible cultural and natural heritage. (UNESCO, 2003)

This interdependence can become problematic where efforts to safeguard ICH as a living practice engage with efforts to preserve related physical artefacts or sites. When British Black dancers became concerned that the dancing of a whole generation of artists was vulnerable and at risk, funding in support of an archives project offered a solution. In the absence of policies to safeguard the legacy of black British dancers as ICH, Deborah Baddoo's aim for the archives is: "*...that they will be experienced in relation with what in both dance and African traditions is an emphasis on oral histories and the embodied experience of learning dancing from elders*" (Carr & Baddoo, 2020, p. 75).

Yet one of the things this project brought into focus was the difference between the assumptions and practices guiding artists and those informing archivists. For example, a costume that might be held in a collection could tell a performer much about how to move and thus be a valuable source of information when re-staging a dance. Yet once archived, or even displayed in a museum, it can be difficult to gain permission to borrow it and more so to wear it. In practice, maintaining links between objects destined for an archive or museum and practices in the real world can be problematic.

Some of those working within the museum sector have called for a closer interplay between tangible and intangible heritage to ensure strategic responsibility for both is 'brought together within the same agencies' (Kaufman, 2013, p. 20). It is not inconceivable to break down such boundaries. Indeed, one example lies at the very heart of a once colonial power: On ceremonial occasions the King of England is able to use items that are otherwise displayed securely in The Tower of London (Historic Royal Palaces, n.d.). If the continued relationship between artefacts and practices evolves into a regular norm of archival and museum practices, artefacts stored—be they a recording of a storey in a Creole language in an archive or an item of traditional dress displayed in a museum—need not become emptied of their lived significance as things belonging to a disappearing heritage but could sustain continuity of embodied cultural experience.

6 Conclusion

We argue, in considering a programme to safeguard Creole and indigenous intangible cultural heritage, it is important to reflect that what is valued as significant in the present has implications for what will be available to future generations. In keeping with the UNESCO Convention (2003) it is vital that it is the values of communities themselves that shape projects to safeguard their cultural practices. This is particularly the case for Creole communities whose cultural identities may be vulnerable to the processes of globalisation and whose cultural practices are largely undocumented. The approach to safeguarding should strive to support the lived significance of cultural practices for participants and recognise the role of continuing tensions between change and tradition as part of a cultural practice's living identity. Projects that are developed should also emphasise how UNESCO's Convention recognises the interplay of tangible and intangible heritage. In developing the means to safeguard intangible cultural heritage, the protection of ways of speaking, doing and making needs to be coordinated with the events that bring people, things and place together. It is through the interweaving of the tangible and intangible—the physical world and embodied practices—that culture thrives. Ensuring this is the challenge for those aiming to safeguard the Creole and indigenous cultural heritage of islands such as Dominica.

References

Avirtualdominica. (2018). Dominica's Independence Celebrations! https://www.avirtualdominica.com/project/independence/

Carr, J., & Baddoo, D. (2020). Dance, Diaspora and the Role of the Archives: A Dialogic Reflection upon the Black Dance Archives Project (UK). *Dance Research, 38*(1), 68–81.

Derrida, J. (1995, Summer). Archive Fever: A Freudian Impression. *Diacritics, 5*(2), 9–63.

Discover Dominica. (2021). Retrieved May 8, 2022, from https://discoverdominica.com/en/events/6/independence

Dominica News Online. (2016, September 24). The "King of Konte", Lawrence Brumant Passes. *Dominica News Online*—Saturday, at 2:54 PM. Retrieved May 8, 2022, from https://dominicanewsonline.com/news/homepage/news/king-of-konte-lawrence-brumant-passes/

Goodman, N. (1968). *Languages of Art: An Approach to a Theory of Symbols.* Bobbs-Merrill.

Historic Royal Palaces. (n.d.). *See the Crown Jewels.* Retrieved May 8, 2022, from https://www.hrp.org.uk/tower-of-london/whats-on/the-crown-jewels/#gs.rfkanu

Kaufman, N. (2013). Putting Intangible Heritage in its Place(s): Proposals for Policy and Practice. *International Journal of Intangible Heritage, 8*, 19–36.

Kirshenblatt-Gimblett, B. (2004). Intangible Heritage as Meta-Cultural Production. *Museum International, 56*(1–2), 52–65.

Labadi, S. (2005). A Review of the Global Strategy for a Balanced, Representative and Credible World Heritage List. *Conservation and Management of Archaeological Sites, 7*(2), 89–102.

McFee, G. (2011). *The Philosophical Aesthetics of Dance: Identity, Performance and Understanding.* Dance Books.

Schneider, R. (2012). Performance Remains. In A. Heathfield & A. Jones (Eds.), *Perform, Repeat, Record: Live Art in History* (pp. 137–150). Intellect Books and the University of Chicago Press.

State of Emergency. (n.d.). Black Dance Archives. Retrieved May 9, 2022, from https://www.surrey.ac.uk/national-resource-centre-dance/projects/british-black-dance-archives

UNESCO. (2003). *Text of the Convention for the Safeguarding of the Intangible Cultural Heritage.* Retrieved May 8, 2022, from https://ich.unesco.org/en/convention

UNESCO. (2015). *Ethics and Intangible Cultural Heritage.* Retrieved May 9, 2022, from https://ich.unesco.org/en/ethics-and-ich-00866

UNESCO. (n.d.-a). *1982–2000: From Mondiacult to Our Creative Diversity.* Retrieved May 9, 2022, from https://ich.unesco.org/en/1982-2000-00309

UNESCO. (n.d.-b). *1946–1981: First Steps.* Retrieved May 9, 2022, from https://ich.unesco.org/en/2000-onwards-00310

CHAPTER 2

Towards Safeguarding Creole Intangible Cultural Heritage: The 2003 UNESCO Convention

Alexis Weedon

1 Introduction

On 17 October 2003 at the UNESCO general conference 120 member states voted in favour of the Convention for the Safeguarding of the Intangible Cultural Heritage (ICH); many other states have subsequently joined and the number has now reached 177. No one voted against it. Such support is a positive endorsement of the need to help the survival of significant cultural activities. Not only in the big institutional arts and cultural organisations where valuable cultural artefacts are preserved, but also the local cultural traditions which bind and have bound communities and societies forging their identities. The Convention spotlights the urgency to safeguard such traditions and requires those seeking inscription to put together a case. A key aspect to the success or failure of an application for inscription, or indeed the wider purpose of safeguarding an

A. Weedon (✉)
University of Bedfordshire, Luton, UK
e-mail: alexis.weedon@beds.ac.uk

V. Cuffy, J. Carr (eds.), *Creole Cultures, Vol. 1*,
https://doi.org/10.1007/978-3-031-24275-5_2

intangible tradition, is the level of support within a national infrastructure. This could be through a combination of researchers, amateur or professional associations, lobbying bodies, and a strong policy and legal framework. They need to unite to construct a sound basis for the protection and sustainability of the ICH. Charlotte Waelde and her colleagues in international law show that legal frameworks for built heritage or intellectual property often pose problems for the extension into intangible culture where ownership and creative input is unclear and the definition of 'public domain' is inadequate (Whatley et al., 2015). The UNESCO Convention therefore places a considerable burden on countries seeking to protect their intangible heritage from exploitation by commercial forces from within or outside the country.

2 Historical Context for UNESCO's ICH Convention

The first essay into this area of cultural protection by UNESCO came in 1972 with the Convention Concerning the Protection of World Cultural and Natural Heritage which lead to the establishment of the World Heritage List. This promoted the preservation and conservation of important monuments and landscapes. Britain has 31 designations, including the Dorset coast preserving the fossil-rich limestone strata of the Jurassic where it comes to the earth's surface, Kew Gardens with its plant-collecting heritage and unique botanical collection (explored in this collection by Carol Sorhaindo), and the Neolithic monument of Stonehenge. In Dominica, the Morne Trois Pitons National Park was designated in 1997 to protect its geomorphic natural features and its endemic and uniquely rich biodiversity among the Antilles. The fragility of the ecology and the vulnerability of communities were demonstrated after hurricane Maria hit Dominica in 2012. Across the island the forest was flattened or stripped bare of its leaves, and plantations and crops were lost and homes destroyed.

After Koïchiro Matsuura became Director-General in 2001, UNESCO started the Masterpieces of the Oral and Intangible Heritage of Humanity programme. It is no coincidence that Japan had in 1950 passed its Law for the Protection of Cultural Properties which distinguished between 'tangible', 'intangible', and 'folk' cultural properties. Examples separate the tangible properties of monuments and landscapes, the intangible properties of performing arts and craft skills, and the folk cultural properties that relate to the rituals of everyday life. Half a century later the UNESCO Masterpieces of the Oral and Intangible Heritage programme listed its first masterpieces. [1] These included Chinese Kun Qu opera; the language, dance, and music of the Garifuna across Central America; the oral heritage of Gelede in West Africa; the Bolivian carnival of Oruro; the Gbofe horn music accompanied by song and dance of Tagbana community in the Ivory Coast, amongst others. Many are in the southern hemisphere where cultures with strong intangible traditions are common. It was hoped that such designations would instigate action and mobilise resources to protect these living traditions and offset the deeply western construct of the World Heritage List which privileges material culture and embedded colonial values. Like the World Heritage List, the Masterpieces programme offered international recognition by naming and conceptually describing the tradition or location and its cultural significance.

The imposing Latinate phrase 'Intangible Cultural Heritage' has a transcultural applicability and status which the more nebulous terms—folklore, traditional culture, community arts—do not have. The issue is in understanding and interpreting its remit. A more convenient definition appears difficult (Kurin, 2004). Defining the term, the Convention states:

> It...includes traditions or living expressions inherited from our ancestors and passed on to our descendants, such as oral traditions, performing arts, social practices, rituals, festive events, knowledge and practices concerning nature and the universe or the knowledge and skills to produce traditional crafts.
>
> UNESCO (2003a)

These may be storytelling practices, puppetry, pilgrimage, culinary traditions, or a community's cosmology. Fundamentally, however, it is the culture of daily life and often of family or community life. It is expressive, often playful, and sometimes irreverent, and it marks transitions in stages of life and reaffirms a community's ontological view.

3 Challenges in Inscribing ICH: Communities, Policymakers, and Researchers

While the intention of the Convention which followed is laudable, the challenges in adopting it are great. The first is in working through what is intangible cultural heritage: the words I have used hitherto—folk, traditional, community occasions, or events—offer wide scope for interpretation especially when transferring them to differing national and cultural contexts. The definition in the articles of the Convention is:

> the practices, representations, expressions, knowledge, skills—as well as the instruments, objects, artefacts and cultural spaces associated therewith—that communities, groups and, in some cases, individuals recognize as part of their cultural heritage.
>
> UNESCO (2003b)

Further precision is given by the continuity and longevity of these practices and their responsiveness to external factors and their purpose:

> This intangible cultural heritage, transmitted from generation to generation, is constantly recreated by communities and groups in response to their environment, their interaction with nature and their history, and provides them with a sense of identity and continuity.
>
> UNESCO (2003b)

This promotion of a sense of social identity—which is often the product of distinction from an 'other' through systemic hegemony, colonialism, tribal or nationalistic forces—is qualified by mutual respect: 'thus promoting respect for cultural diversity and human creativity' (UNESCO, 2003b). And there are exclusions:

> For the purposes of this Convention, consideration will be given solely to such intangible cultural heritage as is compatible with existing international human rights instruments, as well as with the requirements of mutual respect among communities, groups and individuals, and of sustainable development.
>
> UNESCO (2003b)

UNESCO requires the practitioner community, researchers, and the national representatives to come together to make the case. There is a requirement too for infrastructure to maintain the continuance of the ICH. So, a substantial resource is needed and more than that, a convergence of positions.

Many communities formed their identity in contradistinction to an oppressor through struggle against colonial rule or through victory over another, and these stories are embedded in their songs of glory, resistance, and martyrdom. Relevant here is the complex and traumatic history of slavery, transportation, and the marginalisation and oppression of indigenous peoples throughout the Caribbean as we see in many of the chapters in this collection. Also, there are festivals which celebrate the reversal of hegemonic social structures or celebrations of moments of liberation and sit alongside festivities marking transitions through life, such as births, coming of age, and deaths. Respecting the authenticity of these experiences and history, and their importance in creating individual and social identity is fundamental to the inscription (Rabess, 1998).

In contrast, the dominant (Western) model of the ethnographic investigator puts the researcher on the outside of the activity and its meaning making, in a position of authoritative outsider. The relationship between 'objective' researcher and the researched often results in a clash of ontologies as a Western notion of 'objective' knowledge is prioritised over other knowledge systems. Postcolonialism has shown us that this is suspect. This has to be negotiated by the researcher who is required to make a systematic recording of the event witnessed and to understand their relationship to it. As ethnographic researchers they must record all contextualising variables such as: ostensible purpose or function, location, and season, whether the company is participative or receptive. They must undertake the not insignificant intellectual challenge to find suitable categories of type of performance or activity, a person's status or role, the category of community and engagement. This is not easy as Trisha Winter intimates when she problematises the concepts of 'preservation' and 'revival', and the 'indigenous' and the 'local' in an age of social movement and migration, reflecting on her fieldwork, interviews, and analysis of dance and music in *Performing Englishness* (Winter & Keegan-Phipps, 2013). Similarly, the categories of 'indigenous' and the 'local' are problematic when traditions have moved with the community across continents and become fused with other local customs. Yet as Penda Choppy says about the folklore of the Seychelles in this collection (Chap. 3),

> [It]is a testimony of the Seychellois people's traumatic experience as a society created out of slavery and colonialism, a testimony of their efforts to adapt and create new identities in the face of changing historical and political landscapes.

Therefore, researchers themselves have to be cognisant of their position in the nexus of interests and values when an inscription is being planned.

One requirement of an inscription is that it is a living practice. Through history there have been many different ways to justify, validate, and secure the continuance of a tradition, from the claim for an 'unbroken' annual repetition of an event to the reinvention (or revival) of a legend or myth, but in many cases the claim needs research to evidence it. Researchers and other stakeholders must join with the policymakers and government representatives who will champion the case to UNESCO and create the infrastructure to continue the ICH into the future, building it into the curriculum of schools and the cultural life of the nation. If there are no pre-existing community associations, lobbying bodies, industries, or other structural organisations, this can be a huge task involving policy and law making to protect the interests of the community—a problem, as we shall see, in the case of Jamaican Reggae (Spence, 2019).

4 Analysis of ICH Inventories

There are three obligations that the Convention puts on a nation: a national inventory of ICHs; the recognition that the community members who practice the traditions should have major responsibility for their safeguarding; and, thirdly, that one national body has the role of developing action-plans to safeguard its intangible heritage. This requires them to integrate it within plans for growth, education and development, and provide national and international legal protection, and a research agenda.

The Convention puts the task of compiling comprehensive inventories on the country's government. This task requires investment of time and money which is diverted from other governmental priorities, and so the implementation has been done with an eye to economy and sharing of resources. Different cultures have approached the need for community engagement and open sourcing in ways which reflect their values. The French have a centralised system and made the *Mission Ethnographie*, the French Ministry of Culture department for ethnographic research, responsible for its development (Bortolotto, 2012). They collated pre-existing ethnographic inventories and added the required national inventory. Their model for participation is based on the three principles 'turn to the public, internet diffusion, action research' which they say means 'research that aims to return to their "owners" the collected data after they have been studied and organized by the researcher' (Bortolotto, 2012). The *Portail du patrimoine culturel immatériel* (PCI) lists ICH practices across the world, and many Creole and Caribbean communities have applied to the list. It features ICH from Martinique and Guadaloupe to Polynesia. Taking a more federal approach, the *Kenniscentrum Immaterieel Erfgeod Nederland* (Netherlands Intangible Heritage Knowledge Center) offers training, support, and research as well as a list which has a threefold structure: the networks where communities, groups, or individuals register an ICH in their own words; the inventory where an independently reviewed assurance plan has been put in place to safeguard its future; and a register of examples of good practice which can be shared with other communities. Aruba, Bonaire, Curaçao, Saba, Sint Eustatius, Sint Maarten, and Suriname have worked together to build capacity supported by the *Kenniscentrum Immaterieel Erfgeod Nederland*, and the first national inventory of Sint Maarten has been published by the Department of Culture and Sint Maarten National Commission for UNESCO (Sint Maarten & UNESCO, 2016). In contrast, although Britain has many inscriptions for UNESCO heritage sites, it has not ratified the ICH Convention, nor has Australia and Canada. In 2017, Lord Ashton said in the British parliament that it was 'necessary to carefully prioritise resources towards those Conventions that will have the most impact on the safeguarding of our heritage'. A waiting list for ratification has emerged as Britain had only just agreed to the 1954 Hague Convention for the Protection of Cultural Property (Ashton of Hyde, 2017). Waelde argues that Britain is therefore in breach of its human rights obligations (Waelde, 2018).

The cost of implementation was directly addressed in Korea where scholars have created Ichpedia, a web-based ICH encyclopaedia and archive, claiming it is 'the least expensive option' and so can 'reduce the economic burden of establishing a highly efficient database system'. While many countries have used a participatory wiki design, Ichpedia goes further. It is a combination of free open source software (LAMP) based on a MySQL database (LAMP) offered so that countries or groups can 'share this system in order to manage and access intangible cultural resources throughout the Web without incurring any extra costs' (Park, 2014). Using such a database facilitates quantitative and qualitative analysis too. Yet while LAMP software is free, there is still a need for set-up and design and so many nations have opted for the route of joining the French or Dutch lists. One interesting variation is that the French have linked their

PCI with Wikipedia as a way of enriching that pre-existing participatory encyclopaedia and created a portal to submit content for evaluation for the country's own registered inventory. The enormous database of *Portail du patrimoine culturel immatériel* (PCI), France, had 939 Wikipedia pages associated with it in June 2021 and an annual call for listing in the PCI itself.

Many other countries have now issued an open call including smaller nations such as Estonia, Ireland, Jamaica, Scotland, and Malta. Jamaica has a Memory Bank website, made by the African Caribbean Institute of Jamaica, with a map to which people can add their images. The ACIJ/JMB site aims to 'facilitate the sharing of information relating to the island's intangible cultural heritage from Jamaicans at home and in the Diaspora' and 'vision to broaden awareness of African and other migrant cultures that make up Jamaica's total culture and way of life' (ACIJ/JMB, 2021). The site is linked to the Jamaican government website on copyright law, and there is an explanation and encouragement about its use for education. In Scotland the association is between the Museum Galleries Scotland and Napier University, who were commissioned to scope Intangible Cultural Heritage in the country and one outcome is a site 'From first footing to Faeries: An inventory of Scotland's living culture' (Scotland, 2011). The public can explore it through a direct search and a map. A similar approach has been taken in Finland and Singapore (Singapore, 2016). By using digital participatory technologies, the dubious method of inventory and its embedded colonial values and atomistic approach can be transformed into something much more democratic.

The taxonomy adopted interprets the UNESCO Convention within the national context. The five domains listed by UNESCO are:

- Oral traditions and expressions, including language as a vehicle of the intangible cultural heritage;
- Performing arts;
- Social practices, rituals and festive events;
- Knowledge and practices concerning nature and the universe;
- Traditional craftsmanship.

UNESCO (2003c)

These have been interpreted and amended within the national inventories. The French PCI has seven categories: traditional physical practices (e.g. falconry, French horse riding), festive practices, music and dances, games, expressions and oral traditions, ritual practices, craft knowledge. Less centralised and with its three-tiered system, the Dutch inventory includes Curaçao and Aruba's Kaha di orgel (a musical instrument that is somewhere between a cylinder piano and an organ) and the Antillian tambú musical culture categorised using the five UNESCO categories. These can be compared with the Korean ichpedia's seven: oral traditions and expressions; traditional health care, agricultural, and fishing knowledge; food, clothing and housing, and traditional customs; performing arts; social practices, rituals, and festive events; folk belief and social rituals; and traditional craftsmanship. Scotland has simple category headings presented in tiles with a map showing the Scottish counties. The effect is rather of a regional tourist guide where you can access interesting facts under the headings of: beliefs; crafts; customs and rituals; dance; festivals; food; games; know how; music; nature and the universe; storytelling; theatre. In contrast, Jamaica resists such generic categorisation and the post-colonial listing, preferring to focus on the particular instances of ICH in nine collections: Etu/Ettu; Candy Making; Hindus; Jonkonnu band; Obeah; Maroons; Rastafari; Kumina; and Revival.

The range of organisations appointed to create and sustain the inventory is wide and each has its own agenda in supporting the ICH work. Government departments or closely related entities host the inventory in Austria where the National Commission for UNESCO accommodates it, and in Finland where a separate government advisory committee has been set up. In Jamaica the government has established an open call site as we have seen. In some other countries, it is placed within heritage bodies: in Estonia the Folk Culture centre administers the site, in Sri Lanka it is the national library, and in Scotland it is the association of Museums and Galleries with a university (Austria, 2018; Estonia, 2018; Finland, 2017; Sri Lanka, 2017). The Dutch site emphasises its research agenda, while others showcase ICH like museum of cultural artefacts, and still others emphasise the touristic potential.

5 Meaning and Language: Identity, Unity, and Harmony in UNESCO's ICH

A comparison of the national ICH websites and UNESCO's inscription shows that the latter provides a gloss using the language of identity, unity, and harmony for the accepted inscriptions. On the UNESCO website the elements inscribed are displayed as a list and on a map. The map, in tints of green, shows the predominance of ICH elements in the southern hemisphere. Roll over the country and the number of elements is shown, but the map leaves blank the countries which have not yet ratified the Convention. (Being able to explore in this way is one of the advances of digital humanities since the advent of the World Heritage List). The list shows the number each year from an accumulation of 80 in 2008 to a more regular 42 in 2016 and 2017. Those who were turned down were often done so because of a lack of evidence of consultation with the community enacting the tradition (Bortolotto, 2012). Acceptance meets with celebration, but only a subset of the seriously endangered receive financial support.

The Convention uses the term 'safeguarding' rather than preserving which raises a number of considerations; if a tradition is endangered then there may be reasons why it is not sustainable, perhaps it is no longer meaningful, or its cultural context is lost and preserving it may simply hasten its demise as a living tradition and ossify it. Safeguarding craft skills is an example in point. For instance, in 2014 Gwoka was added; Gwoka is singing in Guadeloupean Creole to rhythms played on the Ka drums and dancing. The nomination included safeguarding the skills of dancing and drum-making, which are learned through families and increasingly through formal workshops and schools in traditional dance and music. 'It strengthens identity and provides a feeling of communal development and individual pride, conveying values of conviviality, resistance and dignity,' says the webpage reflecting the values of UNESCO embedded in the Convention (UNESCO, 2017a). But sustainability is unpredictable and so an assessment has to be made by researchers and educators. In 2017 Uilleann piping from Ireland was inscribed on the list and is a useful illustrative example. Uilleann 'is a musical practice which uses a particular type of bagpipe … it offers an important way of socializing and plays an integral role in life events such as marriages and funerals, where it provides a sense of rootedness and a connection to the past' even in a 'diasporic community'. Master-to-student instruction and 'modern methods such as video and DVD tutorials and the internet' keep the tradition living. 'Through a programme of research, publications, tuition and training, the Na Píobairí Uilleann group of pipers [NPU] has contributed to a huge increase in the use and appreciation of the instrument and its music, resulting in a flowering of the art in modern times, with more players than in any previous period' and so the ICH is sustained (UNESCO, 2017b).

These examples show that the Convention requires intellectual work by educators, cultural historians, curators, and researchers to ensure that the ICH is meaningful and sustainable and has a significance in the cultural context. They are positioned as 'verifiers' of its significance and of the claim that it should be taught to future generations. Through their work, Museum Galleries Scotland became 'the first UK organisation to become accredited as an expert NGO advisor to UNESCO' on the Convention (Scotland, 2018). One particularly tricky case was the safeguarding of the Turkish whistling language and expertise was called upon to help with the inscription to avoid opening the list to *all* languages. This work refines and deepens understanding in the interpretation and application of the Convention.

The appropriation of living traditions can go further than the architects of the Convention envisaged. They undoubtedly saw ICH nominations arising from a community definition of a meaningful tradition and were more focused on preservation than evolution. Yet in an age of regional diaspora and when our neighbourhoods have been reconfigured in what Benedict Anderson (1983) calls 'imagined communities', intangible cultures have proliferated. This is pertinent to Jamaica where the success of Reggae is such that it is recognised, played, and enjoyed worldwide. However, its creative origin in the music scene in Jamaica in the 1970s has not been given the same recognition and cultural status (as we shall see). Today people live in a remix culture and take from their heritage what is meaningful to reuse. Many cultural practices have been developed and sustained through social media such as gaming and cosplay, story retelling through fan sites and Instagram, online rap or pop jams, and karaoke. Look hard at some of these and you find they have grown from earlier forms of traditional play, the marking of life events, and rituals of family and community bond making. These modern forms are ruled out of the Convention which is unfortunate when intangible cultural heritage is a repository of a community's creativity and is a source of inspiration for new cultural expressions. For example, Victor Ukaegbu's work on reclaiming of the oral history of Black British voices preserved on audio tape in the archive for his stage performance, is a great example of the value intangible cultural heritage has for developing modern forms of creative expression and community voice (Ukaegbu, 2017) and Brenda Choppy, in this volume, reveals how young Seychellois musicians rework their Creole heritage within the contemporary music scene.

Social memory is also a significant factor in the ICH tradition. Memory, as we know, does not record the past, it re-forms what is meaningful in it to help us in the present and to prepare us for the future. It is not a means to preserve, it empowers us to adapt. The cultural memories within the ICH have a similar role in our societies. Research shows that some of them derive from a moment where adaptation or social agility has been necessary for a community, critically relevant in a postcolonial society where trauma is deeply embedded in social history and remains a defining factor in the community's marginalised identity. For example, the Creole-speaking Palenque de San Basilio community in Columbia still vividly describes itself to tourists as the only free town in America, 'free from Slavery, free from Spanish rule'. While the Bolivian carnival of Oruro celebrates indigenous Andean dances and traditions which recall pre-independence resistance to Spanish rule. Our memories help us to be adaptable, so too without our memories we are untethered and misplace our sense of self within society. Can the process of ICH inscription be used to address political identity and social inequalities?

While UNESCO hopes an inscription will give rise to pride in an indigenous heritage which may have been devalued, ICH emphasises continuity with the past and this risks retaining the old bondage of colonial ties as in the francophone PCI. The process of putting together an inscription can also raise issues of contested ownership, and external and internal exploitation of creative rights, which has happened with Jamaican Reggae as we shall see next. Similarly, there are tensions between museum preservation of the tangible objects associated with intangible performance and living heritage and the enactment of the performance itself. Some derive from the exploitative nature of colonial collection. Others from the static, decontextualised exhibition of the artefacts which, in the case of costumes for example, were made for movement, dance, or procession. Curators and museum directors might offer place of portage for cultural artefacts and practices in the stormy seas of globalisation and displacement, but despite their critical friendship, these traditions must be living and breathing. In cultural terms, the link with the past must be liberating and relevant to the next generation.

6 ICH Inscription and Tourism, Branding, and Regulation

In 2013 the Jamaican Tourism Board (JTB) produced a brand and campaign guide underpinning the 'Brand Jamaica' Campaign. The idea was to provide a platform and identity where Caribbean products on the world market can be identified with their homeland and to foster the desire for an 'authentic' experience or cultural product among the global public. The resulting revenue stream would be channelled back into the national and regional economy (Ferdinand, 2017). As Gabrielle Ferdinand points out not everyone is in favour of brands. One representative from the music industry that she interviewed suggested as an alternative that 'our mission must be to establish ourselves as the magnet, or the home base where all these come if they want to connect', for claims of ownership of indigenous music can 'deter expansion and stifle growth' (Ferdinand, 2017, p. 169). Ferdinand observes:

> the region has adopted a defensive position whereby brand has become a way to mark and label cultural outputs, so as to ensure that they cannot be pilfered by foreign entities
> Ferdinand (2017, p. 164)

This defensive position became central to the policy decisions before the Jamaican application.

Interviewing ministers, producers, and artists in the Jamaican music industry in the first quarter of 2016, Kim-Marie Spence comments that the politics of identity formation in postcolonial countries remains central in such preparations and argues that 'hegemonic dominance is still embedded within Jamaican cultural policy practice' (Spence, 2019, p. 51). Jamaica's National Cultural Policy (NCP) acknowledges Jamaican's African identity and the importance of its culture in economic development (Spence, 2019). The *Jamaica Observer*, covering Culture, Gender, Entertainment, and Sport Minister Olivia Grange's speech, reported the revision of the NCP 'ensures an increase in the number of growing small and medium-sized businesses and the "legitimisation" of all cultural and creative business activities' (NCP 2017–2027) (Anon, 2017).

This is a welcome move in a country where copyright law failed to protect the rights of performers, omitted in the 2015 Copyright Act amendments. Spence argues that this is an 'important oversight in a country practicing creative industries development. It also demonstrates the subordinate position of reggae in relation to other bases of power in Jamaica' (Spence, 2019, p. 52). Jamaica's first cultural policy in 1963 addressed arts competitions and performing arts but not the social and racial inequalities which were in increasing debate in the country's 90% Black population. The Afrocentric Rastafari religion and its 'philosophy of peace, unity, repatriation, and reparations and represents cultural resistance' appealed to the disadvantaged Jamaicans and were a way of refusing the dominant narrative of protestant European cultural heritage (Spence, 2019, p. 48). Rastafari, its concept of collectivity or *levity,* and Reggae, the music which emerged from Trench Town, linked politics and people in the 1970s. Bob Marley and The Wailers became international musical stars of the genre and with its neo-colonial attitude and Afro-diasporic appeal, Reggae music spread globally. Yet insufficiently protected, its performers have not received the rewards of their creativity, and due to its cultural low-status, Reggae's origins have been insufficiently acknowledged by the US and UK pop industry (Vilanova, 2019). It was these issues which lead to the Jamaican Minister Olivia Grange to lead a bid for its ICH inscription.

Like many countries, Jamaica applied to UNESCO's World Heritage List prior to considering making any application for intangible cultural heritage, and the Blue and John Crow Mountains were inscribed in 2015. They followed it with an application for Creative City. The first ICH application was the inscription of the Maroon Heritage of Moore Town, Jamaica, which was successful in 2008. The application for the inscription of Reggae was passed at the 13th Session of the ICH Committee in Mauritius in 2018, and Jamaica was elected to the ICH committee. The *Jamaican Information Service* press release quoted Minister Grange expressing her thanks in a way which shows how cooperation amongst the Caribbean islands had led to this achievement:

> Jamaica expresses its sincere thanks for the overwhelming support we have received. We are heartened by the show of camaraderie particularly by St. Kitts and Nevis, who withdrew and, in the end, provided full backing for Jamaica to sit on the Committee. We do not take this level of support for granted.
>
> JIS (2018)

When Jamaica opened the ICH committee as chair, they received an ovation for the inscription of Reggae (Snapes, 2018). Academic commentators Hubert Devonish and Karen Carpenter view the move as a means of 'blocking appropriation' and ensuring that others are adopters or adapters of Reggae and not owners or originators of the music. It is, they conclude, a 'well thought through' manoeuvre. Spence, on the other hand, says that much still needs to be done:

> Recognition of economic value has been enough to enact economic policy initiatives for the music industry, but not policy documents (Economic Growth Plan), or to revamp the status of artists beyond the entertainment sphere, but the security policy remains unamended.
>
> Spence (2019, p. 56)

A group of researchers and supporters of Creole intangible cultural heritage, *Creoles cultures/Kiltir Kreol/Cultures creoles*, have proposed an alternative definition of Creole ICH which resists commercialism and branding. They identify in Creole cultures the dominant values of solidarity, hospitality, and tolerance and promote working together 'with a sense of celebration'. 'Creole' comes to stand for peace and harmony through dialogue and compromise.

Distinctively, they assert it has a 'profound, "umbilical" link with Nature, mother earth and the ancestors'. As Marc Links phrases it, Creole is defined as a feeling and an action:

> 'Kreolitude' would be defined as an **action**, That of understanding the Creole fact and Knowing what it can bring to other people.
>
> It aims today at offering an alternative to the current "Merchant" civilization.
>
> Lints (2019)

The difficulty of collating a representative portfolio of examples for the inscription of 'Creole Cultures' which this group suggests is huge. Individual ICHs have however been accepted; the language of the Garifuna in Belize, Guatemala, Honduras, and Nicaragua (2001), the music and dance of the Capoeira circle in Brazil (2014), Cuba's Rumba (2016) and the Tumba Francesca (2003), the Maloya from the Réunion Island (2009), and ICH from Mauritius and Jamaica already mentioned. All these separate Creole ICH inscriptions have been supported by their communities and national commissions; so, the idea of cooperation beyond nation states to create a distinctive Creole platform, intimated by Grange on the Jamaican election, and again by the *Creoles cultures/Kiltir Kreol/Cultures creoles* association, is ambitious and visionary.

7 Implications for Creole Nations

The argument in Richard Florida's *The Rise of the Creative Class* (2002) that creatives can become the economic drivers in a global economy has led to greater attention being given by policymakers to their cultural and artistic heritage. The economic threats to immaterial culture and the economic reasons that justify the preservation of ICH have become more apparent. However collective and community cultural production has lacked the protection of property rights assigned to the individual. The Jamaican example illustrates the level of stakeholder development needed to apply for an inscription: three museums, the backing of the recording industry, performers, lawyers, policymakers, government ministers, Jamaican UNESCO commission—and even collegiate islands. While it has helped having the experience of previous applications, knowledge of the processes and resources is a key component in achieving any level of inscription. ICH inscription draws attention to the issues of sustainability, longevity, and significance and offers a platform of shared expertise and experience rather than solutions. It is a point Tiziana Cuccia makes as she questions the real enforcement capacity of UNESCO Conventions and the resilience of the arising local and national structures to global economic flows (Cuccia, 2020).

ICH often privileges the audience or community above the originator or even performer and puts emphasis on co-creation between the society and the individual (Weedon, 2020). This is a reversal of Western concepts of authorship and ownership and the legal rights which emerged from it in copyright and patent law. Jamaica's response was the 'Brand Jamaica' campaign as means of resisting appropriation of their cultural heritage. It remains to be seen if the 'well thought through' manoeuvre redirects sufficient revenue from reggae's worldwide popularity. Kreolitude's resistance to branding offers an alternative set of values on which to build a global network, although without a sustainable economic base it remains a cultural rather than a social movement. A Creole cultural platform would, however, move the work of safeguarding ICH beyond embedded colonialist political and linguistic structures. It is a farsighted and imaginative proposal which might also offer a way to combine its values with a

Creole identity or brand in the way that other diasporic nations have successfully done.

Commentators have observed that both reggae and other areas of Black and Creole heritage are nonteleological and require a different approach to heritage and time. John Vilanova's discussion of Revival which is next on Jamaica's ICH agenda for inscription, shows how this musical genre's 'complication of linear time and history' puts forward a different vision, one in which the 'contemporary collective makes space for events, sounds, and people of the past' (Vilanova, 2019, pp. 4088–4089). Making the wider point that UNESCO's heritage listings skew towards physical space and European history, Kenyatta McLean acknowledges ICH's role in redressing the weight of built heritage, although he says it is not enough. He argues that we need to look at the values and approaches to non-linear time taken outside traditional preservationist networks to address the discriminatory exclusivity of historic preservation. In Mauritius postcolonial discourses which valorised Creole heritage as a national identity were deeply rooted in the memory of slavery and had internalised negative values which subsequent Creole discourse sought to stand against, as Didier Michel and Daniella Police-Michel document in their chapter. So, we can see that Euro-centric concepts of time, the colonial legacy, and the underprivilege of Caribbean and Creole culture are a more entrenched problem than the issues of policy and law.

8 What Are the Lessons to Be Learned from These Examples?

Not everyone wants the full UNESCO ICH inscription, for some communities simply registering local traditions and uploading photos on a database is enough. For others the benefits of the international recognition are great and a prize worth having and will want to consider the following recommendations:

1. Look for the experience that is on offer. If UNESCO is offering to run workshops, or the *Kenniscentrum Immaterieel Erfgeod Nederland* will provide examples of good practice in setting up safeguarding strategies, get them in. Utilise the experience of other UNESCO inscriptions.

2. Do it your own (cultural) way. It is fundamental premise of UNESCO's Convention to safeguard the *diversity* of ICH and protect the living tradition within the community. So, while there are other models, one size will not fit all.
3. Work with stakeholders. The disparate concerns and fears of stakeholder groups may make it difficult to find a common goal. Resisting the external threat of cultural imperialism or commercial exploitation often gives back the energy to unite community stakeholders.
4. Have a clear goal what you want to do with the ICH inscription. As we have seen smaller nations like Jamaica and Ireland have strong cultural identity and significant reach through their diasporic culture. Claiming heritage is a means of ensuring that culture is reinforced within an era of globalisation.

Acknowledgements My thanks to Dr Cuffy for inviting me to give this keynote at the Creole Fest: Building Bridges Across Borders, November 9–10, 2018. The conference was supported by AHRC grant (PI Dr Violet Cuffy and Co-I Dr Jane Carr) Dominica as a Centre of Excellence for the Preservation & Celebration of the Creole Culture through Language, the Arts & its Indigenous Kalinagos. AH/R004498/1

Note

1. Male authorship implicit in the use of the term 'Masterpieces' is problematic.

References

ACIJ/JMB. (2021). *Jamaica Memory Bank*. Retrieved June 25, 2021, from https://memorybankja.org.jm/terms-of-service.

Anderson, B. (1983). *Imagined Communities: Reflections on the Origins and Spread of Nationalism*. Verso.

Anon. (2017, May 31). Revised National Culture Policy Drafted. *Jamaica Observer*. Retrieved June 25, 2021, from https://www.jamaicaobserver.com/latestnews/revised_national_culture_policy_drafted

Ashton of Hyde, L. (2017) *Convention for the Safeguarding of the Intangible Cultural Heritage: Written question—HL6360*. Department for Culture, Media and Sport. Retrieved June 25, 2021, from http://www.parliament.uk/business/publications/written-questions-answers-statements/written-question/Lords/2017-03-27/HL6360/

Austria. (2018). Immaterielles Kulturerbe: Bräuche, Wissen, Handwerkstechniken. Retrieved June 25, 2021, from https://www.unesco.at/kultur/immaterielles-kulturerbe/artikel/cat/12/

Bortolotto, C. (2012). The French Inventory of Intangible Cultural Heritage: Domesticating a Global Paradigm into French Heritage Regime. In A. Eggert, R. F. Bendix, & A. Peselmann (Eds.), *Heritage Regimes and The State* (pp. 265–282). Göttingen University Press.

Cuccia, T. (2020). Intangible Cultural Heritage. In R. Towse & T. N. Hernández (Eds.), *Handbook of Cultural Economics* (3rd ed.). EdgarOnline.

Estonia. (2018). Eesti vaimse kultuuripärandi nimistu. Retrieved June 25, 2021, from http://www.rahvakultuur.ee/vkpnimistu/

Ferdinand, G. D. (2017). *Brand in the Caribbean: A Cultural Analysis of the Regional Creative Economy*. University of Warwick.

Finland, Finnish Ministry of Education and Culture. (2017). *Intangible Cultural Heritage: Implementation in Finland*. Retrieved June 25, 2021, from http://www.aineetonkulttuuriperinto.fi/en/implementation

Florida, R. (2002). *The Rise of the Creative Class*. Basic Books.

JIS Ministry of Culture, Gender, Entertainment and Sport. (2018, June 6). Jamaica Successful in Bid for Seat on Another UNESCO Committee. *Jamaica Information Service*. Retrieved June 25, 2021, from https://jis.gov.jm/jamaica-successful-in-bid-for-seat-on-another-unesco-committee/

Kurin, R. (2004). Safeguarding Intangible Cultural Heritage in the 2003 UNESCO Convention: A Critical Appraisal. *Museum International, 56*(1–2), 66–77.

Lints, M. (2019). Inscription of Creole Cultures to the Intangible Cultural Heritage of UNESCO, Slide Share. Retrieved June 25, 2021, from https://europa.eu/capacity4dev/creoles-cultures-kiltir-kreol-cultures-cr-oles/wiki/inscription-creole-cultures-intangible-cultural-heritage-unesco

Park, S. C. (2014). ICHPEDIA, A Case Study in Community Engagement in the Safeguarding of ICH Online. *International Journal of Intangible Heritage, 9*, 70–82.

Rabess, G. (1998). Popular media and policy in the Eastern Caribbean. *International Journal of Cultural Policy, 4*(2), 431–453.

Scotland, Museums and Galleries. (2011). *From First Footing to Faeries*. Retrieved June 25, 2021, from ichscotland.org/

Scotland, Museums and Galleries. (2018). Intangible Cultural Heritage (ICH). Retrieved June 02, 2019, from https://www.museumsgalleriesscotland.org.uk/projects/intangible-cultural-heritage/

Singapore, National Heritage Board. (2016). *Roots: Inventory of Intangible Cultural Heritage*. Retrieved June 02, 2019, from roots.sg/ICH

Sint Maarten, Department of Culture & Sint Maarten National Commission of UNESCO. (2016). *Intangible Cultural Heritage Inventory*. Retrieved June 02, 2019, from http://www.sintmaartengov.org/government/ECYS/Pages/Intangible-Cultural-Heritage-Inventory.aspx

Snapes, L. (2018, November 29). UN Adds Reggae Music to List of International Cultural Treasures; Jamaica's Distinctive Beat has Furthered "International Discourse on Injustice", Says Unesco—While Devotees Praise it for Breaking Down Colonial Race Barriers. *The Guardian*.

Spence, K.-M. (2019). When Money is not Enough: Reggae, Dancehall, and Policy in Jamaica. *The Journal of Arts Management, Law, and Society, 49*(1), 45–60.

Sri Lanka. (2017) *National Inventory of the Intangible Cultural Heritage of Sri Lanka*. Retrieved June 25, 2021, from http://www.natlib.lk/home/ich_ni.php

Ukaegbu, V. (2017). Post-Colonialism and Performance: Political, Cultural and Pedagogic Legacies and Constraints. *Repertório, Salvador, 20*(29), 12–34.

UNESCO. (2003a). *What is Intangible Cultural Heritage*? Retrieved June 25, 2021, from https://ich.unesco.org/en/what-is-intangible-heritage-00003

UNESCO. (2003b, October 17) *Convention for the Safeguarding of the Intangible Cultural Heritage 2003*, Retrieved June 25, 2021, from portal.unesco.org/en/ev.php-URL_ID=17716&URL_DO=DO_TOPIC&URL_SECTION=201.html

UNESCO. (2003c). Intangible Heritage Domains in the 2003 Convention. Intangible Heritage Domains in the 2003 Convention—Intangible Heritage—Culture Sector—UNESCO. Retrieved March 12, 2018, from https://ich.unesco.org/en/intangible-heritage domains-00052

UNESCO. (2017a). Gwoka: Music, Song, Dance and Cultural Practice Representative of Guadeloupean Identity. Retrieved March 12, 2018, from https://ich.unesco.org/en/RL/gwoka-music-song-dance-and-cultural-practice-representative-of-guadeloupean-identity-00991

UNESCO. (2017b). Uilleann Piping. Retrieved March 12, 2018, from https://ich.unesco.org/en/RL/uilleann-piping-01264

Vilanova, J. (2019). "Kingston Be Wise:" Jamaica's Reggae Revival, Musical Livity, and Troubling Temporality in the Modern Global Music Industry. *International Journal of Communication, 13*, 4087–4106.

Waelde, C. (2018). ICH and Human Rights: ICH, Contemporary Culture and Human Rights. In C. Waelde, C. Cummings, M. Pavis, & H. Enright (Eds.), *Research Handbook on Contemporary Intangible Cultural Heritage: Law and Heritage*. EdgarOnline. https://doi.org/10.4337/9781786434012

Weedon, A. (2020). Restructuring the Knowledge Production Value Chain in Publishing in UNESCO Education Sector (ed.), *Humanistic Futures of*

Learning: Perspectives from UNESCO Chairs and UNITWIN Networks (pp. 203–206). Retrieved June 25, 2021, from https://unesdoc.unesco.org/ark:/48223/pf0000372577/PDF/372577eng.pdf.multi

Whatley, S., Waelde, C., Brown, A., & Harmon, S. (2015). Validation and Virtuosity: Perspectives on Difference and Authorship/Control in Dance. *Choreographic Practices, 6*(1), 59–83.

Winter, T., & Keegan-Phipps, S. (2013). *Performing Englishness: Identity and Politics in a Contemporary Folk Resurgence*. Manchester University Press.

CHAPTER 3

The Rejuvenation of Arts and Culture Through Folklore

Penda Thérésia Choppy

1 Introduction

Folklore, or orature, has been linked to group identity and homogeneity (Peek & Yankah, 2005). In each specific society, folklore is functional, not just for entertainment. This functionality is even more important in the context of Creole societies because they have been formed from disparate groups of people in situations of dominance and resistance, exploitation and retaliation. This is evident in the different genres of oral expression: the twist in the tale of the anti-hero, which subverts power to the underdog, the verbal repartee of proverbs and riddles, which creates innuendoes of everyday life, the loaded messages of popular songs. This is creolization in action—the latent power of a cultural revolution. It is the coming together of different groups and, in the face of adversity, forming a new unity through the necessity to adapt, and subsequently, to survive.

European civilization is deeply woven into the fabric of Creole culture; but in European paradigms, folklore has for a long time been associated

P. T. Choppy (✉)
University of Seychelles, Victoria, Seychelles
e-mail: penda.choppy@unisey.ac.s

V. Cuffy, J. Carr (eds.), *Creole Cultures, Vol. 1*,
https://doi.org/10.1007/978-3-031-24275-5_3

with an earlier and more primitive stage of civilization (Bascom, 1953). Folklore is marginalized in the twenty-first century (Haring, 2018). Since Creole culture derives from the folklore and folk life of different marginalized groups, it may be embraced by them as a source of identity creation. Alternatively, they may reject it as a source of stigma. Yet, from the perspective of a modern, globalized (European-influenced) world, it may also be seen as irrelevant. Alternatively, if in fact, Creole folklore or orature remains functional, it might be a source of rejuvenation for contemporary Creole culture. In this chapter, the enduring functionality of Creole orature is illustrated through several examples from Seychelles.

2 Orature as Palimpsests of the Creole Experience

Creole orature is like an onion. It consists of layers of expression and cultural practices, inherited from the Old World and recreated or adapted to suit new situations and environments in the New World (Choppy, 2018). For example, in his discussion of West-Indian oral art forms, Kamau Brathwaite makes clear links between what he calls 'this belly/drum centred performance' in the Caribbean Anansi narrations and the Anansi of the Akan and of the Ashanti (1993, p.75). As such, orature, in Creole societies, might be compared to an archaeological site; the etymologies of words, the contexts in which they are used, the people to whom they refer, and interactions they describe, reveal different layers of historical experience and significance, placed on top of one another like a palimpsest.

It is for this reason that I disagree with some Caribbean theories that Creole orature has been cut off from its roots because of slavery. Caribbean creolist, Raphael Confiant says that the solid foundation of mythology preceding history is lacking in the Creole cultures of the New World, both in the Americas and the Indian Ocean (Confiant, 1998, p. 13). By this, he means that Creole cultures lack the specific rituals and practices that Ngugi Wa Thiong'o, as an African writer, for example, identifies as grounding his own culture (Ngugi, 1986, pp. 10–11). In Ngugi's tradition, songs, proverbs and other folkloric practices were associated with specific rituals that dated back to antiquity.

In early Creole societies, different genres of orature were also attached to specific traditions and rituals that gave them significance, even though they could not of course, be used in the same way that they had been used in the Old World. For example, people were regaled with proverbs, riddles and folktales at traditional wakes in both the Caribbean and the Indian

Ocean. The older generation also taught the younger generation traditional values through these art forms (Carpooran, 2013; Confiant, 1998). In the Old World, especially the Old World of the slaves, these art forms had had a specific function. Ngugi, for example, describes African drama as 'having its origins in the human struggle with nature and others' (Ngugi, 1986, pp. 36–37). He mentions rites performed during harvests, at births, deaths and during the struggle against natural disasters and human invasions as well as against internal enemies such as idlers or evil doers. He notes that the media by which they were acted out included oral forms such as songs, mimes, poetry and stories. Ngugi also emphasizes the important role of orature in language development: 'Our appreciation of the suggestive magical power of language was reinforced by the games we played with words through riddles, proverbs, transpositions of syllables, or through nonsensical but musically arranged words' (Ngugi, 1986, p. 11). From Ngugi's viewpoint, language is the essence of culture; and orature, which nourishes language, might be seen as the manure that feeds cultures and situates them firmly with roots in a particular tradition. This is illustrated in the example given by Brathwaite of the Ashanti's creation stories involving Anansi the Spider Man (1993, p. 75).

The sad fact, however, is that in many cases, Creole slave descendants have come to alienate themselves from such mythical heroes as Anansi because the hero has become the anti-hero: in their psyche, the slave has replaced the hero. This is possibly why Creole societies often reject oral traditions as a source of culture. In the Caribbean, Brathwaite feels that the folk tradition inherited from Africa or created locally is marginalized because of the valorization of Euro-American cultural forms. He sees this attitude as difficult to counter or erase:

> The resistance to the calypso and related West Indian indigenous forms by West Indians is and continues to be, it seems to me, a very real and pervasive thing.
>
> Brathwaite (1993, p. 730)

He cites the criticism against the growing popularity of the calypso in the 1950s, which dismissed such traditions as 'debased', 'hybrid', or peripheral, 'formless' forms (1993, p. 73). What seems to most concern him is the reason given for the objection to oral forms that were seen as being 'belly-centred bawdy' (Brathwaite, 1993, p. 74): this being the fear of attack on the moral standards of the middle class. Referring to a statement made by Derek Walcott and reported by George Odlum (1967), Brathwaite suggests that the declaration that 'we must teach our philosophy to reach above the navel' represents just such a middle-class fear (Brathwaite, 1993, p. 74).[1] Yet, it is this very 'belly-centred bawdy' of Caribbean folklore and cultural practices that give well-known Caribbean writers and performers, such as Miss Lou and Sparrow the Calypsonian, their vitality and creativity. It is for this reason that Brathwaite proposes indigenous African and Caribbean folklore as an alternative to the English Romantic/Victorian traditions (Brathwaite, 1993, pp. 72–74).

This is why the Martinican creolists identified Creole orature as 'the wicks capable of bringing sparks to our obscurities' (Bernabé et al., 1990, p. 887). In spite of being firm believers in the Creole's ability to create his own myths (after having had his original myths amputated by slavery and French cultural domination), they acknowledge the role of the orature buried deep within the slaves' memories, in the birth of what they call a truly Caribbean literature:

> This situation is not imputable to the mere political domination; it can also be explained by the fact that our truth found itself behind bars, in the deep bottom of ourselves, unknown to our consciousness and to the artistically free reading of the world in which we live.
>
> Bernabé et al. (1990, p. 886)

Gilbert Gratiant's *Fab Compè Zicaque* (1958) is such an example. Gratiant is praised, along with other writers of his era, as the 'precious keepers' of 'the disarranged pieces of pottery, of the lost drawings, of the distorted shapes: of this ruined city which is our foundation' (Bernabé et al., 1990, pp. 886–888).

3 Tapping the Power of Orature

In spite of the wariness with which the different aspects of oral traditions are approached in various Creole societies, they still have a fundamental role to play in the everyday lives of Creole people. They are there in the jubilance of jazz, the music of the freed Negro, as Brathwaite suggests (1993, p. 55). They are there in the lamentations and jubilations of the Seychelles 'moutya', in the rhythm of Creole poetry and in the rhetoric of politicians.

The latent power of language in the written tradition is often exploited and the same can be said for orature in its diverse forms—'in political language, ethical language and, most particularly, didactism, all of which involve an attempt to make the listener think or act in a certain way' (Furniss, 2008, p. 132). This is evident in the appropriation of oral forms by the state, corporate organizations or social groups for specific purposes to suit their own agenda. The praise song, for example, may be 'in an instant, transformed into innuendo or vilification', so that the subject, who is usually acted upon, becomes the wielder of power (Furniss & Gunner, 2008, p. 6). Even the more ordinary forms of orature have this power. Furniss and Gunner refer to John W. Johnson's discussion of Somali work songs, which in the Somali tradition, are supposed to help only in doing work. Nevertheless, such a song was played on the radio at an crucial moment during parliamentary votes, influencing the mood of the MPs and leading to a change of Prime Minister (Furniss & Gunner, 2008, p. 11).

The Caribbean calypso may be used to wield a power of this kind as in the vote-them-out calypsos of the 1980s. An example is Cro Cro's 1988 hit song, 'Three Bo Rats', sung at the Dimanche Gras.

> My predictions were great now I could sing bold
> Ah know that 3 big bo rats could never live in one hole Ah tell them clear the air
> The public say that they want to hear
> If yah doh end like we on them racial affairs I demand that you call elections this year.
> Greaves (1998)

The point Cro was making was that: (i) he was right that the three leaders of former political parties could not coexist peacefully in one party with one leader, (ii) the leaders should stop the racial fighting among themselves, or the people will demand a new election. Likewise, opposition politicians gave the ruling party in Seychelles a warning after the introduction of multi-party democracy in 1993 by using a moutya song as propaganda: *Sa ki anler i kapab desann, sa ki anba i kapab monte* (Those who are on top can come down, those who are at the bottom can go up). In the 2020 general elections, they made good on this promise, winning a majority in both the National Assembly and the Presidential election, which gave them both legislative and executive power.

4 Seychellois Orature and Its Origins

Seychellois society, though comprising of one of the world's smallest populations, is nevertheless one of the most intensely creolized cultures today. The creolization process began with the introduction of slavery in the eighteenth century, when a wide range of people of African ethnicities, from Eastern, Central and even Western Africa were brought in as slaves by French settlers. The slaves also included Malagasies, already creolized from their source, having mixed Bantu origins and original Malagasy tribes (Michaelis et al., 2013; Baker, 1982). Since the slaves were obliged to mix with the white settlers culturally (and inevitably, genetically), having to serve them, and work for them, and thus having to use their language, the result was an amalgamation of cultural practices and folklore.

The Seychelles Culture Department lists the following French oral forms as part of the Creole cultural heritage: 'romans' (old French folk songs), 'ronn' (from French, 'rondes', being folk songs danced in a ring) and some lullabies. To this list, can be added wedding speeches and some French expressions that have entered the Creole language whole-piece. 'Semafot', 'c'est ma faute' in French, is one such example (It's my error—used to express regret and accompanied by the gesture of pressing a closed fist to the chest thrice whilst reciting the expression). Some Creole forms include 'zistwar' (stories), fab (fables), 'bersez' (lullabies), 'zedmo' (riddles) and 'proverb' (proverbs), of mixed French and African origins. In addition, there are dance genres including European-influenced kontredans (country-dance). While the 'sega' (a dance where the feet are placed close together with emphasis on hip movements), 'moutya' (a dance where the feet are placed wide apart with emphasis on the movement of the backside), 'sokwe' (masked dance) and 'tinge' (martial arts dance) are all of African origins (Mahoune, 2007).

In the language of the Seychellois people, that is, Kreol, though strongly dominated by a French lexicon, some words betray their Malagasy or Bantu origins: for example, 'kanbar'(yam) from kambara in Malagasy and 'toto' from 'mtoto' (child) in Swahili (Michaelis et al., 2013). Bollée's etymological dictionary (1993) gives some samples from Hindi, for example, 'zonblon' from 'jambūla', meaning 'rose apple', and from Cantonese, 'siav' from 'shi yau', meaning soy sauce. In contradistinction to the argument that Creole societies lack connection to mythical sources of prehistory due to their erosion during slavery, a glimpse of this prehistory is found in some African or Malagasy words in the Seychelles Creole lexicon.

The D'Offay/Lionnet dictionary, for example, defines Boya as a traditional dance for raising the dead (1982, p. 58). Indeed, a cultural animator of La Digue Island, Mr Andreix Rosalie, confirms that the dance evolved from a myth about a man called Boya who was resuscitated. The dance was performed in the 1980s by the La Digue Cultural Troupe on National TV.

These examples demonstrate how the slave has not only assimilated the language of the master but has transformed it in his own recreation of myths and customs from his original culture, giving it a local flavour.

5 Some Samples of Seychellois Culture and Their Evolution

The Seychellois kontredans is believed to be an adaptation of the French quadrille and other European 'court dances' brought in by European settlers (Valentin, Keven, 2004, pp. 1–2). It represents a transformation that took place over the course of the population's history in that it is now danced by descendants of slaves, white settlers and other ethnicities. This is not only due to the dissolving of social barriers, but also because of the genetic and cultural mixing that has formed the population. The instructions in the songs have remained in French—'*en avant les deux cavaliers*!', or 'dos a dos, pas a pas'—but they have been embellished by witty Creole inserts: 'Pardon manman, zanmen mon a fer ankor zot!' (Forgive me Mother; never will I do it again). These inserts are thrown in during lulls when the dancers are following a specific instruction, for example, during 'la *chaine des dames*' when the ladies weave their way around their male partners (Valentin, 2004, p, 8).

In the folktale genre, the Seychellois trickster hero, 'Soungoula' originates from the Swahili 'Sungura', which means 'Hare' (Choppy & Salomon, 2004). This character has also been traced back to the Yao and Nyanja peoples (Baker, 1993, p. 145; Haring, 2005, p. 294). Haring claims that at least 45 folk tales recorded in Seychelles are of African origins (2003, p. 4). These include versions of the most well-known trickster tales like the Tarbaby and a widespread East African story which Haring calls 'The Defiant Girl' but is known in the Western Indian Ocean Islands as 'Tizan, Zann ek Loulou' (Little John, Jane and the Wolf) (Haring, 2005). The stories of the Seychellois trickster hero, 'Soungoula', are of two types. There are those closest to the original African versions, for example, the Tarbaby, which in Seychelles is the story of the Hare who bathed in the King's pool (Choppy & Salomon, 2004, pp. 25–31). There are also those invented in Seychelles that show distinct aspects of Seychellois society; for example, the story of 'Soungoula' in the guise of a Canadian businessman who calls himself, Greyboy Mr Grey (but whose real name is Gribouy Mistigri). This modern 'Soungoula' enjoys the luxury of hotel living for one whole week and speaks of his vast empire of car factories and airlines, before making his escape back to his tree hole in the forest, leaving his bill unpaid (Creole Institute, 1990, pp. 33–45). In adapting the African trickster hero to a modern Seychelles, this story illustrates the fact that 'Soungoula' has managed to escape the confines of the traditional plantation environment of early Creole societies and is thus evidence of a dynamic Creole culture.

The merging of cultures in the historical and physical environment of Seychelles resulted in an orature that reflects the adoption and adaptation in the New World, of languages and cultures from both European and African continents. Rites, customs, music, song, dance and different forms of expression remembered from the Old World continued to play an important role in the lives of both colonizers and slaves, and people who did not fit neatly into either category.

6 Folklore and Seychellois National Identity

The folklore of Seychelles is a testimony of the Seychellois people's traumatic experience as a society created out of slavery and colonialism, a testimony of their efforts to adapt and create new identities in the face of changing historical and political landscapes. In the decolonization period of the country's history, especially with the accession of the Second Republic in 1977, folklore was closely associated with national cultural identity. In the 1980s, as part of the effort to address the problem of cultural alienation common to post-slavery Creole societies, the Seychelles government made a conscious effort to collect a considerable amount of folklore through the Oral Traditions Section in the Department of Culture. One of the earliest publications of folklore of that period discusses elements of the Seychellois folkloric heritage that were suppressed under the colonial government, namely genres originating from Africa and Madagascar. These were promoted as part of the national cultural heritage (Diallo et al., 1981). This went hand in hand with the promotion of the medium of expression of these formerly suppressed genres: the people's language, Kreol. This is exemplified by its recognition as a national language and the Seychellois mother tongue in 1981 and, most importantly, its introduction in formal education in 1982 (Choppy, 2005).

In spite of the early association of folklore with cultural identity, this aspect of culture appears to have lost ground with time. Because of the fast pace of social change in Seychelles, many Seychellois are becoming less aware and less knowledgeable about the cultural traits that make them who they are, especially, how their folklore interacts with their everyday lives. By the start of the twenty-first century, the practice of folkloric traditions had petered off considerably and the large repertoire of folkloric data collected during the enthusiastic years was collecting dust in little used documentation centres (Haring, 2003).

7 Orature and Folklore as a Source of Modern Culture and Cultural Rejuvenation

As for the theory that orality is dissociated from modernity, Herbert Chimhundu cites several instances of proverb-like song titles on the contemporary Shona music scene that seem to explode that myth (Okavango Boys, Patrick Mukwamba, The Bhundu Boys). He suggests the updating of proverbs as an example of the continuation of oral traditions:

> Proverb coining by singers may also be compared with what happens in slang when young people substitute lexical items in older proverbs with new ones to incorporate new imagery reflecting a new environment and changed circumstances [...]. In this way, a symbiosis is established between lexis and ecology.
>
> Chimhundu (2008, p. 153)

Although in Seychelles, there are indications that folklore is often associated with backwardness (Choppy, 2018), there is an increasing tendency among Seychellois artists to use different forms of folklore as sources for new, popular forms of culture. Younger artists often engage with the older generation of artists, or tap into oral sources, to enrich their work, or simply revamp existing oral expressions in new, exciting ways that are enticing to the younger generation. This development provides new possibilities for earlier forms of Seychellois culture to evolve and survive, even in the midst of globalization. Some examples are given in the following case studies.

Case Study 1: Seychellois Proverbs

Proverbs are being used as a source of cultural rejuvenation in Seychelles, mainly in the music scene. Older musicians often suggest that the younger generation's imitation of rap, raga (for instance), is a danger to our traditional culture. However, young composers are engaging their own generation in the local culture through their adaptation of modern black music forms to Seychellois contexts, for example, in the use of old proverbs. Rapper Jarimba used several proverbs in his song *Tou lekontrer* (All the contrary) on his new album *Douler Lo Zot* (Tough on Them) (Jarimba, 2016). *Pa tou bon lezo ki tonm dan lagel en bon lisyen* (Not every good dog gets a good bone) and *Si ou kras dan lezer i a tonm lo ou menm* (If you spit up, it will fall back on you) are two such proverbs used in this song. Both are well-known Seychellois proverbs though they were not commonly used among the youths until Jarimba renewed their popularity. Jarimba was using these proverbs to pass on a message to fellow youths in his circle, as well as people perceived as power-wielders in society. In an interview with Seychelles News Agency (SNA), he also says that he taps from Seychelles Creole because it is his identity and it is what makes his songs unique, and he advises younger artists that this is how they can be original and be themselves (Bonnelame, 2017). Similarly, popular rapper, Elijah, also created a jingle out of an old proverb, *Delo lo fey sonz* ('Water on a taro leaf'—being equivalent to 'water off a duck's back' in English), to pass on a message to a perceived rival. Both artists participate in a developing tradition of renewing older forms of Creole in a medium, that is, popular music, that will help the survival of the language and culture rather than killing it. Without music, Creole would lose much of its relevance to a good part of the younger generation. In spite of the heavy influence of English in contemporary popular culture (e.g., videogames, international popular music, blockbuster films, etc. are mostly in English), youth music is a medium by which young people relate to each other in Creole.

Case Study 2: Seychellois Riddles

A second example of cultural rejuvenation through orature is the Creole Institute's creation of new Creole riddles, using old Creole expressions as the main source. The Creole Institute of Seychelles was created in 1987 to promote and assist the development of Seychelles Creole (SC) in all its dimensions (Bollée, 2007, p. 15). One of its enduring programmes is a series of language activities targeting primary and secondary pupils to improve their knowledge and use of kreol. Orature is included in their annual quiz programmes for secondary school students. The following examples show how Kreol expressions can be played with to create enigmas.

Example 1

> Mon premye i sant kat-r-er bomaten (kok) Mon dezyenm i esansyelpour en vwalye (ma) Mon trwazyenm i fer letour parey lalyans (ron)
>
> *Mon tou i pa en poulayer. Lekel mwan? (* ***Kokmaron*** *)* (Creole Institute, Seychelles)

> My first sings at four o'clock in the morning (The cockerel) My second is essential for the sailing ship (The mast)
>
> My third goes round like the wedding ring (A round shape)
>
> My all is not a family man. Who am I? (A bachelor/playboy [in kreol, wild cockerel])

In this example, the concept of 'maron', which in Seychellois expression is associated with the wild (referencing the escaped 'maroon' slaves of the past) is extended to simply being the opposite of the domesticated. In English, this riddle does not make much sense, because it relies on a phonetic and semantic play on words in Kreol. The answer to the first part of the enigma is the cockerel ('kok'), with the question establishing a well-known phenomenon of the Creole world, that is the cockerel that sings at four o'clock in the morning, waking up fishermen and labourers who need an early start on the day. The second part is the mast ('ma'), without which a sailboat cannot move. The third part is the shape of the wedding ring, which is round ('ron'). Ironically, this part of the question also alludes to the final answer: 'Fer letour' also connotes infidelity or going around (contrary to the symbolism of fidelity in the closed ring), the opposite of what should happen when one is wearing a wedding ring. The answer to the enigma is in the amalgamation of all three syllables in the order in which they have been given, and a final clue is offered by giving the opposite concept of the answer, which in this case is 'poulayer' (the domesticated cockerel or family man). The answer thus is the bachelor or playboy, which in traditional Creole terms is the wild cockerel ('kok maron'). In Kreol/SC, a 'poulayer 'is a cockerel that stays in the 'poulaye' (chicken coop) and does not go wandering around like the wild cockerel. Everything about this enigma reveals the creolization process during the plantation or homestead era when concepts about everyday life were established. There were the domesticated aspects of the homestead, as in the animals and plants, and their opposites in the wild. These local concepts were soon borrowed to refer to human beings and their behaviour. The most common use of 'poulayer' and 'kokmaron' was on the outer islands in the pre-independence era when the men who had wives were known as 'poulayer' and those who didn't and thus sought sexual release from house to house, were coined, 'kokmaron'. The existence of the 'kokmaron' has become an accepted part of everyday life in creole society, without retaining the original connotation of maroons in a slave society, in the root word, maron.[2]

The second example is a play on the term 'gran nwanr'.

> Mon premye i azout ek sif pour dir ler (er) Mon dezyenm pa o (ba)
> *Mon trwazyenm i en fler (lis)*
> *Mon tou i en* ***grannwanr*** *ki sonny dimoun*
> *Lekel mwan? (****erbalis****).* (Creole Institute, Seychelles)

> My first is added to a number to tell the time (hour) My second is not high (low)
> My third is a flower (lily)
> My all is an old sage who heals people. What am I? (Herbalist).

'Grannwanr' literally means the big/tall/great black. Both editions of the Lionnet/de St. Jorre dictionary (1982, 1999) have only one definition for grannwar: male adult. The following riddle illustrates this context: Pti ki mon pti, mon fer taye grannwanr? → Mous zonn (Diallo et al., 2001). (As small as I am, I can scatter big men? → The wasp). The contextual meaning is clear: the little wasp can scare grown men. The paradox of size emphasizes the fact that the subject being acted upon, that is, the grannwanr, is an able-bodied man, or an adult who should normally be capable of coping with fear or pain. This meaning applies to every male adult, irrelevant of colour, class or race, and it is the first important difference in the scope of meaning between 'gran nwar' and 'gran blan'. 'Gran blan' is limited to the white propertied upper class, preferably with direct unsullied links to France (de Commarmond & Gillieaux, 2004, p. 10).

However, gran nwar is hardly used in its literal context, and it has eventually come to mean all male adults.

Grannwanr has also come to connote an old sage or a man of wisdom. This is in fact the first listed meaning in the Creole Institute monolingual dictionary: grannwanr 1 n (i) a man of wisdom and knowledge. The well-known herbalist, Mr Charles Zialor, is known as a 'grannwanr' decades after his decease because of his knowledge of herbal medicine (Wilks, 1998). As the first definition of the monolingual Kreol/SC dictionary, this represents the link to the idea of greatness or influence as found in 'gran blan'. It connotes a sense of respect for an individual. It probably emerged as a term of respect for older black males who showed a certain amount of wisdom but has gradually come to apply to all men of wisdom, irrespective of race. It is probably the consciousness of this meaning of grannwanr that influenced the Creole Institute's coining of the riddle.

Thus, the answer to the first part of the riddle is 'er' (hour), or more specifically, it is the equivalent of o'clock when telling the time, for example, 'enn er', 'senk er' (one o'clock, five o'clock). The second part represents the opposite of high, which in kreol/SC is 'ba' (low). The third part refers to the most well-known flower of the French empire, the lily (in kreol/SC, lis). The three together form the syllables of the herbalist in kreol/SC, 'erbalis'. However, in this study, the most significant aspect of this riddle is its description of the herbalist as a grannwanr (old sage) 'ki sonny dimoun' (who heals people). The use of the term 'grannwanr' defines the riddle and grounds it firmly in the Seychellois cultural context in a riddle that enhances the Seychellois traditional folklore. Its use in language activities with secondary school students, who might otherwise not have made much use of it in their everyday interactions, ensures its rejuvenation in the younger generation.

Case Study 3: Folktales

Another aspect of folklore that inspires artists and promoters of local culture in modern Seychelles is the folktale genre. Theatre and visual arts are two genres that have tapped from this source. During the 1995 Creole Festival, local playwright and theatre director, Christian Servina, staged a play based on a folktale entitled 'Sen Disparet' (The Disappearing Saint) (Lemiel, 2008). Marie-Therese Choppy, another well-known playwright also wrote a play in 2007, based on our well-loved trickster hero, 'Soungoula', exploiting the story of the soiling of the king's pool (Choppy

& Salomon, 2004, pp. 25–31). It won a local literary award and was staged during the Creole Festival, in 2009. The popularity of this story, which is one of the oldest forms of this genre, is reflected in its appearance even in the visual arts, through Colbert Nourrice's renditions of the high points of the story, as illustrated below.

Both Figs. 3.1 and 3.2 are bordered by a running 'Soungoula', which reflects his tendency to always be able to escape his fate. Figure 3.1 shows 'Soungoula' stuck on Brer' Tortoise's back and being judged by the king. It is significant that the inner borders depict him as being surrounded by his captor, Brer' Tortoise, and the king's soldiers. However, the outer border shows him on the run as usual, which might signify his final escape. Figure 3.2 again shows 'Soungoula' being judged by the king, whilst he is stuck on Tortoise's back, but he is the dominating feature in the painting, with his diversion tool, which is a bottle of homemade honey liquor, which knocks the guardian of the pool out cold. This is the most convoluted and by far, the most loved of all 'Soungoula' stories in Seychelles. Its immortalization in Colbert Nourrice's paintings guarantee a good source of reference for the story.

Fig. 3.1 Soungoula's capture by Brer' Tortoise and his judgement at the King's palace, followed by his escape (Source: Colbert Nourrice)

Fig. 3.2 Soungoula's temptation of the guardian at the King's pool (Source: Colbert Nourrice)

Case Study 4: Music

Coming back to music, this time in its own right as a form of oral expression, it is in this genre that cultural rejuvenation, through the use of folklore and orature is most effective. Apart from youths tapping into oral traditions to enrich contemporary and less traditional productions, an evolved form of traditional music has emerged through remakes of older and very traditional versions of old songs and music by popular traditional artists. Take for example, the music of celebrated traditional musician, 'Ton Pa' (Jacob Marie, 1908–1994) who is best known for his mastery of ancient instruments of African heritage, the 'bobre' and the 'zez', which are now no longer in use (Parent, 2018, p. 28). His music is rejuvenated through popular singer and musician, Jean-Marc Volcy. The song 'Kanbar maron' (wild yam) is now quite popular on the local radio and is also circulated via CD sales. In 2018, Volcy's and Ton Pa's renditions of several of the latter's songs were the subject of a television programme which reacquainted current generations with Ton Pa's lyrics and type of music, thus allowing them to appreciate it. This appreciation of the traditional genre might not have been possible without Volcy's remake—but tapping from the traditional source has also permitted Volcy to create his particular brand of traditional music that has earned him his current popularity. This type of rejuvenation occurs even among the Seychellois diaspora, as exemplified by Grace Barbé's rendition of the 'Mardilo' song. Barbé is very popular in the Seychellois community in Australia and is often active in the Australian version of the Seychelles Creole Festival. The 'Mardilo' song is associated with traditional group 'Masezarin' from the island of La Digue (the third most populated island in Seychelles). The modern remake of the song not only exploits the lyrics and rhythm in a new way but also includes the traditional version of the original song. This mix of the modern and the traditional not only allows the new generation to enjoy a form of music that they can identify as their own but also allows them to sample the more traditional version. This would otherwise not be accessible to the ordinary layman except on special occasions such as the Creole Festival, and even then, only if it happens to be featured in a particular programme. The Mardilo song, which is also a game that is danced, might be said to have been a lost tradition from the 'Old World', that is, pre-slavery, pre-settlement era. In a television programme in 2017, the matriarch of the 'Masezarin' group, Mrs Fernande Ladouce, said that she remembered the dance from childhood, and she passed it on to her daughter, Molly. The 'Mardilo' song and dance then became emblematic of Masezarin's cultural performances, both for the local and the tourist audience. Grace Barbé's reinterpretation of this song gives it a new dimension that makes it more likely to survive in a society that is constantly buffeted by the effects of modernization and globalization. Such is the power of orature if it is properly used.

8 Conclusion

As observed by Kriel, 'oral literature is not at all that traditional and static but living and changing all the time' (Kriel, 1971, p. 18). In that respect, one might say that orature may be considered as revealing layers of the postcolonial experience like a palimpsest. In borrowing from the oral tradition that is more ancient, contemporary culture in postcolonial societies, inclusive of the written tradition, is also a palimpsest (Choppy, 2018). The use of this invaluable source by artists, academics and cultural practitioners in current Creole societies will not only inspire their creations but also ensure the continuity of the Creole heritage. This is especially important in an age when globalization and technology are helping to erode traditional culture in the global south. This erosion is what will ensure that the global south, as Cohen puts it, remains at the peripheries of the global north, from whence the more dominant metropolitan trends and technological advancement are emerging (Cohen, 2007). Creole societies, especially Creole societies that are also small island states and more subject to westernization because of their colonial past and history of slavery, stand to lose more by allowing their sources of oral literature to dry out. In global markets, the only way that such societies can compete with the metropoles of the world and other 'destinations' similar to their own particularities is by tapping into their oral traditions. Since tourism features largely in most of these societies, they can transform their oral traditions into an economic advantage—both locally and abroad. This will help in the endeavour to ensure cultural and economic sustainability. Even though Cohen says that 'Creolization is a never-ending process, and cultural innovation is inevitable' (2007), this process should encompass each society's peculiarities, more often than not, represented by their oral traditions. This is the heritage that must be passed down to the younger generation, thus ensuring both diversity and uniqueness.

Notes

1. Brathwaite refers to a meeting of The Caribbean Artists Movement in April 1967, London, during which George Odlum made these declarations. Source—CAM tapes, 1967.
2. The agglutinated word in the Creole Institute dictionary is defined as the bachelor or playboy, whilst the compound noun written in two words is defined as the wild cockerel.

References

Baker, P. (1982). *The Contribution of Non-Francophone Immigrants to the Lexicon of Mauritian Creole*, PhD Dissertation, School of Oriental and African Studies, University of London.

Baker, P. (1993). Assessing the African Contribution to French-based Creoles. In S. Mufwene (Ed.), *Africanisms in Afro-American Language Varieties* (pp. 123–155). University of Georgia Press.

Bascom William R. (1953, October–December). Folklore and Anthropology. *The Journal of American Folklore, 66* (262), 283–290.

Bernabé, J., Chamoiseaux, P., & Confiant, R. (1990). *In Praise of Creoleness* (Mohamed B. Taleb Khyar, Trans.). *Callaloo, 13* (4): 886–909, *The Johns Hopkins University Press,* (Online). Retrieved April 05, 2014, from http://www.jstor.org/stable/2931390

Bollée, A. (1993). *Dictionnaire étymologique des créoles français de l'Océan Indien.* Buske Verlag.

Bollée, A. (2007). *Beiträge zur Kreolistik.* Helmut Buske Verlag.

Bonnelame, B. (2017, May 29). Up Close With Best Male Artist from the Seychelles Cable Tune Awards. *Seychelles News Agency.*

Brathwaite, K. (1993). *Roots.* University of Michigan Press.

Chimhundu, H. (2008). Sexuality and Socialisation in Shona Praises and Lyrics. In G. Furniss & L. Gunner (eds.), *Power, Marginality and African Oral Literature* (2nd edn, pp. 147–161). Cambridge University Press (Online). Retrieved October 16, 2016, from www.cambridge.org/9780521480611

Choppy, P. (2005). Les Créoles face aux défis de l'éducation pour tous et de la mondialisation: Les Seychelles. Paper Presented at *XIème Colloque International des Etudes Créoles;* November, Cape Verde.

Choppy, P. (2018). *Attitudes to Slavery and Race in Seychellois Creole Oral Literature.* Masters dissertation, University of Birmingham, U.K. Retrieved January 05, 2019, from https://pdfs.semanticscholar.org/a576/1bd65390e4e26a90843d7b653d5c295cb62d.pdf.

Choppy, P., & Salomon, N. (2004). *'Soungoula' ek Bann Konper.* Creole Institute.

Cohen, R. (2007). Creolization and Cultural Globalization: The Soft Sounds of Fugitive Power. *Globalizations, 4*(3), 369–384.

Confiant, R. l. (1998) *Dictionnaire des Titim et Sirandanes.* Ibis Rouge Editions.

D'Offay, D., & Lionnet, G. (1982). *Diksyonner kreol-franse.* Kreolisch Bibliotek.

De Commarmond, O., & Gillieaux, C. (2004). *Memories of Slavery* (unpublished). Seychelles: Ministry of Education.

De St. Jorre, D., & Lionnet, G., (1999). *Diksyonner kreol – franse,* Bamberg: Imprimerie Difo-Druck.

Diallo, A. et al. (1981). *Zistwar Sesel* (Folk Tales of Seychelles). Seychelles: Oral Traditions Section, Culture Division.

Diallo, A., Rosalie, M., Essack, G., and Labiche, E., (2001). *Zedmo Sesel.* Victoria, Seychelles: National Heritage Research Section.

Furniss, G. (2008). The Power of Words and the Relation between Hausa Genres. In G. Furniss & L. Gunner (Eds.), *Power, Marginality and African Oral Literature* (pp. 130–144). Cambridge University Press.

Furniss, G., & Gunner, L. (2008). *Power, Marginality and African Oral Literature* (2nd edn). Cambridge University Press (Online). Retrieved October 16, 2014, from www.cambridge.org/9780521480611

Gratiant, G. (1958). *Fab Compè Zicaque*. Martinique: Editions Horizons CaraYbes.

Greaves, G. (1998). 'Call-response in Selected Calypsos of Political Commentary from the Republic of Trinidad and Tobago', *Journalof Black Studies, 29* (1) September, 34–50.

Haring, L. (2003). African Tales in Seychelles. In Paper Presented at the *International Society for Folk Narrative Research (ISFNR) Conference;* 13–17 August, Visby, Sweden.

Haring, L. (2005, Summer). Eastward to the Islands: The Other Diaspora. *The Journal of American Folklore, 118*(469), 290–307.

Haring, L. (2018). Among the PALMS. *Humanities, 7*(2), 44. Retrieved May 20, 2021, from https: Humanities | Special Issue: The Challenge of Folklore to the Humanities. https://www.mdpi.com/2076-0787/7/2/44

Jarimba. (2016). *Douler Lo Zot.* Extra Big Studio.

Kriel, A. (1971). *An African Horizon.* University of Cape Town Press.

Lemiel, J. (2008). *Kont ek Lezann, 9* (Tales and Legends 9). Creole Institute.

Mahoune, J. (2007). *Traditional Dances/Games of the Republic of Seychelles.* Ministry of Tourism and Culture. Retrieved October 09, 2016, from http://www.pfsr.org/seychelles-traditional-dances-games/traditional-dancesgames-of-the-republic-of-seychelles/

Michaelis, S., Maurer, P., Haspelmath, M., & Huber, H. (Eds.). (2013). *The Atlas of Pidgin and Creole Language Structures.* Oxford University Press.

Ngugi, W. T.'. O. (1986). *Decolonizing the Mind: The Politics of Language in African Literature.* Heinemann.

Odlum, G., (1976). Meeting of the Caribbean Artists' Movement, April 1967, London, UK.

Parent, M. (2018). Le moutya à l'épreuve de la modernité seychelloise: Pratiquer un genre musical emblématique dans les Seychelles d'aujourd'hui (océan Indien), phd dissertation Sociétés, Humanités, Arts et Lettres, Laboratoire Interdisciplinaire Récits, Université Côte d'Azur. Retrieved October 19, 2019, from https://tel.archives-ouvertes.fr/tel-01788777/document

Peek, P. M., & Yankah, K. (Eds.). (2005). *African Folklore: An Encyclopedia.* Routledge.

Valentin, K. (2004). *Annou Aprann Dans Kanmtole* (Country Dance Manual), Seychelles: Creole Institute.

Wilks, I. (1998). An Asante Pharmacopeia. *Ghana Studies Council, Newsletter* (11). Retrieved August 14, 2017, from http://www.ghanastudies.com/gsa/gsc98wilks.html

CHAPTER 4

Valorisation of the Intangible Creole Heritage in Mauritius: A Case Study

Didier Michel and Daniella Police-Michel

1 Introduction

The definition given to intangible cultural heritage in Chapter 1, Article 2 of the 2003 UNESCO Convention is as follows:

For the purposes of this Convention,

1. The "intangible cultural heritage" means the practices, representations, expressions, knowledge, skills—as well as the instruments, objects, artefacts and cultural spaces associated therewith—that communities, groups and, in some cases, individuals recognize as part of their cultural heritage.

D. Michel
Faculty of Law and Management, University of Mauritius, Reduit, Mauritius

D. Police-Michel (✉)
Green Reparations Foundation, Rose Hill, Mauritius
e-mail: dan.pmichel@greenreparationsfoundation.org

V. Cuffy, J. Carr (eds.), *Creole Cultures, Vol. 1*,
https://doi.org/10.1007/978-3-031-24275-5_4

In fact, 'practices, representations, expressions, knowledge, skills…' are signifying practices that refer to the concept of discourse as developed in the work of Foucault (1966, 1969).

Threadgold (1997, pp. 58–59) presents as follows, the concept of discourse in Foucault's work which has a sociological and political dimension:

> What Foucault's work did was to insist on the controlling, positioning and productive capacities of signifying practices, denying in the process the primacy of signification itself and radically unsettling common theoretical assumptions about the ways in which signifying practices operated. His work also explicitly connected the discipline of the body, the production of knowledge and the making of subjectivity.
>
> In this context, the term discourse has come to mean something that was precisely not limited to, or by, the categories of linguistics or semiotics. A discourse is a way of categorising and limiting, but also producing, the objects of which it speaks: for example, the discourse of childhood, the discourse of gender, and so on. In this broad definition of 'discourse', a discourse might be said to consist of all statements—visual, verbal, bodily—that might be made about childhood, for example.

The concept of discourse seems to be the best approach to present the uplifting of the Creole heritage in the colonial, postcolonial and Creole socio-discursive contexts.

The first part of this chapter is on the meaning of the word 'Creole' in the Mauritian context which is fundamental to understand the dynamics of the three social discourses that led progressively to the valorisation of the Creole heritage. The other three parts are on the valorisation of the Creole heritage within respectively the colonial, postcolonial and Creole discourses. In part 2, emphasis is laid on the fact that during the pre and post-independence periods (1950s to 1960s), the colonial discourse remained predominant in the Mauritian context. However, Creole music would be used as a local cultural asset to promote the tourist industry of the new state. Part 3 deals with the postcolonial discourse as developed by the Marxist and socialist political movements which valorised Creole heritage as a national heritage (1970s–1980s). The Creole discourse presented in part 4, refers to the struggle of the Mauritian descendants of African enslaved people that began in 1968, the year Mauritius acceded to independence. Their political movement for their rights and acknowledgement led to some important achievements regarding valorisation of Creole heritage.

2 On the Meaning of the Word 'Creole' in the Mauritian Context

The word 'Creole' has specific meanings that have to be underlined when referring to a specific context (Carpooran, 2002, pp. 1–14). In the multiethnic and multicultural context of Mauritius, 'Creole' (used as a noun or an adjective) designates mixed descendants of enslaved people of the country and their cultural practices. It also means the first spoken language in Mauritius. Both the language and cultural practices have emerged through slavery. It is difficult to understand Creole culture without referring to how Mauritius has been colonised. The island was originally uninhabited. It was colonisation that set the path for the emergence of a new culture inculcating practices, representations, expressions, knowledge and skills. Mauritius has known three types of colonisation.

Holland was the first European power to colonise Mauritius from 1598 to 1710 (Truth and Justice Commission, 2011, p. 59). They brought to the island slaves from South Africa. However, those slaves escaped and sought refuge in the woods.[1] The Dutch, in a rather erratic manner, used Mauritius as a base. They regularly used Mauritius as a port of call. It was only in 1638 that Holland decided to colonise Mauritius owing to the decision to exploit the ebony forests for export and to the threat of British occupation (Truth and Justice Commission, 2011). In 1710, the Dutch abandoned the island primarily because of frequent attacks from runaway slaves. When the Dutch left, the runaway slaves remained on the island. They were the origins of Creole heritage in Mauritius.

During French occupation from 1710 to 1810, the French settlers brought to the island (then called 'Isle de France') people mainly from Madagascar and Mozambique to work as slaves in the sugar cane fields in order to develop the island's economy (Allen, 2006, p. 54). The first settlement was completed during that period with a slave population of around 63,000 (Truth and Justice Commission, 2011). In 1810, when the British took over the island following a naval defeat of the French, there was another wave of settlement of slaves brought from Africa as England gained monopoly of the sugar market across the world. In 1835, slavery was abolished in all British colonies. This rule was applied in

Mauritius too. However, under the new colonial rule, indentured labourers were brought mainly from India in order to replace the former slaves who had previously worked on the sugar cane fields.

As a result of these waves of settlements under colonial rules, the Mauritian population became multi-ethnic and multicultural. There were people with European origins mainly the Franco-Mauritian who are still the economic elite (Salverda, 2013). The descendants of slaves with African ancestry are categorised as Creoles. The indentured labourers came from India during the Apprenticeship period[2] (Truth and Justice Commission, 2011) and also from China, due, mainly, to the communist regime.

It is undeniable that Creole culture finds its origin in slavery. In other words, they are strongly linked to each other. Creole culture, namely practices, representations, expressions, knowledge and skills—as well as the instruments, objects, artefacts and cultural spaces—emerged from the cruelty engendered by this system. Creole language and culture emerged during the French colonisation within the enslaved population as a result of their contacts with the dominant group and also due to the fact that they came from different African language communities. The enslaved people had to develop their own way of living as their original oral cultures could not be maintained due to their heterogeneity and their harsh living conditions: the slaves were ruled by the Code noir which compelled them to be baptised and given a new identity. On top of which they were considered chattels meaning they were not human beings but property that belonged to their masters (Sala-Molins, 2007, p. 178). It was a condition where the master had unilateral rights towards his slaves whose legal status were that of moveable properties. It meant that depending on the market price the slave could be bought, sold or bartered. The slaves could also be traded for if their masters ran into bankruptcy.

The classification of the population under British administration was a political strategy for the elite Franco-Mauritians to control both the ex-apprentices and Hindu immigrants. This became apparent two years after the abolition of slavery in 1837: The population was divided into three categories namely the Free Individuals, Hindus and Apprentices (Carmignani, 2019, p. 29). In 1841, there was a reclassification of the population in four categories which were as follows: Mauritius Population, Indian Labourers, Chinese and Malagasy. The first census of 1846 redesigned the population in Mauritius into three categories: General Population, ex-apprentices and Hindus. Then in 1861 the ex-apprentices were included in the category of General Population. This inclusion was considered as a move to counterbalance the Hindus who had become the majority on the island (Carmignani, 2019, p. 29).

The 1968 Constitution of Mauritius, in the year the island gained its independence, classified its population into four communities but not as decided 127 years earlier in 1841. The classification became a constitutional provision. In other words, all public institutions are bound by this constitutional principle. The classification is provided by Schedule 1 paragraph 3 of the Constitution in the following terms:

> For the purposes of this Schedule, the population of Mauritius shall be regarded as including a Hindu community, a Muslim community and a Sino-Mauritian community; and every person who does not appear, from his way of life, to belong to one or other of those 3 communities shall be regarded as belonging to the General Population, which shall itself be regarded as a fourth community. (Constitute, 2016)

The definition of 'General Population' is extremely intriguing as it cannot be defined appropriately. It includes in fact: the Franco-Mauritian elite; the coloured community (this community emerged from those slave-owners who were having extra-marital affairs with their female slaves) who can be classified as forming part of the middle class; and the Creoles-descendants of the enslaved Africans, who occupy the bottom of the ladder.

The Mauritian constitution does not refer to the Creoles, descendants of slaves who form the second ethnic majority of the population. Neither can it explain or define the classification of *General Population*. In the case of Parvez Carrimkhan v Tin How Lew Chin and Ors (2000), the issue to be determined by the Supreme Court was mainly about the classification of ethnic groups in the Republic of Mauritius for candidates taking part in general elections. It is mandatory that all candidates declare his or her community on the nomination paper as provided by paragraph 3(1) of Schedule 1 of the Mauritian constitution in the following terms: 'Every candidate for election at any general election of members of the Assembly shall declare in such manner as may be prescribed which community he belongs to and that community shall be stated in a published notice of his nomination'. In the case mentioned above, the litigants have refused to mention to which community they belong to on their nomination papers.

As a result of this, their nomination papers were declared null and void by the Office of the Electoral Commission and due to this impropriety could not stand as candidate. They applied to the Supreme Court praying it firstly to declare the unconstitutionality of paragraph 3(1) of Schedule 1 of the Mauritian constitution. Secondly, the litigants prayed that the Court defines the legal meaning of General Population. The Supreme Court, in its judgement confirmed that every candidate must declare to which community he or she belongs, and it agrees that paragraph 3 (4) of Schedule 1 of the Constitution contains a legal lacuna because it is difficult to define how an individual by his way of life can be considered to be part of the General Population (Parvez Carrimkhan v Tin How Lew Chin & Ors, 2000).

3 Valorisation of the Creole Heritage by the Colonial Discourse

Creole identity, culture and language have been considered as a marginalised, shameful and poor heritage in the Mauritian context due to the colonial discourse that has forged the cultural discourse of the country. In this context, two periods must be distinguished in order to understand the negative impact brought to the valorisation of the Creole heritage. Firstly, there is the pre-independence period and secondly the post-independence (Eriksen, 1988, p. 150).[3]

The Pre-independence Period

As demonstrated above since 1841, ex-apprentices have been included in the General Population category. This category that can neither be defined from a sociological perspective nor can a legal meaning be ascribed to it. In this context, it was therefore difficult to support the valorisation of the Creole heritage.

From the early 1950s to mid-1960s a consociationalism strategy was developed by the main political leaders in Mauritius (Eriksen, 1988, p. 150). According to this theory, in order to keep a stable regime and to avoid dictatorship, especially in a highly ethnicised society, each ethnic group who is considered to be a minority ethnic group must be placed at the head of a public institution (Eriksen, 1988, p. 150). The objectives of consociationalism are that each ethnic group must be adequately represented. For example, the office of the Commissioner of Police, the head of the Civil Service and other public institutions must be shared across ethnic minority groups in order to maintain stability. The end result of the consociationalism strategy is that it has had a drastic effect on the valorisation of the Creole heritage which is still visible to date. Recruitment figures for the civil service reveal that in the year 2000 there were around 85,000 civil servants, out of which there were around 3000 civil servants who were descendants of slaves (Michel, 2019, p. 378). To date there are around 87,000 civil servants, but the proportion has remained the same in terms of the descendants of slaves.

The Post-independence Period

This period may be considered as a continuation of the processes undermining the Creole identity. The provisions of the Mauritian constitution were unilaterally decided by the officials of the Colonial Office. These officials were Professor S. A. de Smith, Sir J. Rennie, the then Governor of Mauritius and Sir A. Greenwood, Secretary of State to the colonies (Colom, 2013, p. 23). The content of the constitution was decided as far back as 1961 (Colom, 2013, p. 21). Those truly concerned with the provisions of the constitution were not properly consulted, with the exception that there were consultation meetings held in Lancaster House, London, from 1961 to 1965 with delegates from Mauritius. However, the Mauritian delegation did not include any representative speaking on behalf of descendants of slaves. The delegates belonged mainly to the Hindu community elite. Despite the fact that not all communities were adequately represented in these meetings, approved by Professor de Smith himself stated that:

> [The] least controversial safeguard would probably be a justiciable set of fundamental rights based on the terms of the European Convention on Human Rights and fundamental freedoms. Provision along these lines has already been made in the constitutions of Nigeria, Sierra Leone and Kenya... The main dangers of fundamental rights provisions are that they may throw a heavy burden on the judiciary which would bring up expectations that cannot be fulfilled. (Colom, 2013, p. 26)

The end result is that in March 1968 the Mauritian constitution had only civil and political rights in terms of fundamental rights. The socio-economic rights were purely and simply set aside as Professor de Smith was opposed to follow the universal declaration of human rights (Colom, 2013, p. 31).

The fact that the Mauritian constitution is limited only to civil and political rights has a negative and direct impact on the descendants of slaves. Because only civil-political rights were protected, this type of constitution is seen as embodying a narrowly individualist version of freedom, blind to social and economic disparities: this narrow view of equality before the law is, in the words of the nineteenth-century French writer Anatole France, 'prohibiting rich and poor alike from sleeping under bridges, begging in the streets, and stealing loaves of bread' (Darwood and Bulmer, 2014, revised 2017, p. 6). Socio-economic rights afford each and every individual equal right on numerous fronts. Therefore, valorisation of the Creole culture had to be achieved through political actions over time: The Convention for the Safeguarding of the Intangible Cultural Heritage of UNESCO was implemented with reference to Mauritian Creole culture in 2019, but that was 50 years after independence.

However, on the eve of political independence, stakeholders of the newly emerging tourist industry, consisting mainly of descendants of the French settlers, acknowledged the local aspect of the Creole music as an asset. The economic elite saw the Creole musical practices, namely the sega dance and music, as a means to attract and entertain tourists coming from mainly France, the United Kingdom and other parts of Europe.

On 24 October 1964, stakeholders of the new tourist industry organised a sega night consisting of a competition between performers of the traditional sega. This date marked the beginning of the valorisation of sega at national level. From then onwards, many unknown artists became famous such as Alphonse Ravaton, called Ti Frer (Little brother), who has become a national icon.

Independence has certainly given a boost to the sega. The marginalised music of the Mauritians of African origin has become a cultural icon of Mauritius which is praised as a paradise island for tourists. Since independence, hotels started recruiting local sega troops to perform on the beaches for tourists; this is still the case nowadays. The troops would also be sent abroad to represent Mauritius at international musical and cultural events. Consequently, though they still have to do other jobs to earn their living, sega artists are motivated to renew their practices. Hence, sega music has constantly adapted to new international music styles adopting new instruments, specific clothes and choreographies.

To summarise, the sega has evolved from a musical practice performed within the Creole population for community building (Des Rosiers, 2004) to a 'show' to entertain the tourists and display the indigenous national culture (Déodat, 2015). This valorisation of the Creole music can be seen as the continuing discourse of colonialism as the music is promoted following a euro-centred worldview of indigenous culture.

4 Valorisation of the Creole Heritage by the Postcolonial Discourse

The postcolonial discourse is defined as a counter-discourse in order to counter the solidly grounded continuing colonial influence favouring an elite. As a first move towards independence, the political party led by the Parti Travailliste *of* the late Dr Maurice Curé, the labour party of Mauritius founded in 1936 can be considered as being postcolonial. Its first mandate was to foster the rights of workers who had no legal protection and especially those working in the sugar cane fields. The sugar industry had an important mass of workers.

However, the independence of Mauritius on 12 March 1968 did not bring any significant change pertaining to the valorisation of the Creole culture. In fact, from December 1967 to January 1968, a couple of months before independence, there were riots in the suburbs of Port-Louis, the capital, between people of the Muslim and Creole communities leading to injuries and fatalities. The death toll has never been revealed. The reaction of the then provisional government was to declare a state of emergency and calling for British assistance to bring back law and order to the country (Michel, 2017, pp. 3–6).

The majority of the political actions pertaining to the postcolonial discourse have used the disadvantaged situation of the Creole community within the Mauritian society in order to justify those actions. Seldom has there been any concrete policy decision to better Creole culture or to contribute to its valorisation. In order to gain some form of valorisation the postcolonial discourse has to be pursued through hunger-strikes, protests march or picket actions. Since independence, the laws and all policy decisions have been geared to favour the French elite so that the latter could maintain its grip on the economic front. Also, independence through 'consociationalism' has led to a strong Hindu influence having the upper hand in all public institutions. As a result of this, the descendants of slaves occupying leading or senior positions in public institutions are barely visible.

To date, this is still a prevailing situation.

In all former slave countries and colonies, the trend is not to reveal the past so that recognition of the slaves' tremendous contribution to the economic success of those countries has not been easily gained. The recognition of this contribution has been made possible through mainly political struggle which took place largely after independence (Rossi, 2018). In this respect, the Mauritian context has been no exception. There has been no real change in the laws in order to allow the valorisation of the Creole heritage. It is important to go through the different post-independence stages in order to understand how postcolonial discourse has led the way to the valorisation of the Creole heritage through the political ordeal. New socialist and Marxist political positions emerged in 1969. Led by the party Mouvement Militant Mauricien, at its contesting phase, the political movement constituted a second postcolonial discourse. One of its main objectives being the cultural emancipation of the Mauritians for nation building, it has valorised Creole language and music as shared national practices against the European cultural practices of the elite. However, the national values of those Creole cultural practices would be put into question when the political movement acceded to power in the 1980s.

One of the main figures of the new political movement, Dev Virahsawmy (1967a, 1967b, 1967c, 1987)[4] had already published in the local press, the first articles on Mauritian Creole as a national language to be taught in schools. These articles led to a passionate debate in the local press due to the colonial scale of values that predominates, even nowadays, in the educational sector. On the other hand, these articles can also be considered as a major breakthrough due to the fact that they go against the tradition that has been developed since slavery was practised in Mauritius in the sense that it was the tradition and rules of the ruling class that prevailed. The impact of slavery on Creole culture did not gain any attention in Mauritian historiography. Instead of being deeply investigated, slavery was rather downplayed by generations of Mauritian historians (Teelock, 1998, p. 6). Most of them belonged to the Franco-Mauritian elite community. It was decided to pay little attention to Mauritian history in order to maintain peaceful ethnic and communal relations (Teelock, 1998, p. 6). The teaching of the history of slavery was thus neglected for many years. This attitude was informed by pre-independence parliamentary debates on the future of history education in the 1950s, which have been detrimental to Creole culture. The parliamentary debates reflected preoccupations which still exist in modern Mauritius. For example, during one debate, Gaëtan Raynal, a well-known political figure, felt it not to be wise and safe to teach the ten-year-old son of a poor black fisherman about the horrors of slavery when next door to him lived a rich white proprietor, hence readily identifiable as the possible descendant of a slave-owner (Mauritius Hansard, 1957). Sir Seewoosagur Ramgoolam, the future Prime Minister, agreed too that it would be better to be silent on certain aspects of the Mauritian history because it might traumatise the youth of the island (Mauritius Hansard, 1957). The various strategies to downplay Creole culture in Mauritius are similar to situations appearing in other former colonial States. This policy decision has led to the fact that many Mauritians have not been made aware of their history. They have remained ignorant of the facts of colonial history. Not many are aware that their ancestors had been subjected to slavery for over a century. They are even less aware that their ancestors were captured and forced to come to work for free and in inhuman conditions in the sugar cane fields. The ex-slaves had to work four additional years in order to buy their freedom. Yet they undoubtedly contributed to the economic success of the island. It was thus important that a new postcolonial discourse uplifted the Creole language and music at national level. Today, no Mauritian will say that Creole language is not his/her language, that is, the language of the people of Mauritius. As for the sega, it has obtained a growing acknowledgement. It is also used to promote the social contest of the postcolonial discourse giving birth to the 'sega engagé' with singers of Indian origins also, as Bam Cuttayen, Ram and Nitish Joganah.

However, at its second phase, after it acceded to power in 1982, this new political movement endured an important scission that gave birth to the Mouvement Socialiste Mauricien (MSM). The successful economic policies developed by this second socialist party would make it be re-elected until 1995. As the ruling party it also promoted a cultural policy aiming at the valorisation of the cultures of origins. The teaching of Indian and Chinese languages, introduced as optional subjects at schools since the 1950s, would be reinforced as ancestral languages, as from primary level.

However, the promotion of Creole culture for nation building had a double counter effect.

On one hand, the promotion of Creole culture at national level, perceived (and still perceived) as the promotion of the culture of the Creole people, has encountered serious resistance. In the case of the Creole language, its official use in the national institutions needs further years of struggle.

On the other hand, the emphasis put by government on cultures of origins of the different ethnic communities of Mauritius, while being valorising for Mauritians coming from India, China and Europe, would have been problematic for the Creole people. For those people who are in an economic and cultural dependency towards the Franco-Mauritian elite, it was the first time in the history of Mauritius, that they would have faced their origins following the example of other ethnic communities. With regard to the negative values inherited from the colonial discourse and internalised through generations, the way back to their African origins would have implied the way back to the memory of slavery deeply rooted under heavy social taboos and a rather total ignorance.

5 Valorisation of the Creole Heritage by the Creole Discourse

Creole discourse is the name that can be given to the discourse developed by the Creole community in their effort to stand up on their own to find their way out of their political, economic and cultural dependency.

In fact, the Creole social discourse emerged in 1968 some months before the postcolonial one, as a pacifist social response to the riots of January 1968 (Michel, 2017, pp. 3–6). These riots opposing Creoles and Muslims were the result of a racist campaign of the general elections of 1967. As a reaction, Creoles of the working class all over the country set up a non-violent NGO called l'Organisation Fraternelle to help the affected families left on their own by the Catholic Church and the authorities. This NGO began from then, the struggle for social justice and acknowledgement due to the former enslaved people of Mauritius. Realising the need for political action, they would be politically active within the socialist movement during its phase of social contest in the 1970s (Michel, 2017, pp. 1–2).

Through the presence of one of its elected representative, Sylvio Michel, in the socialist opposition party (1974–1981), and also through an annual rally organised on 1 February, the NGO advocated for a public holiday to commemorate officially, on that date, the abolition of slavery.

However, members of the NGO did not wait for a governmental decision: in 1976 they set up a first monument in the public garden of the capital, to commemorate their enslaved ancestors (Michel, 2017, pp. 25–28; 76–81).

L'Organisation Fraternelle would turn into an independent socialist party in 1984 before becoming definitely a green party in 1987 named Verts Fraternels (VF). Its political discourse for social justice and reparations to the Creoles, descendants of the former enslaved people of Mauritius, would become particularly relevant in the 1990s. In fact, at that time, Mauritius was experiencing an economic crisis after the economic success of the 1980s that would affect a majority of Creoles forming part of the working class.

In his speech on the occasion of the commemoration of slavery, a Catholic priest, Roger Cerveau, raised the issue of the exclusion the Creoles, contrasting their plight with the economic improvement of the other ethnic groups, as a 'malaise créole' (Creole uneasiness) (Piat, 1993; Boswell-Laville, 2003). This expression would act as a catalyst, mobilising the newly born sociocultural NGOs and many Mauritian academics.

However, in the context of the electoral campaign for the general elections of 2000, the NGOs found themselves divided due to their political affiliation. More fundamentally, the riots that burst out following the death of the famous seggae singer named Kaya in prison would result in the acknowledgement of the Creole issue by the Mauritian elite and the setting up of policies for the valorisation of the Creole language, identity and music (Police-Michel, 2007a).

The official status of the Creole language on the radio and TV news of the Mauritius Broadcasting Corporation has become a reality following the case lodged in court by the leader of the Verts Fraternels against the national broadcasting corporation for the application of the MBC act. Today the MBC news in Creole has the highest audience in Mauritius and government has set up a Creole channel.

The introduction of the language at school has been possible after more than 40 years of national debates, through Daniella Police-Michel's proposal supported by the Verts Fraternels to teach the language as an optional language to respect the right of the children for whom Creole is a language of origin (Permal, 2004; Hookoomsing, 2004; Police-Michel, 2007b). The proposal has also been supported by activists and academics who have been struggling for the promotion of the language since 1968.

These two claims in fact have opened the door for an official acknowledgement of the language as a national language.

As for identity building which recognises Creole cultural origins, this has been established mainly with reference to the period of slavery. The public holiday of 1 February obtained in 2001, again after 40 years of struggle, is the consequence of an electoral agreement of the Verts Fraternels with the parties that won elections in 2000 (MSM-MMM, 2000; Police-Michel, 2007a, p. 143). While the Le Morne Mountain, a maroon site in the Mauritian landscape, became a World Heritage site following the struggle by NGOs and the annual rallies of the VF on 1 February to protect the mountain against an Integrated Resort Scheme (Lowe & Gopauloo, 2010).

The setting up of a Truth and Justice Commission (TJC) in November 2008 by the then government of Mauritius was a response to the claim of the VF. The TJC is unique in the world compared to other colonies or former colonies that have known the system of slavery. Its mandate was to assess the consequences of slavery and indentured labour during the colonial period up to the present (Truth and Justice Commission Act 2008, Section 3(2)). The TJC was also empowered to conduct inquiries into slavery and indentured labour in Mauritius during the colonial period and, for that purpose, gather information and receive evidence from any person. The TJC Act allowed the Commission to make recommendations so that appropriate reparative measures could be extended to descendants of slaves and indentured labourers (Truth and Justice Commission Act 2008, Section 3:2).

The Truth and Justice Commission in its report submitted 290 recommendations to the then government in November 2011 as means of resolving the aftermath of slavery in the Mauritian context. The areas covered by the recommendations ranged from historiography issues to illegal land acquisitions, educational reforms, the provision of new accommodation for the needy ones, that is, the descendants of slaves, economic measures in resolving poverty, social justice, racism, ethnicity, culture, memory and identity. Other recommendations were related to the outer islands of Mauritian territory. In its report the TJC allocated a whole chapter on the memorialising of slavery. A whole unit was entitled 'A better and increased protection of Mauritian Heritage' (vol. 1, p. 399). Below are the recommendations that were made:

General recommendations:

34. There is a need for national policies to be formulated that are based on full public and professional consultations and to cover cultural and natural, tangible and intangible. This would set the base for the development of an integrated management of heritage in Mauritius.
35. The population should be consulted to consider their vision of heritage considering Mauritian diversity.
36. The creation of a green paper fostering consultations with all segments of the population would be an initiative enabling to gather views on values invested in heritage by all Mauritians.

    The policy for heritage would support the reinforcement of the legislation for the protection and promotion of museum collections and heritage;

    This to allow for an optimal management and also the integration of existing policies for Tourism, environmental and cultural.
37. To privilege the scientific approach for the documentation of heritage and museum collections in order to recreate a link to the past.

    The scientific approach supports the appropriation of the past by the population at large.
38. Promote history and other disciplines involved in heritage documentation and research to provide the nation with scientific vision of the past thus allowing the dissemination of knowledge.
39. An independent audit of heritage which has disappeared, stolen or entered private domain.
40. The continued destruction and dispersal of Mauritian heritage to cease.
41. No projects to be undertaken without a proper cultural heritage impact assessment and a scientific evaluation.
42. Better supervision and physical protection and policing of sites: Of documentary and intangible heritage;

    Customs Personnel to be trained to detect cultural theft.

Specific recommendations:

43. There is an urgent need for trained resources and professional management of Mauritian heritage.

    The current management of museums and heritage sites shows the necessity to consolidate, if not create, a strong technical pool empowered to preserve, manage and promote heritage.
44. Training of all staff and capacity-building to create a national technical pool of technicians in heritage field and Museum management and conservation. The administrative management of heritage institutions should be complemented by strong technical competence to optimize the functioning of the institutions; it would also ensure the sustainability of heritage institutions and an optimal preservation of national heritage.
45. Heritage and museums need to be managed by a scientific and technical personnel having clear knowledge and experience in this field.
46. Such institutions would benefit from a better development and organisation by empowering the technical and scientific staff to become managers of such institutions instead of the traditional administrative line of authority, not versed in such specialised fields.
47. Revalorization of the heritage field by providing better conditions to employees:
48. There should be a valorisation of technical and scientific staff as they are the appropriate resources to manage heritage places or museums, thus leading to an optimal management of resources and a better management of heritage sites and museums.
49. To create an integrated management system for heritage which is to be led by a pool of technicians centralizing all heritage data and ensuring the coherence of projects undertaken for effective results and optimise resource management.

(Truth & Justice Commission, 2011, pp. 399–400)

These achievements are the manifestation of a positive appropriation of the memory of slavery by the Creoles and Mauritian population: this period of the national history is no more a taboo.

With the yearly Creole Festival, there is an effort from the tourist industry to move from the use of Creole culture as entertainment only to promote a better understanding of the Creole culture. The nomination of the Mauritian and Rodriguan segas as intangible heritage is a good starting point for further improvement.

6 Conclusion

Concerning the postcolonial discourse, the one promoted as from 1982 inviting Mauritian population to valorise their cultures of origins has, in fact, in the Mauritian context forced the Mauritian population, and particularly the Creoles, to become more aware of their cultural values.

As for the Creole discourse, it reveals that the ethnic struggle of the Creoles has in fact led to the promotion of the Creole culture (mainly the language) at national level.

As compared to any other country that has been colonised and has known the harsh slavery system, Mauritius does not appear as an exception. The fact is that the situation of the descendants of slaves in all former colonial countries has remained unchanged. But the Mauritian situation pertaining to the valorisation of the Creole culture becomes a relevant case study due to the fact that it has been able to overcome several obstacles which have strived to keep those of African ancestry at the bottom of the ladder culturally, economically and socially. This has been made possible on the basis of its political discourse during the post-independence era.[5]

In terms of achievements for the recognition of Creole culture, Mauritius has outweighed other powerful countries such as France and England. Since 2001, 1 February is an official bank holiday to commemorate the abolition of slavery on the island. However, it took more than 25 years to reach that step: there had to be an electoral agreement between Les Verts Fraternels and the MSM. The very first commemoration of the abolition of slavery was held in 1976 by the Organisation Fraternelle (which became Les Verts Fraternels in 1989). In France, 10 May of every year since 2001 is only decreed as a commemorative day of the abolition of slavery in French colonies. England does not commemorate officially the abolition of slavery.

A Truth and Justice Commission was set up in 2008 to study the impact of slavery in modern Mauritius. In 2011, the Commission submitted its report to the then Government containing 4 volumes with 290 recommendations as means of repairing the past. Although the Commission did not recommend any form of pecuniary reparations, it has suggested strong means to change the Mauritian society. Such a Commission is unique in the world compared to other colonies that practised the system of slavery. As mentioned above, the Commission has made a number of recommendations on how to valorise Creole culture in Mauritius. However, those recommendations are highly dependent upon the will of the policymakers. Since submission of the report, the recommendations have yet to be implemented.

As demonstrated above, Les Verts Fraternels promoted strategies to overcome the lack of recognition of Creole as a language so that it has become a means of communication in the evening news and as a medium that can be taught in schools at primary and secondary levels.[6]

These achievements have contributed towards the valorisation of Creole culture in Mauritius. However, the recognition of Creole culture is in total contradiction with the Constitution which is the principal law of the country because it does not recognise Creole culture. The Constitution is expected to contain and protect values of its citizens in a State. The Mauritian Constitution does not follow that spirit. It is clear that the category *General Population* is outdated. It must be repealed and replaced by another that acknowledges the descendants of enslaved Africans in order to reflect Mauritian reality.

It must be noted that achievements had to be made through a long political battle. They have been achieved without having recourse to violence. However, there is still a long way to go.

To conclude, we would add that due to the valorisation of the Creole heritage by a colonial discourse still prevalent in the tourist industry, there is a need to educate the performers working for the tourism sector to become aware of the histories and values that motivated their Creole practices.

This awareness could lead to the recognition of those values by the new generation and a more proactive participation to the demands of the tourist industry which is informed by a postcolonial discourse. Currently, most performers have to learn by themselves, and the passing on of experiences and skills cannot be done appropriately. Relevant training will be a useful means to maintain the sustainability of Creole practices in a manner which continues to valorise Creole heritage.

Acknowledgement The authors are ever grateful to Dr Jane Carr for her valuable advice, comments and support during the review process of this contribution.

Notes

1. Runaway slaves were named as maroons.
2. Slavery in Mauritius was abolished on 1 February 1835. However, the ex-slaves had to work four more years as Apprentices in order to buy their freedom to become free individuals afterwards. This was called the Apprenticeship period. The ex-slaves were officially released on 1 April 1839.
3. Mauritius became independent on 12 March 1968.
4. These articles are related to the Diploma-dissertation submitted by the author at the University of Edinburgh: *Towards the Re-evaluation of Mauritian Creole*, 1967.
5. It can be considered that the post-independence era ended in March 1992 when Mauritius became a Republic.
6. A different situation appears at tertiary level as Creole language was already taught at degree level at the University of Mauritius.

References

Allen, R. (2006). *Slaves, Freedmen and Indentured Laborers in Colonial Mauritius (African Studies)*. Cambridge University Press.

Boswell-Laville, M. J. R. (2003). Le malaise Créole: A Critical Study of Ethnic Identity in Mauritius. PhD dissertation, Vrije Universiteit Amsterdam, The Netherlands.

Carmignani, S. (2019). *Mémoires de l'Esclavage et Créolité, Le patrimoine du Morne l'Ile Maurice*. Éditions Karthala et Ciresc.

Carpooran, A. (2002). Créole, créolité, créolisation: les contours d'une terminologie floue. *Revi Kiltir Kreol, 1*, 1–14.

Colom, J. (2013). L'Écriture Dirigée par le Colonial Office de la Constitution mauricienne de 1968. In J. Colom (Ed.), *Le Développement Constitutionnel dans les États du Sud-Ouest de l'Océan Indien* (pp. 23–42). PUAM.

Constitute. (2016). Mauritius's Constitution of 1968 with Amendments through 2016. Constituteproject.org. https://www.constituteproject.org/constitution/Mauritius_2016.pdf?lang=en

Darwood, A., & Bulmer, E. (2014). Social and Economic Rights: International IDEA Constitution-Building Primer 9. Institute for Democracy and Electoral Assistance, 9 August 2014 (revised 2017). Social and Economic Rights (idea.int). Retrieved June 20, 2020.

Déodat, C. (2015). Les métamorphoses du pouvoir dans le séga mauricien: de la 'danse des Nègres' au patrimoine 'créole national'. *Recherches en danse, 4*. https://doi.org/10.4000/danse.1062

Des Rosiers, B. (2004). Le chant à l'île Rodrigues: rites, rires et sanctions. In Y. S. Live & J. F. Hamon (Eds.), *Kabaro, 2*(2–3), 257–270.

Eriksen, T. H. (1988). Communicating Cultural Difference and Identity: Ethnicity and Nationalism in Mauritius. *Occasional Papers in Social Anthropology*, 16 Department of Social Anthropology, University of Oslo.

Foucault, M. (1966). *Les mots et les choses: une archéologie des sciences humaines*. Gallimard.

Foucault, M. (1969). *L'Archéologie du savoir*. Gallimard.

Hookoomsing, V. Y. (2004). *A Harmonized Writing System for the Mauritian Kreol Language, GrafiLarmoni*. Retrieved June 20, 2020, from http://www.potomitan.info/bibliographie/harmonized.php

Lowe, C., & Gopauloo, N. (2010). *Le Morne Cultural Landscape: History, Symbolism and Traditions*. Le Morne Heritage Trust Fund.

Mauritius Hansard. (1957). Debate on the Education Bill, 10 December, Mauritius Hansard number 33/1957, Port-Louis.

Michel, D. (2019). Socio-economic Rights: Useful Ways of Dealing with the Aftermath of Slavery. In J. Colom, S. Rohlfing-Dijoux, & G. Schulze (Eds.), *The 50th Anniversary of Mauritius Constitutional Development* (pp. 377–390). Nomos Verlagsges.

Michel, S. (2017). *Combats Fraternels: Premiers pas d'une diaspora africaine vers les réparations*. Dir Eko, Rose-Hill.

MSM-MMM. (2000). *Programme gouvernemental: Anou redress nou pays*. Mauritius: Quad Printers.

Parvez Carrimkhan v Tin How Lew Chin & Ors, 2000 SCJ 264.

Permal, J.-D. (2004, March 10). Les Verts Fraternels en désaccord avec le gouvernement. *L'Express.mu*. Accessed January 10, 2021, from https://fr.allafrica.com/stories/200403100893.html

Piat, M. (1993). *Réflexion sur le malaise créole*. Diocèse de Port-Louis.

Police-Michel, D. (2007a). Les Discours sur l'exclusion et l'esclavage dans la société mauricienne. In S. Bunwaree & R. Kasenally (Eds.), *Rights and Development in Mauritius—A Reader* (pp. 123–130). OSSREA Mauritius Chapter.

Police-Michel, D. (2007b). Pour un partenariat cohérent français/anglais/créole dans le cursus du secondaire à Maurice. In A. Carpooran (Ed.), *Appropriation du Français et pédagogie convergente dans L'Océan Indien* (pp. 203–221). l'Université de Maurice/Agence Universitaire de la Francophonie.

Rossi, B. (2018). *50 Years of African Studies: Concepts, Methods, Politics 1968–2018*. Paper presented at the International Conference: Between Slavery and Post-slavery Citizenship, Dependence and Abolition in African and Indian Ocean Societies, 10–12 April, University of Mauritius, Mauritius, University of Birmingham UK and SLAFNET.

Sala-Molins, L. (2007). *Le Code Noir ou le Calvaire de Canaan* (Quadrige Grands Textes). Presses Universitaires de France.

Salverda, T. (2013). Balancing (Re)distribution: Franco-Mauritians Landownership in the Maintenance of an Elite Position. *Journal of Contemporary African Studies, 31*(3), 503–521.
Teelock, V. (1998). *Bitter Sugar, Sugar and Slavery in 19th Century Mauritius*. Mahatma Gandhi Institute.
Threadgold, T. (1997). *Feminist Poetics*. Routledge.
Truth & Justice Commission. (2011). *Report of Truth and Justice Commission* (Vol. 1). Government Printing.
Virahsawmy, D. (1967a, August 12). Pour un parler national. *L'Express*.
Virahsawmy, D. (1967b, September 8). Defense of Orthography. *L'Express*.
Virahsawmy, D. (1967c, September 18). Has Morisyê No Syntax? *L'Express*.
Virahsawmy, D. (1987, December 29). Le créole, langue mauricienne. *L'Express*.

CHAPTER 5

The Spirit of Koudmen: The Genesis of Identity, Community and Cooperation in Saint Lucian Society

Rhyesa Joseph

1 Introduction

The discourse on ***koudmen***, a form of self-help found within Saint Lucia attempts to contextualise the significance of this endogenous cultural form in the process of development, by examining not only its cultural contribution but crucially its significance in shaping social, human and political development. This is done by framing the emergence of ***koudmen*** within the context of colonialism which imposed power structures that advanced the dominance of European ideals, systems and strategies while simultaneously endeavouring to dismantle the native cultures and identities of colonised peoples. The aim is, therefore, to evaluate the contribution of ***koudmen***, in theory and practice, as a feature within the community and as part of citizen action in response to their societal needs and as a part of their internal worldview.

R. Joseph (✉)
University of the West Indies, Cave Hill Campus, Bridgetown, Barbados

V. Cuffy, J. Carr (eds.), *Creole Cultures, Vol. 1*,
https://doi.org/10.1007/978-3-031-24275-5_5

Further, an exposition of its historical roots is undertaken to highlight the possible linkages with Amerindian and predominantly African inheritances. An attempt is also made to understand the worldviews and social tools transported into the West Indian environment that served as a tool for resilience for colonised peoples. Consequently, an evaluation of the principles undergirding ***koudmen*** is undertaken, as well as how ***koudmen*** is operationalised within the Saint Lucian context. As such the merit of ***koudmen*** as a cultural form and value system is explored.

Essentially, the chapter proffers the political and cultural power of this endogenous practice and seeks to broaden the understanding of how colonised peoples sought to assert their own independence and carve out their own way of life under colonial circumstances. Additionally, it attempts to challenge the narrative that colonised peoples had no culture, thought or civil organisation save for their exposure to European ideals (Lewis, 1987, p. 4).

2 Culture as a Source of Resistance

Within the academic discourse on citizenship, civility, culture and civilisation in formerly colonised spaces like the Caribbean, there is a gulf of erudite writings on what these meanings constitute in indigenous and creolised terms, and how they are manifested within mainstream literature. This is not because they do not exist, but because the lenses from which they are examined, often do not appreciate indigeneity, preferring instead a replication of what is accepted as Western models and standards. Thus, it is necessary to employ a mind-set of decolonisation, where a concerted effort must be made to see and to think from the perspectives of the formerly colonised.

This is necessary to understand what has always existed in plain sight but, has been relegated to the periphery and branded as simply ornamental 'folk tradition' based on inherited colonial hierarchies, preferences and attitudes that remain intact. In the discussion surrounding creolisation pertinent questions emerge about the sources from which Caribbean identity and thought sprout. Consequently, critical questions emerge, "What were Afro-Caribbeans like before creolization? What were their thoughts, values, political ideologies before crossing the Atlantic and subsequently arriving in the Caribbean? Were these ideas and values important contributors to the beginnings of Caribbean Thought?" (Henry, 2015, p. 20).

The study of ***koudmen*** attempts to bridge the divide between what these antecedents were, and to illustrate how they contribute to the developing tapestry that is Caribbean thought and identity. In like manner, it recognises Caribbean thought more explicitly and highlights its latent potential in shaping Caribbean development if valued, respected and integrated more strategically into a Caribbean vision plan.

Fundamentally, evaluating the spirit of ***koudmen*** and its impact on identity, community and cooperation in Saint Lucia is subsumed within the broader dialogue of what Rex Nettleford so aptly articulated as 'The Battle for Space' which remains an ongoing journey. The endeavour of the colonised to create civilised life was antithetical to the aims and objectives of the colonisers. In many ways, 'The Battle for Space' euphemises what is and continues to be an ongoing war not just for space but the right to maintain that space against attack, and the ability to actualise one's humanity, legitimacy and dignity. This polemic is succinctly framed as "...tensions between European and creole hegemony became the basis for a cultural dissensus between Europe and Africa within the emerging Caribbean creole identity. The colonisers wanted a white, European identity for Caribbean society, not a creole one" (Henry, 1996, p. 6).

The space that ***koudmen*** comes to occupy, proffers the pre-eminence of African identity influences, how these influences shape self, assert agency and act as a fillip for human, social and community development. In this way, the value of identity can be grasped on a cultural and symbolic level, and pivotally in its efficacy as being indispensable to political change. ***Koudmen*** is a response to the 'call for renewal' and the fulfilment of a Caribbean society yet to be fully realised due to a political culture of authoritarianism that has been planted within the democratic soil of the region. Indigenous thought is the umbilical cord that sustains a political system (Grenade, 2010, pp. 35–36; Hinds, 2008, p. 391). It severs the cleavages that facilitate the subordination of one civilisation to another. It also circumvents the chaos which ensues from transplanting foreign elements into native spaces, particularly by means of force. In carving out space for themselves in new societies, Caribbean people tended to marry physical revolution with philosophical ones. The latter created the architecture for how these new societies were to be actualised on their own terms and legitimised the ideals of the people who were to live within them. "Against... various myths and misconceptions, the truth is, rather, that both in geographical and sociocultural terms the Caribbean has possessed and still possesses its own distinctive and idiosyncratic characteristics" (Lewis, 2004, p. 2). Consequently, our responsibility is to discover what these idiosyncrasies are and make them legitimate parts of society and the formal political fabric.

Emancipatory Thought and Practice—Countering Cultural Imperialism

To speak of independent thought is to speak of the transformation of society. Enslavement and the colonial condition created a particular society, commonly regarded as a plantation society. It is unsurprising, therefore that the plantation was a principal site for independent struggle (Beckford, 1983, p. 3). The plantation was undergirded by supportive institutions and ideas that did not vanish with the emigration of colonial authorities from the Caribbean neither with their replacement by local leaders. For this reason, independent development is interpreted as incomplete as "the colonial project in the Caribbean was not only about the political economy or political colonial relationships" (Bogues, 2003, p. 145). It constitutes a mental universe that must be dismantled and renewed as it created, "not just a place of work" but also a way of life (Beckford, 1983, p. 54).

This is critical as quantitative modifications have created the façade that the fundamental challenges of colonialism have been overcome. The vestiges of imperial power which remain evince a contradictory reality. Presently, what obtains is a politics of limited participation and the maintenance of colonial power relations (Bogues, 2003, p. 146; Lodge et al., 2015, p. 11). Breaking this continuity requires spurning the ideological baggage which Gordon Lewis contends the Caribbean took with it into the twenty-first century (Bogues, 2008, p. 170).

A paradigm shift must occur where independent thought emerges. This can be realised according to Lloyd Best through decolonised thought and intellectual reimagining. Ergo, "If we are to act for change, our philosophers and our theorists have first to understand how we relate to ourselves and to the wider world in which we live" (Best, 2003, p. 24).

Similarly, the pillars of the colonial Caribbean were material and immaterial and were glued together by a political culture that influenced the economic, political, philosophical and psychological. Consequently, cultural emancipation must also be adopted. This responds to the Caribbean challenge, "…of creating coherent civil societies guided by a sustainable measure of a volunté générale of shared interests and shared objectives which would facilitate rather than obstruct Caribbean freedom" (Henke,

2003, p. 128). Essentially, the quest is to construct a society where the socio-cultural and ideological tools utilised are reflective of its people and their idiosyncratic beliefs, culture, practices and ideals.

Fostering holistic emancipation is concerned with institutional formulations, and the theoretical and cultural pillars that sustain them influencing political power and social life. This transformation is rooted within the political culture which is conceptualised as "the seasoning" of the political system (Emmanuel, 1993, p. 3). There is a symbiotic relationship between political culture and the political system "as anatomy is related to physiology (and psychology)" (Emmanuel, 1993, p. 3). Therefore, bringing indigenous theory and cultural practice into a realm of legitimacy and utility which centres Caribbean independent development is paramount.

This necessitates relinquishing colonial legacies and instruments that preserve an authoritarian colonial character within the Caribbean Westminster political system, despite its outward features of democracy, that have often produced illiberal and contradictory outcomes. This is pellucid in Caribbean constitutions which "incorporate crucial elements of traditional authoritarianism in the ways in which official power is organized" (Emmanuel, 1993, p. 4). Notwithstanding the ascription of states within the region as Westminster democracies, such claims continue to be hollowed due to fear of the state apparatus (Henke, 2003, p. 131).

So, our focus shifts to the "inner plantation" that is preoccupied with "cores and kernels: resistant local forms: roots, stumps, survival rhythms; growing points" (Bogues, 2008, p. 169). Within this sphere, there are prospects for change and the declaration "We are human too" (Best, 2003, p. 25). It is acknowledged that ignorance of our history has been detrimental to taking advantage of indigenous thought as exemplified in our failure, "to measure, the volume of *sou-sou* transactions though so much of the population deals in them" (Best, 2003, p. 21).

Koudmen is a representation of Creole cultural identity. *Koudmen* is defined as "a cooperative self-help practiced in St. Lucia. It consists of a group of co-operative workers who give voluntary help to members of their own communities and sometimes neighbouring communities upon special request" (Foklo, 1992a, p. 42). However, deeper investigation reveals that it is more. *Koudmen* frequently referred to as a cultural spirit is essentially a Caribbean Creole worldview that shares historical ties predominantly with African legacies, but assumes its own character within the Caribbean environment. It presents a definition of identity that connects individual and community and serves as an impetus for social agency and development. Crucially, its impact is revealed in shared values and precepts that constitute the foundation of other Saint Lucian cultural forms and practices, as well as the genesis of many indigenous movements, actions and institutions.

Unravelling Saint Lucian ***koudmen*** is the rediscovery of a world outside the realms of the plantations which was resistance and survival. Based on the varied antagonisms of colonial society it arose out of what some describe as a "culture of survival" linked to *créolité*, that is, the idea that survival was possible through creolisation (Dahomey, 2003, pp. 92–93). Though many definitions of creolisation abound, Rex Nettleford's exposition is apt, "Betwixt and between them all there was the added necessity of adjustment and adaptation since different tribal groups met in circumstances which forced on the encounters a dynamic interplay of differing customs, social forces, and compassions. All these in turn had contact with different types of Europeans… to shape the new creolised cultural being who now stalks these Caribbean Islands… The creolising process in facts continues. We are, in fine, the inheritors of a richly textured ancestry which in turn determines the claims to an indigenized 'Caribbean' ethos" (Stoddard & Cornwell, 1999, 219).

'***Koudmen***' is a Kwéyòl word that is often linked to variations such as the French '***coup de main***' or '***coudmain***'. Its etymology reveals the impact of French colonisation on language development. The history and development of ***koudmen*** illustrate the transplanting of cultural and political tools from the Old World to the New World, to form what essentially became a Caribbean Creole creation. One of the first official documentation of ***koudmen*** in Saint Lucia was made during the nineteenth century by John Quinlan who observed, 'The peasants of St. Lucia are the only set of planters to whom it would be safe to make loans; they can work with their own hands, and small plots of land they offer as security are unencumbered. They are united, one willingly helps the other; they work for each other under a system called coup de main or help for which no money is paid'.[1]

Quinlan's observation is insightful as it underscores issues of identity, work, cooperation and unity. The use of the term 'system' is pertinent as it alludes to a measure of organisation and one that is distinguished by the absence of monetary payment or endorsement. The epoch and association with the peasantry suggest that ***koudmen*** is not a recent phenomenon and may have developed over time. Beyond the acknowledgement of people engaged in unremunerated work, is a sociological mapping of the social class of economically dispossessed people who have a cooperative philosophy shaped by partnership, solidarity and identity.

A more thorough delineation of *koudmen* is provided by folklorists, cultural activists and historians. The Monsignor Patrick Anthony Folk Research Centre, Saint Lucia's premier institution on folk culture and heritage conservation, provides a contemporary and more focused attempt to document *koudmen* expansively, connecting it to the cultural heritage of Saint Lucian society and its people. *Koudmen* is viewed as foundational to community life and impactful due to its utility in a range of activities and causes such as food cultivation and harvesting, boating building and the provision of home construction (Foklo, 1992a, p. 43). Cooperation, volunteerism and community are common threads tied to *koudmen* thinking and action.

Moreover, though closely identified with activity centred on work, integral elements of *koudmen* are based on artistic cultural expressions of song and dance that speak to social solidarity and the recognition of the importance of diverse members of the society to fulfil specific objectives. Consequently, it is noted that in *koudmen*, "workers work hard, zealously and diligently for many hours, keeping up their spirits by singing, joking or calling out challenges or words of encouragement to each other" (Foklo, 1992a, p. 13). Such activity can also involve storytelling and drumming (Weekes, 2014, p. 9). Notably, the role of the performing arts was both functional and symbolic, and there are similarities to African customs. Such thought is supported by the elucidation, "Music and dance though recreational, were functional as well. Slaves, as in Africa, danced and sang at work, at play, at worship, from fear, from sorrow, from joy. Here was the characteristic form of their social and artistic expression" (Brathwaite, 1974, p. 17). It is, therefore, unsurprising that music, dance and storytelling are elements of *koudmen*, and by extension what constitutes the societal rhythm of Caribbean society.

Koudmen presents a stark contrast of what economic life and thought constituted for formerly colonised peoples in spaces governed by capitalism. During an economic and historical paradigm that gave birth to modern-day capitalism entrenched in the imperial objectives of colonialism, many distinctions can be made. Unconventional ideas concerning the economy, remuneration, and labour are demarcated. *Koudmen* is a voluntary act that is devoid of any monetary compensation. It operates on what can be termed as an 'economy of reciprocity': "The payment for an individual's efforts or labour is not money, but a return in kind of one's benevolence".[2] This is because, "No one is ever paid, nor does anyone even expect to be paid in hard cash at the end of a koudmen, although each organizer should always be ready to give payment in kind i.e., join a koudmen whenever he is especially asked by a next organizer" (Foklo, 1992a, p. 43). What was provided materially was sustenance to fulfil the requirements of work. Accordingly, an organiser of a *koudmen* provided, food, rum and music for individuals who participated (Foklo, 1992a, p. 43).

It is practical to understand a moneyless economy for a class whose monetary income was virtually non-existent. But beyond pragmatism, it represents a conscious choice and a tradition that values reciprocity, the significant recognition of the individual's responsibility to the collective and interdependence. Had this practice been simply expedient, other methods could have been adopted like trading one's labour for food. Additionally, it would be possible for the practice to die once money became a more prominent feature in the lives of Saint Lucia's peasant class.

Crucially, attention is drawn to the ability of the colonised to optimise human and social capital. This is indispensable to the process of community building, as reciprocity in *koudmen* reveals "the spirit of volunteering towards community development" (Charles, 2018). *Koudmen* theoretically is conceptualised as a "co-operative work attitude" which has undergirded "St. Lucian Community life for generations" (Foklo, 1992a, p. 2). It is also deemed a "spirit of cooperation" (Wever, 2011, p. 59) which has "a strong historical tradition of community solidarity and self-help in the form of Friendly Societies and 'Coudeman' [Koudmen] groups" (Trist, 1986, p. 20). The emergence of this 'spirit of cooperation' underlies an instructive past that continues to shape Saint Lucian society.

Koudmen evinces the politics and resilience of Saint. Lucian citizens during the colonial era. That period was beset by oppressive working conditions and inequality for a landless majority whose toil "always profited others" (Foklo, 1992a, p. 1). Following this experience, the people whose lives still were characterised by economic challenges and restricted access to land tenure (Foklo, 1992a, p. 1) cultivated their ethos and action. In so doing, they claimed space for themselves by creating "special skills and approaches to work" to improve their livelihoods by providing "more options within the difficult economic environment" (Foklo, 1992a, p. 1). This was illustrated in "Koudmen and other forms of cooperative work like Jan Jounen, Jounen Pwété, or Self-help which have…been an important aspect of life in…St. Lucian communities" (Foklo, 1992a, p. 1).

In *koudmen* citizens exercise political power in shaping society through a collective social agency. This is buttressed by the ideology that "Work builds character, work builds relationships, Work builds community" (Foklo, 1992b, p. 1). Thus, whereas before labour translated into exploitation and advantage for others, it was usurped to create opportunity and development for self, identified in the interpersonal and communal rather than solely the individual sense. This provides a new platform for understanding and advancing nation-building. Sidney Mintz (1994, 1996) opines due to slavery the "great tasks of culture-building, society-building, and nation building...[which] required creativity and resourcefulness that have led to unique solutions-ways of life-often termed and even celebrated as creole" (cited in Wever, 2011, pp. 71–72).

Based on the clasificaction and the use of *koudmen* a veritable case can be made for *koudmen* as a cultural resource. Accordingly, questions arise surrounding the genesis of *koudmen*. The adoption of cooperativism, operationalised through self-help as embodied through *koudmen*, should not be viewed superficially as simply a response to colonial conditions or a historical accident. The legacy of *koudmen* provides an understanding of civilisation transplanted, adapted and determined to obviate oppressive conditions by using political and cultural tools. *Koudmen* is a window into the life and political development of people whose perspectives were silenced and regarded as factors of production without vision, voice, virtuosity or intellect.

The value placed on the collective and the significance of *koudmen* in multiple areas of community life speaks to its reliability, utility and embeddedness in the Saint Lucian reality. Critically, *koudmen* is an idiosyncratic Caribbean cultural element that should not be reduced to western ideas of charity that are often transactional. It is an indigenous Caribbean expression that draws from a particular value system and concept of community and civic duty tied to collective responsibility. Thus, *koudmen* is not an adopted western model. This is evident as it shares distinct similarities with other regional variants like *koudmen* in Dominica (Honychurch, 2018) and maroon in Grenada. Yet, greater enlightenment can only be realised by surveying the ancestral linkages that buttress *koudmen* and by exploring how *koudmen* came to function as the umbilical cord of the community, influencing its conscience, concept of self-individual and collective, and philosophy towards work and other actions.

3 The Historical Roots of Koudmen

Unravelling the historical roots of ***koudmen*** shines light on the identities of varied groups whose stories became dispensable components of the Trans-Atlantic enslaved experience and subsequently the machinations of the colonial project in the West Indies. Defining Creole identities like ***koudmen*** assists in piecing together a kaleidoscope of forces, peoples and social realities that transform transplanted practices and philosophies into creolised Caribbean legacies. Cultural identity is not a historical accident and presents conscious and consistent efforts to promote particular ideas, and values, to produce a particular kind of society.

The Caribbean's first known inhabitants were indigenous Indians referred to as Amerindians. Amerindians had their civilisation and political structures that directed their governance, relationships, livelihoods and social interactions. Examining some of the core elements of ***koudmen*** reveals some links to Amerindian practices. Amerindian life was demonstrative of communalism, particularly in the home building practices of the Kalinago (Honychurch, 2018). Other historical Amerindian practices have been attributed to Caribbean society. In Dominica, for example, it is noted that "it was the Arawaks who first started to process foods and the methods which they employed are still followed by those farmers who grow and process cassava or manioc today. The main product now is cassava farine and the main tools for its production are cassava grater, cassava canoe, palette, press and platine" (Honeychurch, 1988, p. 34).

Importantly, the practice of ***koudmen*** has been used in farine making (Foklo, 1992a, p. 43 Robertson, 2018, p.176.) in Saint Lucia. Additionally, it is stated that a ***koudmen***-type practice used by Amerindians in the construction of huts employed collective work, which involved the preparation of food and drink (Williams, 2018). However, due to the European genocide of Amerindian populations and an absence of more substantive literature on their lives further referencing cannot be made as to the gamut of their influence.

Nevertheless, more thorough connections can be made with ***koudmen*** and African ancestral survivals. This is grounded in the belief that "the African heritage is the strongest element of Saint Lucian culture" (Foklo, 1992b, p. vii). Further, it is asserted that "Koudmen is really an African heritage experience…of working together. It comes from the concept of life in the village, the village or tribal life, you know in which the tribe or village is in charge of the person, so that community is defined by that kind of environment" (Anthony, 2018). Beyond these elucidations lies historical and cultural evidence that ***koudmen*** is a product of African ancestral survivals.

Indigenous language development underscores the African presence and influence in Saint Lucia which is linked to Africans from the Senegambian region (Dalphinis, 1980, pp. 52–54). Establishing these origins is fundamental in delving into the African philosophical contributions of specific groups and regions. Generally, it is opined that African philosophy is hinged on ideas of communalism and grassroots participatory practices. There is also a significant environmental element that defines African thought. Through socialisation, "members learn about ways to manage and interact with their social and ecological environments and struggle to maintain their way of life for future generations" (Ali, 2014, p. 145). The relationship between community and environment is cemented by collective responsibility and solidarity. This ethos helps consolidate identity and the promotion of communal values which "serve as moral guiding principles that promote social responsibility, collective ethical conduct, and interconnectedness to the well-being of the community" (Ali, 2014, p. 148). Such views underscore commonalities with the ***koudmen*** experience which possesses aspects of environmentalism, collective responsibility and community at its core.

Ties to African influences can be found in Igbo society and Ghanaian philosophy. The Igbo culture reflects the African worldview that denotes the interdependent relationship between individual and community and differs from the notion of the atomised self which is one of the pillars of Western thought. As Donatus Nwoga explains, "the Igbo concept of the human person is expressed in terms of multiple relationships between humans" (Ezenwa, 2017, p. 22). Additionally, participation in community life enables the individual to attain full identification. To the Igbo people, this orientation towards the communal is considered beneficial to all individuals (Ezenwa, 2017, p. 32). Added to this, communal work is perceived as facilitating the improvement of the quality of life of the individual and the community. For various clans, this safeguards their interests and affords essential needs (Ezenwa, 2017, p. 52).

In like manner, Ghanaian philosophy consolidates many of these ideas and values. It proffers the sharing of political power (Wiredu & Gyeke 2010, p. 105) and exemplifies the African socio-ethical thought of community, collectivity and solidarity. Dissecting the principle of communitarianism makes it pellucid to see the similarities between ***koudmen*** and

African influences, and comprehend why ***koudmen*** functions as it does in Saint Lucian, and ideas of community are so central. With ***koudmen***, the idea and practice of giving to the community and being one with the community are accepted and applied to a range of social experiences. *Koudmen* came to define what a community was and what it did, that is a Saint Lucian way of life.

4 A Comparative Analysis of *Dòkpwê* and *Koudmen*

Still, the most vociferous case for the plausible impact of African heritage in the Creole formation of ***koudmen*** is presented in the system of ***dòkpwê*** in Dahomey. The people of the West African Kingdom of Dahomey and their practice of ***dòkpwê*** provide a crucial channel for reconnecting to Afro-Caribbean foundations and transcending casual theorisations. The anthropological work of Melville J. Herskovits establishes the significance of the Dahomean people to the creation of the New World and the people of African descent. It is opined, "For those interested in the background of New World Negroes, the importance of Dahomean culture derives from its situation at the very center of the long coastal belt where the most intensive slavery operations were carried on" (Herskovits, 1938, p. iv). Importantly, a link is made where the physical presence of the Dahomean people within the region is recognised, as well as their role as a cultural reservoir. Hence, Dahomean culture becomes a site of analysis that can present a coherent and concrete example of an African survival whose legacy is seen in a Caribbean creolised form (Herskovits, 1938, p. iv).

Dahomean society is characterised by self-help and cooperativism and has been defined by, "a rigidity of structure that manifests itself in a consciously close organization of society" (Herskovits, 1938, p. 29). This consciousness permeates every layer of the society and is emblematic of Dahomean culture and thought. "The Dahomean love of organisation is perhaps best exemplified in the numerous associations for mutual self-help which characterise all phases of life. These include such diverse types of societies as those for cooperative farming, for the production of tools and weapons, for subsidizing the cost of funerals, marriages, and other ceremonies which exact large expenditures from the individual" (Herskovits, 1938, p. 63).

In like manner, there are similarities within the Saint Lucian context of an affinity to cooperative work in all aspects of life. In circumstances of death, burials, farming, weddings, cultivation, processing and home building cooperation is a tradition. In short, "...St. Lucians come together and stay together in everything that matters" (Foklo, 1992a, p. 42). A more in-depth analysis of ***dòkpwê*** and ***koudmen*** reveal more profound connections.

The institution of ***dòkpwê*** was an activity performed by young men. It was a cooperative organisation guided by an attitude of pleasure and was not determined by social class (Herskovits, 1938, p. 64). This attitude of pleasure within ***dòkpwê*** could be likened to ***"bonne volonté"***, that is, "the spirit of lending a helping hand" (Weekes, 2014, p. 15) which is an enabling factor within ***koudmen***. ***Dòkpwê*** was also a marker of individual identity and community belonging, and also presents itself as a social glue, in that "...to be a member of a ***dòkpwê*** [meant] that a man is a full-fledged Dahomean, and his expression of pride in his membership is an expression of pride in being a Dahomean" (Herskovits, 1938, p. 64). With ***koudmen*** Patrick Anthony draws a parallel noting, "There was a sense of solidarity. Your personhood was defined by community" (Anthony, 2018).

Additionally, like ***koudmen***, ***dòkpwê*** is complemented by feasting, singing and competition which was used to enhance the experience of work. The centrality of ***dòkpwê*** to social life is underscored by the testimony of a Dahomean chief, in which it was declared, "It is for everyone; whether you are a chief or a common man, the ***dòkpwê*** will help you. If you need a house, it will build one for you; if you have a field to cultivate, it will break your ground. When you are sick, it helps you; when you die it buries you. Every man must show respect for the head of the ***dòkpwê***; when he comes here, I take off my chief cap to him" (Herskovits, 1938, p. 64).

It is important to note that power-sharing arrangements are based on equity. In Dahomey, the timeliness of a request for ***dòkpwê*** usurps the prioritisation of those who have greater socio-economic standing. Consequently, a notion of mutual respect, power and dignity is advanced. Embert Charles articulates this status of equality among individuals within the society in ***koudmen***. Charles notes, "The value of respect for individual contribution to the community that would be a fundamental value...the power did not reside in one or two people; the power was shared. The contribution of the ***koudmen*** was equal" (Charles, 2018).

While there are many intersections between ***koudmen*** and ***dòkpwê*** there are also significant departures. ***Dòkpwê*** is an ancient institution that predates the existence of kings and chiefs within Dahomean society (Herskovits, 1938, p. 65). The ***dòkpwêgą*** possessed unquestioning obedience and had authority over the burial ceremonies of all members of his village (Herskovits, 1938, p. 65). This speaks to the social and political organisation of the Dahomean society which differed greatly from social and political hierarchies in Saint Lucia. Added to this, it is necessary to examine the factors that cement the practice of ***dòkpwê*** and the distinct social arrangements that sustain it. Foremost among these forces is kinship. Kinship ties involving the family, extended family and patrilineal sibs were seminal. They were complemented by the arrangement of kinship dwellings that nurtured the "consciously close nature of society" (Herskovits, 1938, p. 29).

In contrast, this unfettered socio-political arrangement did not exist in the Caribbean. In many ways a dual society of power and organisation was obtained: one whose archetype was a plantation model of domination and exploitation, the other was a subversive organisation that endeavoured to be despite the plantation, but which was impacted nevertheless by this overarching nature of the colonial project. The demands of plantation and post-plantation life, the complexity of people of diverse geographical backgrounds, different languages and other cultural dynamics are exigencies that were instrumental in the formation of ***koudmen***. There is also the loss of orthodox political leadership in the form of village chiefs or kings, societal fragmentation and increased social change that contributed to the nuances of ***koudmen*** which embrace gender inclusion, novel and less hierarchical forms of leadership and expand beyond the conventions of home construction, agriculture and occasions of death and burial.

Conventional and Contemporary Expressions

In communities throughout Saint Lucia ***koudmen*** built the social, economic and political character of the society. ***Koudmen*** supported a way of life that permitted cooperative work and living. It is asserted that ***koudmen*** is a "self-help initiative by people in communities" which was based on "each one help one kind of concept" (Jn. Pierre, 2018). Jn. Pierre adds that ***koudmen*** proffered a concept of reliance on the benevolence of one's neighbour or community for survival (Jn. Pierre, 2018). This reliance was based on the trust that the people had in the system. As Williams observes, "they trusted it, because they [knew] tomorrow when I am going to do my ***koudmen*** you're gonna come" (G. Williams, 2018). Without trust, the proclivity to volunteer, participate and reciprocate, the spirit of ***koudmen*** would be debilitated. Since ***koudmen*** is based on self-help its continuity depends upon trust in forging a social contract between members of the community.

In its modern dispensation, *koudmen* maintains elements of traditional forms but also has assumed new forms. These contemporary forms have involved the mobilisation of civil society-based organisations, community-based groups and development agencies. For instance, civil society groups in Saint Lucia collaborated to launch a campaign termed '758 Koudmen' with the associated slogan, "It's the Lucian thing to do". Project Manager of '758 Koudmen' Bennet Charles asserts that the movement was geared towards the promotion of volunteerism among young people, without being affiliated with an organisation (Charles, 2018). The branding of the initiative as '758 Koudmen', according to Charles, was due to the symbolic value of *koudmen* and also its role in national development, "we wanted St. Lucians to recognise a word that they could connect with and for us that was the thing. When you say volunteer…it is an English word, but I think it does not create the same spirit than when you use that actual Kwéyòl word koudmen. It really means giving back in a St. Lucian way and being a St. Lucian and understanding that when I give back, you are not doing it just to volunteer but you are doing it because you are a St. Lucian, and you are giving back and supporting St. Lucia" (Charles, 2018). This example testifies to the relevance of *koudmen* and its versatility in meeting evolving needs.

Despite these realities, there are many challenges associated with research on *koudmen* that inhibit identifying its dynamism. Many may subconsciously use *koudmen* without being aware that they are using it. This is due to a failure of cultural knowledge transfer from older generations to younger generations outside of and within the formal education sector. In like manner, due to the prevalence of Western terminology, it may be referred to as simply volunteerism without further probing or inquiry. In the absence of more long-term documentation and research on *koudmen* there may be limitations on how it is conceptualised and therefore identified in other variations. Furthermore, social change brought about by endogenous factors like economic mobility, changing value systems, competing political cultures, new ideas of community and community formations, as well as foreign influences, necessitate broadening how *koudmen* is defined. There is, as well, a tide that relegates *koudmen* to the confines of ornamental or dead culture, stymieing not only more thorough investigation but also diminishing its value.

5 Towards an Indigenous Caribbean Governance Frontier

Significantly, bringing what is the Caribbean in cultural practice and thought into a place of legitimacy becomes an imperative for survival and holistic development. It is also integral for ensuring the compatibility of the political system with the society in which it operates. As José Martí philosophises, "The spirit of the government must be the spirit of the country. The form of government must be in harmony with the country's natural constitution" (Allen, 2002, p. 209). Similarly, it draws on a reimagined political society whose configuration and actors spurn orthodox hierarchical, authoritarian and exclusive structures and relationships to ones of greater partnership and participation. To this end, ***koudmen*** provides an alternative governance form rooted in community practice, cultural values and the lived experience of Saint Lucian folk and the generations which followed and mirrored their political example. It affords a decentralised view of power that is citizen-centric, culturally conscious and reflects the social, economic, historic and Creole character of the society.

Through ***koudmen***, the community is provided an outlet for defining purpose, positive engagement and the transferal of skills, values and experiences that iterate the importance of the individual and the community. The practice of ***koudmen*** beyond traditional definitions of home construction and agricultural production incorporates a significant social value as the basis for cultural, religious and sporting activities. These created relationships which were safeguards for community security and the accomplishment of varied tasks such as the creation of clubs, rehabilitation of churches and playing fields and fundraising support for vulnerable individuals. Added to this, it created a sense of belonging and purpose for those who were involved.

Koudmen has also been a catalyst for economic development within communities, tied to the formation of financial institutions like credit unions and banks and through cultural economic practices like 'society' which continues to function today as an indigenous burial scheme. Regrettably, little focus has been placed on how these economic developments tied to ***koudmen*** practice have contributed to enabling internal economic resilience and social stability and how these may aid the government in their development objectives by utilising internal sources of revenue and investing in endogenous growth spurred on by community enterprise.

Political engagement with the community through ***koudmen*** in consultation and implementation of policy prescriptions can result in the realisation of development that translates to more genuine human and social well-being. Additionally, its employment can usurp the narrowness of social impact assessments and present more efficient and congruent solutions which draw from local experiences and community agency. For example, the provision of costly road networks in the context of a weak government fiscal space can be surmounted by partnering with community members who collectively provide material resources and or labour for its construction. Equally, the government can engage in ***koudmen*** providing the plan, technical expertise and material, with citizens volunteering their labour and other skills. This engagement would be mutually beneficial for the community, government and by extension national development.

Furthermore, what is evident with ***koudmen*** is an innate ethos and capacity of resistance that confront many of the historical continuities of colonial society. There is an internal resilience to dependency and a counter to the narrative that denies the existence of Caribbean Philosophy while reaffirming the status of colonial thought. As Paget Henry asserts, there is a Caribbean intellectual tradition notwithstanding its position of relegation relative to the established status quo (Meeks, 2012, p. 158). The responsibility, therefore, becomes ours to reform a society that reflects and legitimises our thoughts and ideals and gives meaning to our actions. To do so the political system which governs us in theory and practice should be our own.

By and large, the experience of the region under Westminster politics is plagued by ambivalence. The growing gulf of social apathy and exacerbating socio-economic concerns dictate a dire need for change. Yet, having examined the missteps during the initial independence process it is evident that this transformation must touch at creating a political system that is compatible with the indigenous political culture, philosophical ideals and objectives of the region and engage in political relationships in which the governing and governed are partners instead of master and servant. A creole governance model in this regard can become the vehicle that gives legitimacy to endogenous forces in devising political strategies to address national concerns.

In assessing the region's strides towards development and a more substantive democracy it is necessary to highlight the linkages between the vision for inclusion and the processes of decolonisation and autonomous political development. Similarly, it is critical to denote the threats posed to the realisation of these objectives are due to historical legacies that planted colonial continuities and strangled fundamental transformation. Consequently, in the post-colonial era confronting the challenges of governance and realising progressive developmental advances are tied to addressing the contradictions of the Westminster political system and reconvening the unfinished business of decolonisation. Moreover, beyond pinpointing the inadequacies which are to be uprooted, new seeds must be planted that are culturally and politically congruent with Caribbean philosophy and people. Therefore, the prospect of Saint Lucian ***koudmen*** as a native philosophy and an alternative governance model grounded in collective agency, cultural and social resilience is proffered for deeper political emancipation and independent development. Its impact on the character of communities, the formation of indigenous economic institutions and the impact of regional variants of ***koudmen*** found in Dominica (***koudmen***) and Grenada (maroon) establish not just theoretical arguments for its utility but lived examples.

Notes

1. Memorandum of John E. Quinlan, Sworn Land Surveyor to the West India Royal Commission, Castries, St. Lucia, 1897 in Report of the West India Royal Commission.
2. Joseph, Rhyesa. "An Investigation on the Political Identity of St. Lucian Koudmen and Its Utility as a Post-Colonial Model of Governance and Social, Economic, and Political Development." Master of Philosophy Thesis, The University of the West Indies, Cave Hill Campus, 2020.

References

Ali Ilmi, A. (2014). 'Rethinking Development: An Indigenous African Communal Approach', Counterpoints, 443, 142–156.

Allen, E. (2002). *Selected Writings by Jose Marti*. Penguin Classics.

Anthony, P. (2018, November 13). *Interview on Koudmen*, interview by Rhyesa Joseph.

Beckford, G. L. (1983). *Persistent Poverty: Underdevelopment in Plantation Economies of the Third World*. Maroon Publishing House.

Best, L. (2003). Independent Thought and Caribbean Freedom. In S. Ryan (Ed.), *Independent Thought and Caribbean Freedom Essays in Honour of Lloyd Best* (pp. 1–34). Sir Arthur Lewis Institute for Social and Economic Studies.

Bogues, A. (2003). Lloyd Best and the Politics of Epistemic Development. In S. Ryan (Ed.), *Independent Thought and Caribbean Freedom Essays in Honour of Lloyd Best* (pp. 145–162). Sir Arthur Lewis Institute for Social and Economic Studies.

Bogues, A. (2008). Writing Caribbean Intellectual History. *Small Axe, 12*, 168–178.

Brathwaite, E.(1974) Folk Culture of the Slaves of Jamaica. London: New Beacon Books.

Charles, B. (2018, November 12). *Interview with Bennet Charles*, interview by Rhyesa Joseph.

Dahomey, J. (2003). Cultural Identity Versus Political Identity. In H. Henke & F. Reno (Eds.), *Modern Political Culture in the Caribbean* (pp. 90–110). University of the West Indies Press.

Dalphinis, M. (1980). 'African Language Influences in Creoles Lexically based on Portuguese, English and French, with Special Reference to Casamance Kriul, Gambian Krio and St.Lucian Patwa.' PhD thesis, SOAS, University of London. Available at: 5. https://eprints.soas.ac.uk/28601/1/10672760.pdf. Accessed May 2020.

Emmanuel, P. A. M. (1993). *Governance and Democracy in the Commonwealth Caribbean: An Introduction.* Institute of Social and Economic Research University of the West Indies Cave Hill Campus.

Ezenwa, P. C. (2017). The Value of Human Dignity: A Socio-Cultural Approach to Analyzing the Crises of Values among Igbo People of Nigeria. Julius Maximillians- Universitat Wurzburg.

Foklo, The Folk Research Centre Plas Wichach. (1992a). A Cultural Calendar of Saint Lucia. Castries: The Folk Research Centre.

Foklo, The Folk Research Centre Plas Wichach (1992b). Cultural Education Resource Kit Work of the Folk in St. Lucia. Castries: The Folk Research Centre.

Grenade, W. (2010). Governance in the Caribbean: Towards Renewal. In S. Lartey & D. Sastry (Eds.), *Governance in the Commonwealth: Current Debates* (pp. 33–40). Commonwealth Foundation.

Henke, H. (2003). Freedom Oddified Political Culture and Public Use of History in Jamaica. In H. Henke & F. Reno (Eds.), *Modern Political Culture in the Caribbean* (pp. 11–140). University of the West Indies Press.

Henry, P. (1996). Rex Nettleford African and Afro-Caribbean Philosophy. *Prepared for Conference on Caribbean Culture.* Kingston: University of West Indies.

Henry, P. (2015). Gordon Lewis and the Writing of Afro-Caribbean Political Thought. In B. Meeks & J. McCalpin (Eds.), *Caribbean Reasonings: Freedom, Power and Sovereignty—The Thought of Gordon K. Lewis* (pp. 14–45). Ian Randle Publishers.

Herskovits, M. (1938) Dahomey: An Ancient West African Kingdom. (2 Vols.). New York: Augustin.

Hinds, D. (2008). Beyond Formal Democracy: The Discourse on Democracy and Governance in the Anglophone Caribbean. *Commonwealth and Comparative Politics, 46*, 388–406.

Honychurch, L. (1988). Our Island Culture. Barbados: Letchworth Press Ltd.

Honychurch, L. (2018) 'Koudmen in Dominica'. Interview by Joseph, R. (2 November).

Jn. Pierre, K. (2018, November 7). *Interview with Kentry Jn. Pierre*, interview by Rhyesa Joseph.

Lewis, G. K. (1987). *Main Currents in Caribbean Thought: The Historical Evolutions of Caribbean Society in Its Ideological Aspects 1492–1900.* The John Hopkins University Press.

Lewis, G. K. (2004). *Main Currents in Caribbean Thought: The Historical Ecolution of Caribbean Society in Its Ideological Aspects 1.* University of Nebraska Press.

Lodge, M., Stirton, L., & Moloney, K. (2015). Whitehall in the Caribbean? The Legacy of Colonial Administration for Post-colonial Democractic Development. *Commonwealth & Comparative Politics, 53*, 8–28.

Meeks, B. (2012). Reasoning with Caliban's Reason. *Small Axe, 6*, 158–168.

Robertson, C. (2018). "Gwan Moun Se Wimed" Elders are Medicine- Life Stories from Twentieth Century. Saint Lucia: Steuben Press.

Stoddard, E., & Cornwell, G. (1999). Cosmopolitan or Mongrel? Reading Creolite and Hybridity via "Douglarisation" in Trinidad. In R. R. Premdas (Ed.), *Identity, Ethnicity & Culture in the Caribbean* (pp. 211–245). School of Continuing Studies, University of the West Indies.

Trist, C. R. (1986). *Participatory Approaches to Development in St. Lucia, West Indies: Learning Processes, Innovation and Collaboration Emergent National Model.* Philadelphia: University of Pennsylvania.

Weekes, Travis. (2014). *Bodies, Memories and Spirits A Discourse on Selected Cultural Forms and Practices of Saint Lucia.* United States.

Wever, J. L. (2011). *Dancing the Habenar Beats (In Country Music) Postcolonial Creolizations in St. Lucia.* University of Iowa.

Williams, G. (2018, November 16). *Interview with Gregor Williams*, interview by Rhyesa Joseph.

Wiredu, K, and Gyeke, K. (2010). Person and Community: Ghanaian Philosophical Studies. Washington: The Council for Research in Values and Philosophy.

CHAPTER 6

Embodying Creole Heritage: The Dominican Bélé

Jane Carr, Delia Cuffy-Weeks, Aristedes Narh Hargoe, Terry Ofosu, and Nii Tete Yartey

1 Introduction: Understanding the Significance of Creole Performance as Living Cultural Heritage

Formal recognition of traditional performance as cultural heritage builds on the World Conference on Cultural Policies in Mexico City (1982) where participants agreed to the changing definition of heritage which '…

J. Carr (✉)
University of Bedfordshire, Luton, UK

Bird College, Sidcup, UK
e-mail: jane.carr@beds.ac.uk

D. Cuffy-Weeks
Konmité pou Étid Kwéyòl, Canefield, Dominica

A. N. Hargoe • T. Ofosu
University of Ghana, Accra, Ghana

N. T. Yartey
Ghana Dance Ensemble, National Theatre of Ghana, Accra, Ghana

V. Cuffy, J. Carr (eds.), *Creole Cultures, Vol. 1*,
https://doi.org/10.1007/978-3-031-24275-5_6

now also covered all the values of culture as expressed in everyday life...' (UNESCO, n.d.). Simultaneously, the term 'intangible cultural heritage' was brought into the official lexicon and later adopted in the UNESCO Convention for Safeguarding of Intangible Cultural Heritage (2003). This convention 'broadened the more traditional view of heritage to include anthropological and sociological points of view' (Duvelle, 2014, p. 28). This has highlighted the cultural significance of performance traditions and the value of safeguarding them as a means to support transmission from one generation to the next (Junko, 2011). However, the binary of tangible and intangible, reliant on an underlying mind-body dualism, is problematic (Iacono & Brown, 2016). Instead, Iacono and Brown propose the concept of 'living cultural heritage', stressing that 'heritage and human beings are indissolubly connected and continually shape each other in an open-ended fluid dialogue' (2016, p. 90). Their approach perhaps better serves UNESCO's concern with how such heritage '... is constantly recreated by communities and groups in response to their environment, their interaction with nature and their history, and provides them with a sense of identity and continuity...' (UNESCO, 2003: article 2.1).

In the field of dance studies, there is a substantial discourse surrounding how movement may be understood as embodying cultural identities that draws on concepts from sociology. For example, Morris (2001), Mitra (2015) and Carr and Lewis (2019)[1] have all referred to Pierre Bourdieu's concept of 'habitus' which recognises the 'differences in gesture, posture and behaviour which express a whole relationship to the social world' (Bourdieu, 1984, p. 192, first published 1979). In the wider field of performance studies, the focus is on the ways in which performance 'functions within a system of codes and conventions in which behaviors are reiterated, re-enacted, re-invented, or relived' (Taylor, 2016, p. 26). A key concern, often related to the concept of 'performativity', is the question of how everyday norms may be both reiterated and challenged in embodied actions (Noland, 2009). This has implications for how identities may be understood as negotiated, particularly in improvised dance performance (Carr & Lewis, 2019). It is important not to lose sight of how the lived experience of performance can move beyond the replication of embodied norms. However, key signifiers may serve to anchor lived experience so that it can be interpreted as meaningful.

The choreological approach to analysis offers one means to analyse performance in order to consider its significance as living heritage. Initially developed to consider (western) dance theatre works, this approach to analysis may not seem the most appropriate lens through which to gain an insight into Creole traditions. However, due to its emphasis on how what is perceived is shaped by the experience of the audience, choreological analysis may be usefully applied to cross-cultural contexts (Alvarez, 2007). It provides a framework to consider the 'strands' of the medium—performer, movement, sound and space—along with their 'nexial connections' or the manner in which the 'strands' are interrelated (Preston-Dunlop & Sanchez-Colberg, 2010).[2] Attention to various sub-strands, such as the dynamic or spatial content of movement, or details of the performer's costume, provides for more detailed analysis of the style and significance of the dance. By considering these components in relation to the cultural context of the performance, important signifiers may be identified and interpreted. Yet this approach to analysis goes beyond attention to the physical details of performance:

> What a choreological perspective proposes is a more detailed examination of how the experience and expression of dance is a result of an intersubjectivity whereby knowledge of ourselves and the world is not self-contained but contingent upon interaction with the other….
> Preston-Dunlop and Sanchez-Colberg (2010, p. 110)

While a choreological analysis reveals semiotic constructions that may be interpreted in relation to culturally accepted codes and conventions, it also recognises how performance is a phenomenon engaged with by both performers and audience. It thus cuts across the binaries of the physical and phenomenological properties of performance that are equally important to grasping its significance. To fully capture the significance of living Creole heritage, it may be valuable to draw on local, European and African perspectives so as to surface the complex of heritages at play.

2 Situating Bélé Within Dominica's Creole Heritage

Dominica's Creole culture draws on diverse influences including the Indigenous Kalinago, African slaves, Maroons (escaped slaves), Europeans who settled on the island during the colonial period as well as freed slaves and indentured labourers mainly of African origins (Honychurch, 1988, p. 5). In part due to its geography, Dominica was the last island in the Caribbean to be colonised. French settlers arrived in the eighteenth century, but they tended to be poor and shared the land with settlers from Martinique and Guadeloupe of African descent or mixed 'race'. French-influenced Creole culture developed, perhaps affected by close relationships between slaves and their owners in small households (Wason, 2010).

According to the historian Lennox Honychurch (1995, 2014), the Maroons used the mountainous inner terrain to evade the grasp of authorities and were able to establish versions of African cultural communities which would continue to provide a haven for escaped slaves. During a period of transition from French to British control, the disruption enabled more slaves to escape to Maroon communities who then assisted the French in recapturing the Island in 1778. The island returned to British rule in 1784, but the strength of French Creole culture continued. While the resilience of Maroon communities was evident in the continued need for the British to resist Maroon uprisings and their lasting influence on the Creole culture of Dominica (Honychurch, 1988, p. 5, 2014, p. 13).

Dominican Creole culture, as in many communities with similar histories, features adaptations of dances from European ballrooms of the colonial period. Their modification to 'local cultural circumstances' was a common feature across the Americas and West Indies (Szwed & Marks, 1988, p. 29). As described in Janet Wason's (2010) seminal account of the Bélé and Quadrille dancing in Dominica, dances such as the Mazook and Quadrille have clearly identifiable European antecedents. However, the precise history of Bélé seems less clear. Wason reports her fellow dance researcher's unpublished findings that Bélé developed in the French colonies of Grenada, Saint-Domingue (Hispaniola) and Guadeloupe, only later travelling to Dominica and other Caribbean Island territories similarly occupied by French settlers (Franco cited by Wason, 2010, p. 231). Gerstin (2010, p. 18) agrees with this account by stating that Bélé is 'associated with the spread of French Creole culture somewhat after the period of initial neo-African transculturations'. There are certainly many instances across the Caribbean of what is termed Bélé which all, according to Camee Maddox (2015), are variants of overlapping traditions strongly influenced by European ballroom dances. They share features which are identified by Maddox (2015, p. 39) as:

> ...dance partners who playfully interact with one another in the center of a circle through intricate foot patterns, dynamic arm movements, turns, and bent-knee, flat-footed body orientation....

In Dominica, Bélé is viewed as drawing strongly on an African diasporic heritage:

> While not many of us can claim to be expert Bélé dancers, yet there is a definite response in the hearts and minds of all good Dominicans towards the African drum-beat, which has survived the great upheaval of our social and historical evolution.
>
> Caudeiron (1988, p. 49)

For Mabel 'Cissie' Caudeiron, Bélé has 'roots' in African 'mating and fertility dance rites' (Caudeiron, 1988, p 62). Wason (2010) reports Dominican elders believe that Bélé was brought to the island by 'nèg mawon' (Maroons) predating the arrival of European settlers to the island. Whatever its foundations, Bélé would have been influenced by a continuing influx of peoples of different heritages. Outside Maroon communities the boundaries between different social groups seem to have been more fluid than in other colonial contexts (Wason, 2010, p. 231). Thus, Bélé could have continued to absorb a wide range of dance influences particularly due to its incorporation of improvisation.

Local cultural expert, Delia Cuffy-Weeks provides further insights into Bélé's cultural significance. She reports how, in some areas, Bélé remained a popular form of entertainment amongst communities who, until this century, did not have access to electricity and contemporary entertainment. In particular, the Grand Bay area was cut off from much of the rest of the island until better roads were built. Here there was a strong sense of a community which was understood to draw upon African cultural heritage. People would gather on moonlit nights in a communal space at the centre of a village. Attracted by the sound of the drum, younger adults would gather to dance and sing. Older folk might sit on steps and chat and tell stories to the children. Until recently Bélé was not deemed a suitable dance for children, at least not before puberty, 'because Bélé is related to fertility rites and sexuality' (Cuffy-Weeks, in conversation with Jane Carr, 2021). There was also a tacit understanding that the drum could summon 'the spirits of the ancestors…, and … other malevolent spirits who may get attracted to the sound of the drum' (Cuffy-Weeks, in conversation with Jane Carr, 2021).[3]

> ...the only way I can really explain it, is that the rhythm of the drum connects with your soul. And it calls to you. So it's almost as if you have to dance.... and it all ties in with when the rhythm of the drum continues for long enough, people begin to really do things that they would not normally do, because they are now possessed by spirits. Cuffy-Weeks (in conversation with Jane Carr, 2021)

As Dominicans first emerged out of the slavery period, the association of Bélé with previously enslaved and Maroon communities led to its perception as holding a lower status than European-based dances (Wason, 2010, p. 235). However, Bélé gained in respectability becoming associated with Catholic feast days such as fete la Saint Pierre and fete St. Isidore (Cuffy-Weeks, 2021). In the lead up to Independence, Creole culture became pivotal to national identity. In 1965, amidst a developing Creole nationalism, Dominica began to formally celebrate its cultural heritage. Then, soon after Independence (1978), the national government instigated the establishment of cultural organisations that now, under the umbrella of the Division of Culture, take responsibility for the 'preservation and promotion of Dominica's cultural heritage and all its various expressions' (Government of the Commonwealth of Dominica, n.d.). The safeguarding of Creole heritage is a core element of their work, the results of which are evident in Bélé performances as part of National Day and Independence celebrations. Cultural officers work with schools to encourage a new generation to participate since children no longer learn cultural forms from their elders in evenings spent together in the heart of a village due to the influence of American TV shows on traditional cultural values (Blank, 2003).

In this context what was once entertainment for the poorer elements of society is now celebrated by all. Today Bélé performances not only play an important role in National Day and Independence celebrations but more generally celebrate important events such as the opening of new health centres (Cuffy-Weeks, in conversation with Jane Carr, 2021). Moreover, communities that have a strong sense of their heritage as liberated slaves are now valued for having a strong cultural base which includes their knowledge of the Bélé (Cuffy-Weeks, in conversation with Jane Carr, 2021).

3 Multi-perspectival Choreological Analysis of Bélé

In order to analyse a tradition that draws on different cultural roots, Jane Carr, a British-based dance academic, entered into dialogue with Delia Cuffy-Weeks, a local expert, and sought input from African academics, Narh Hargoe, Terry Ofosu and Nii Tete Yartey (thereafter Hargoe et al.) to support analysis of a recorded example of Bélé performance (Commonwealth of Dominica Cultural Division, 2020). The former provides invaluable information about Bélé practices and traditions, while the latter consider how Bélé shares common movement thresholds with some Ghanaian dance forms.

Our findings are synthesised into a multi-perspective analysis which draws upon the above contextual information to support interpretation. In what follows Delia Cuffy-Weeks' contributions are highlighted and reported verbatim so as emphasise the significance of her lived experience of Bele.

The Space

Originally Bélé was performed in an outside setting within a circle of people who might be both audience and participant. Due to the geography of the island, separate Bélé traditions developed in different areas: even to this day knowledgeable practitioners can distinguish drumming rhythms as belonging to different locations. It is possible that the different varieties date back even to different Maroon communities (Cuffy-Weeks, in conversation with Jane Carr, 2021). What defines the space is the drummer and performers who frame the dancing performed by the main couple: the kavalyé (male) and danm (female) (see Fig. 6.1). However, for many events, as in the video analysed, it is now presented on the stage and the circle is opened up so that the audience in front of the stage can watch the dancing.

Hargoe et al. consider Bélé to draw on the African-type of setting, which is often demonstrated by its circular gatherings during performances. This form of imagery in dance is influenced by the African philosophy of continuity which is based on the cyclical continuum between the living and the dead. For the African, the circle represents an unbroken connection between the living and the dead who continually interact in a cyclical manner: this is what Jacqui Malone (1996, p. 11) describes as 're-enacting ancestral patterns that have been in existence for centuries'. In

Fig. 6.1 Bélé dancers, Dominica. (Photo courtesy of Delia Cuffy-Weeks and Lennox Honychurch)

most African dances, the performance space is a circular one, with drummers often placed within the circle and surrounded by dancers and singers, as evident in the Bawaa of the Wala, the Adowa of the Akans and Apatampa of the Fante people, all Ghanaian. Hargoe et al. attribute the current semi-circular form of the performance space to the restrictions posed by the conventional proscenium stage. This phenomenon is also currently experienced within the African performance space where it is assumed that the audience and/or camera (fourth wall) complete the performance circle. They observe that the spatial organisation of Bélé could have been solely gotten from an African/Caribbean 'arch of mutual inspiration' (Osumare, 2012, p. 1) because the Western approach, often found in orchestral arrangements, places their drummers behind the singers, whilst the opposite happens in West Africa.

It is evident from this analysis that the nexial connections between place and performer are integral to Bélé performances. This is not only due to different Bélé traditions being attached to specific communities, but also because Bélé connects Dominicans to a sense of heritage through the spatial organisation of participants.

Performer

On first viewing, it is the costumes the performers wear which signify Creole heritage by drawing on recognisable elements of national costume.[4] Males and females have distinct clothing in which the simple long white chemise for females, and plain trousers for males, are embellished by a patterned over-skirt (jip) for females and shirt for men. These are often of a checked 'madras', or bright flowered material that became popular in Dominica at the end of the eighteenth century and remains an important element in national dress worn during Independence celebrations. The female participants also wear a headkerchief, often of the same material.[5] For females the over-skirt is used to support the motion of the dance as the performer holds the edges of the skirt at each side. For the males, loose fitting mid-length trousers and a loose cut shirt allow for freedom to perform more virtuosic actions. This careful distinction between male and female costume reinforces traditional gender roles, just as in the formal ballrooms of the past. Although they both retain connections to the dress codes of a European-influenced past, clothing for both males and females worn for Bélé is less cumbersome than that worn for the more European-based dances such as quadrille. This lack of restriction is emphasised by bare feet which suggests a direct African influence.

Hargoe et al. reflect that the Bélé costume also has antecedents in the Ghanaian Sokedee dance. This dance is performed amongst the people of Brong Ahafo situated in the middle belt of Ghana, en-route to what was the popular slave market called Salaga Market in the Northern Region of Ghana (about 500 kilometres from the capital, Accra). Sokedee costumes depict the flamboyance and pageantry of the peacock. The dance is performed by both males and females. The costume is a piece of cloth tied around the upper torso, so it drapes behind the dancer. The dancer then holds the hems of each side (right and left) at the thigh level (demi second arm position) and opens his/her arms with elbows pointing outwards. The posture and costume give the dancer a spatial volume and peacock-like aesthetic just like the Bélé.[6]

The Sound

Bélé commences with the sound of the drum. There is only one drum, the tambou, which was traditionally made by stretching goat skin over a hollowed tree trunk (Caudeiron, 1988). A metal bell provides a beat while the lead female singer, or chantwèl, introduces a simple melodic theme that is answered by a chorus or lavwé. The singing provides a melody that adds to the overall aural texture while it is the drum patterns that accompany the rhythms of the dancer's steps.

Sources agree that the drummer is guided by the dancer (Wason, 2010; Commonwealth of Dominica, 2020). The African perspective of Hargoe et al. emphasises the role of the drummer who interprets the dance by creating appropriate synchronous rhythmic patterns to exhibit his/her dexterity. On the other hand, the dancer gives a visual interpretation to the rhythms provided by the musicians. In practice there seems to be a competitive relationship between drummer and dancer.

> ... you never know what is coming. And even if you have a very rhythmic song going along, you cannot ... even say, well, okay, I'm going to do this when they sing in the chorus, or I'm going to do this... the rhythm of the song has nothing to do with what is going on between the dancer and the drummer.

There are evidently strong nexial connections between performer, movement and sound. While the dancing and drumming can be easily seen to correspond in terms of the basic beat, it is difficult for Carr's western orientated ear to fathom more details of this relationship. Here the input to the analysis from Hargoe et al. supports how the drummer provides the rhythmic impetus, keenly following the dancer's movement in order to give the performance colour and emphasis. From their perspective the music organisation is quite unique in nature but its structure, even though minimal in set up, can be understood as strongly retaining its African ancestry by relying on idiophones (piece of metal and a rattle or shaker), a membranophone (drum) and body percussions such as clapping. The most important rhythmic foundation of the ensemble is provided by a simple metal piece. This rhythmic foundation is coloured by the rattle (shaker) made from a gourd filled with beads or seeds.

Analysis from a West African perspective also reveals how the drum patterns have striking semblance with the Ghanaian Fumefume, which also relies on intricate leg movements just as in Bélé. The Pitjé bell pattern is a variation of the 6/8 pattern as exists in the Ewe Agbadza, Agbekor bell structure, whereas in the Soté, the bell closely mimics the 4/4-time signature of the Kpatsa, Klama (Hargoe, 2017) and Tokoe of the Ga-Dangme people of the Greater Accra region of Ghana.[7] While it is rare to find such scanty music accompaniment as in Bélé in Ghanaian ensembles, this aspect can be attributed to the abrupt nature in which Africans were captured into slavery and the possible restrictions that they experienced. Early Dominicans had to improvise with what resources they had based on the memories they carried along with them.

Bélé musical performance retains the African call and response pattern or cantor and chorus mode of singing where the lead cantor raises a tune, and the chorus responds. In African traditions, the lyrics of the songs are mostly based on historical facts, heroic exploits or local narratives as found in the Akan nyomkoro.[8]

Cuffy-Weeks (in conversation with Carr, 2021) adds that in Dominica, during the slavery period, songs might be used to communicate important news at distance to slaves in a separate household. However as with the masquerade tradition that later drew upon Bélé practices, the songs might also call out concerns of the time ranging from a 'wayward' husband to the impact of a fire (Caudeiron, 1988, pp. 49–50).

Alongside what have become traditional songs, new ones develop. Today they may provide political commentary, using song to 'sensitize people about different things or reference a catastrophe' (Cuffy-Weeks, in conversation with Carr, 2021).

> *...so sometimes you may hear a song for the very first time.... if you listen carefully, then you know all that is what they're singing about. ... it would be no great*
> *surprise if maybe for the next Bélé season we hear them lambasting Trump and telling him to go in a corner because Biden has the chip.*
> *Cuffy-Weeks (2021)*

Movement

The chorus have simple moves, side to side steps in time to the beat. They also sing in response to the chantwèl and frame the dancing of the main couple. In informal settings the audience and chorus may interchange (Wason, 2010), but this is not evident in the formal stage presentation recorded.

It is generally agreed that the Dominican Bélé has a set structure through which the kavalyé and danm perform solos before dancing together (Caudeiron, 1988; Wason, 2010; Commonwealth of Dominica, 2020). The steps, style and speed with which they are performed vary depending on different forms of the Bélé. Today the main forms are Bélé pitjé and Bélé soté; the latter being danced faster is possibly similar to Bélé djouba and there is also Bélé rikitik which is mostly practised in the Woodford Hill area (Wason, 2010).

Steps such as the 'pitjé' (or pitchay) and the back-foot emphasise footwork in which the flat foot grounds the movement. The rhythm created is enhanced by the use of the hips in a manner commonly associated with dancing of the African Caribbean. Similarly, an Africanist sensibility can be seen in a more grounded quality and relaxed torso than found in either western ballroom or Caribbean quadrille dancing. In keeping with many African diasporic dance traditions in the Caribbean, the dancing has a competitive edge in the manner in which male and female interact with each other and with the drum (Gerstin, 2010). However, their efforts are not emphasised in sudden dynamic changes but integrated so that jumping actions are performed within the ongoing flow of the dancing. This flow may be momentarily disrupted by the 'stop' in which the dancer, bending the knees, brings the heels up and down to firmly signal a change of rhythm to the drummer.

From a western perspective, Carr found many foot patterns that are reminiscent of western dance. For example, the 'travelling step' is a little like a balancé but performed with more sense of momentum in duple rather than triple time (rather like a step ball change in jazz dancing). The 'gwiji' found in the Bélé soté is a basic step which uses the ball of one foot to momentarily release the weight off the supporting leg to allow the other foot to travel. According to Wason (2010, p. 234), this step can also be found in the quadrille, but it is an action found in many dances.

The 'cut' seems similar to the structure of a pas de bourrée as it travels side to side. Local Bélé performers however recognise the cut as a means to signal to the drummer that they are transitioning from one part of the dance to another. While analysis from Hargoe et al.'s perspective further suggests how, in Bélé pitjé, the 'cut' movement has its antecedent in four notable religious dances in Ghana. The first is the Akom dance of the Akan ethnic group, the second and third are the Kple and Klama dance of the Ga-Dangme. The fourth, on the other hand, is Tigare/Tigali, a religious dance that originated from the northern part of Ghana but has found its performance habitat among the Ga of Greater Accra. While in Bélé, the 'cut' step is placed behind one foot, the Akom, Kple and Klama 'cuts' are usually parallel or in front of the second foot. The Tigare/Tigali usually has its 'cuts' in front and sometimes these 'cuts' are used as preparatory positions for turns. The kinaesthetic aesthetics and the timing are however the same. It is the positioning of the foot on which the final emphasis or the stress is placed that marks the difference.

The Bélé soté also has semblance to several dances in Ghana. The dancers' movements that use the ball of one foot to momentarily release the weight off the supporting leg to allow the other foot to travel also pertain to Ghanaian dances such as Gome, Kpatsa and Kpanlogo of the Ga-Dangme. The Gome dance is a 'creative dance drama' (Younge, 2011) and can sometimes be presented in the form of a flirtatious dance like the Bélé. The female basic movement is a spitting image of Bélé soté. The accentuated side to side hip movements of the female dancer and her traversing across the dance floor are also typical of the Gome dance. In Gome dance, unlike in Bélé soté, the male dancer performs a different movement that emphasises his masculinity and bravado, whilst in Bélé soté the male dancer at this point replicates the female movement. However, elsewhere in Bélé performance, during his solo, the male dancer chooses movements that demonstrate his physical prowess.

For both males and females, the arms may be brought inwards with the hands resting on the hips as in a traditional hornpipe, suggesting some European influence. However, more often, the arms move loosely and freely with the movement. At times they open out sideways in an expansive manner to assist both male and female with balance in turns or travelling. This also allows the female dancer to hold out her skirt. At other times, the sides of the skirt are drawn forwards and back in closing and opening actions or swept back more forcefully to punctuate the dance, embellishing the dynamic qualities of her movements and revealing the important connection of costume and action as a feature of the female's role. As discussed, this has antecedents in the Ghanaian Sokodee dance. In both

Bélé and Sokodee dances, the essence of wearing costumes that circumscribe the direction dictated by the body can be explained by what Yartey (2013) refers to as loco-aesthetic.[9]

The above breakdown of Bélé movements reveals similarities to several dance styles that can be found in Ghanaian traditional dances. These traditional dances cut across the various regions of Ghana. That Ghana (formally known as the Gold Coast due to its huge gold deposits) was one of the major centres of the slave trade in West Africa makes it likely that its influence is strong in the Caribbean.[10] This emphasises how the movement strand also carries traces of diasporic identities.

Improvisational Parameters

In keeping with African diasporic traditions, Bélé can be understood as a combination of dancing, singing and drumming. The songs by continuing to respond to current events help provide for the continued relevance of tradition. Similarly, the dancing, by virtue of being improvised within parameters provides leeway for individual expression, especially by the main dancers. These improvisational and responsive aspects are evident in Cuffy-Weeks' testimony which also highlights the strong nexial connections between performers, movement and sound.

> *... we allow for inclusion... So you may ...introduce a new style, which other people may copy. Or if it doesn't really fit into the dance, then there's the possibility that the people may boo you and you may decide, well, okay, I'm never going to do this... because it just doesn't fit....*
>
> *What is important is that the basic story that is told during Bélé remains the same. So if, for example, the person who does the 'moonwalk' is the male... he's showing off his prowess at that time when he is dancing. So he is free ... to do whatever he wants to impress that woman that he's trying to catch her attention...And if he can do it, within the rhythm of the dance, then it's okay...And that may become his signature....*

The sense of improvisation that absorbs influences from other dance forms is a recognisable feature of diasporic practices elsewhere that provide for their continued relevance in changing social contexts. Bélé has drawn on many influences. Individual variations or incorporations of new steps may be understood as the product of negotiation within a collective experience which reinforces the sense of individuals within a community. In this way improvised diasporic dance practices become a tacitly understood embodied discourse. At times, such as when one young man introduced Michael Jackson style 'moonwalking', this discourse spills into language to debate what is permissible (Wason, 2010). Carr and Lewis (2019) have argued how dance improvisation provides a site for dialogue between tradition and innovation that can be understood to have significance in relation to embodied cultural identities. As a form in which improvisation plays an important role, Bélé may be understood as significant in terms of how Creole identities are asserted in ways that engage with wider cultural changes without losing a sense of connection to the past. This may be contrasted with the more European-based dances.

> *The steps within the European based dances... are very set—You may play a little bit with the choreography of them... but there is not so much more that you can do, that will not cause the dance to change what it is.... But with Bélé ... you have a wider scope... So, for example, within a European dance, you may have a four count or an eight count. What may happen within Bélé dance is that the dancer may do a four count, followed by a three, then followed by an eight, then followed by a 16 or something. So the drummer cannot really determine what you're doing. So they have to follow you. ...It's like a battle of wills. The drummer trying to prove how good a drummer he or she is and the dancer, also testing that drummer.*

4 The Significance of Bélé as Creole Living Heritage

The multi-perspectival analysis suggests how the performer, movement and sound strands can be seen to have strong nexial connections to a sense of place which, while strongly referencing a national Creole culture, also carry embodied connections to a sense of diasporic heritage. For those drawing from an African perspective, Bélé is significant for its representation of the African elements of Creole cultural heritage. It can be understood as an amalgam of different Africans who have been moved from their place of origin and placed in another environment due to several factors, including slavery. The collective muscle memory of movements, soundscapes of drumming and singing orchestrated by nostalgia might have triggered the creation and performance of Bélé. People moved from different regions of Africa, with different ethnic backgrounds, were put together in a foreign land where they began to form a community of their own. Within such communities, the embodied dance movements could be put together to create a new kind of artistic form.

Yet Bélé can also be understood as referencing western ballroom dances such as quadrille, or at least their creolised versions. More research is needed to establish if a European influence is more apparent in forms of Bélé danced in other islands. Yet even in Dominica the dancing and elements of dress seem to reference the French and British ballrooms of the nineteenth century.

Perhaps this is key to understanding how Bélé embodies Creole identities. As a product of Creole culture, it plays between the codes and conventions of both European and African traditions.

Through a sense of improvisational play, aspects of movement, sound and costume manage to reference both African and European traditions—turning one into the other—and back again. While Béle's continued relevance as living cultural heritage can be seen in the manner in which it continues to include new influences and respond to contemporary events to continue to assert a strong Creole identity that can adapt to the challenges of a changing global context.

5 Conclusion

A multi-perspectival choreological analysis can be applied to Creole performance traditions to further understanding of their significance as living cultural heritage. The example of Bélé has revealed how Creole performance traditions can be understood as sites for the continual play between the complex of influences that have shaped them. Such living traditions continue to change in response to new influences, although the parameters within which changes take place may be contested. In safeguarding such traditions, it is important to recognise the full range of embodied interactions between participants (whether danced, drummed, sung or spoken) through which living cultural heritage is constantly being re-created in order to remain a vital part of culture. From this perspective arguments about what is allowable are part of a living cultural tradition, the significance of which is understood through the ways in which it is brought into life. Those cultural organisations who recognise this will be best placed to encourage new generations to connect with their heritage in ways that help them to make sense of their Creole identity in a fast-changing global context.

Acknowledgements This chapter would not have been possible without the efforts of Dr Violet Cuffy and Akosua Boakye to put the authors in touch and to guide us towards understanding of the complexities of Creole cultures and their diasporic heritage.

Notes

1. Carr and Lewis (2019) draw on the existential phenomenology of Maurice Merleau-Ponty to explore embodiment in ways that are similar to Iacono and Brown (2016). However, Carr and Lewis place more emphasis on Merleau-Ponty's analysis of human embodied experience as both object and subject.
2. In contrast to some other forms of dance analysis, it considers all these 'strands' as equally relevant. This is important when considering traditions that, in contrast to western theatre dance, do not necessarily prioritise the movement above sound, costume or even the experience of the participants.
3. Hargoe (2017) equates this with African experience of the role of the drum.
4. In Preston-Dunlop and Sanchez-Colberg's method of choreological analysis, costume is analysed as part of the performer strand.
5. Made of traditional material from India this is known as the mouchoir madras. When made of other cheaper materials it is known as 'imite' (Caudeiron, 1988, p. 57).
6. In Sokodee, the draping costume is worn over a pair of knickers (locally termed Adasa) for the men. The women on the other hand wear Kaba (a short dress made from African wax print that truncates at the hip line) and slit (long fitting skirt-like dress with a slit from the hem to the knee level also made out of the same wax print). The women also carry a piece of the wax print, held at the hem with both hands as they wave it from one side to the other in praise of the male dancers (interview with Nana Baffour, Kyeremanteng, April 2021).
7. It is important to note that these music and dance practices are a preserve of the Dangme, in whose territory (Prampram township) exists a slave fort/trading post by name Fort Vernon built in the year 1742 (Hargoe, 2017).
8. Akans are the most populous ethnic group in Ghana several of whom may have ended up as slaves in the Americas.

9. A similar situation can be inferred from the Damba dance among the people of Dagomba of the Northern Region of Ghana. In the Damba dance, the costume worn (large smock worn over loose pantaloon) is designed in such a manner that it dictates or suggests the flow and direction of movements as activated by the dancer (Yartey, 2013).
10. Those contributing to this analysis from an African perspective have relied on some Ghanaian ethnic dances. They emphasise this is not to suggest that Ghanaian dances represent the totality of African dances but rather to propose that Bélé shares common movement thresholds with some Ghanaian dance forms. Based on the historical accounts of slavery in the Caribbean, much of what is central to Bélé could not have come from any other continent but from Africa, more especially the West African Coast.

References

Alvarez, I. (2007). Cultural frontiers of expressive strands in dance performances. International Congress of Aesthetics: Aesthetics Briding Cultures, Middle East Technical University, Ankara, 9-13th July.

Blank, S. (2003). Socialising a Nation's Youth: The Influences of American Cable Television in Dominica. In S. Courtman (Ed.), *The Society for Caribbean Studies Annual Conference Papers*, Vol. 4 (3).

Bourdieu, P. (1984). *Distinction* (R. Nice, Trans.). Routledge (first published 1979).

Carr, J., & Lewis, I. (2019). Improvisational Practices in Jazz Dance Battles. In V. Midgelow (Ed.), *The Oxford Handbook of Improvisation in Dance*. Oxford University Press.

Carr, J. (2021). The Negotiation of Significance in Dance Performance: Aesthetic Value in the Context of Difference. In R. Farinas & J. Van Camp (Eds.), *The Bloomsbury Companion of Dance and Philosophy*. Bloomsbury Academic.

Caudeiron, C. (1988). Music and Songs of Dominica. In H. Lennox (Ed.), *Our Island Culture*. Letchworth Press (First Published 1982).

Commonwealth of Dominica: Division of Culture. (2020). *The Bélé Dance of Dominica*. Retrieved March 28, 2021, from https://www.facebook.com/125415637795211O/videos/149126973175437

Duvelle, C. (2014). A Decade of Implementation of the Convention for the Safeguarding of the Intangible Cultural Heritage: Challenges and Perspectives. *Ethnologies, 36*(1–2), 27–46.

Gerstin, J. (2010). Tangled Roots: Kalenda and Other neo-African Dances in the Cirum-Caribbean. In S. Sloat (Ed.), *Making Caribbean Dance: Continuity and Creativity in Island Culture* (pp. 11–34). University Press of Florida.

Government of the Commonwealth of Dominica. (n.d.). *Division of Culture*. Retrieved March 28, 2021, from http://divisionofculture.gov.dm/

Hargoe, A. N. (2017) *Performance Aesthetics of the Klama Dance of Gbugbla (Prampram), Ghana*. PhD Dissertation, University of Cape Coast, Ghana.

Honychurch, L. (1988). *Our Island Culture*. Letchworth Press (First Published 1982).
Honychurch, L. (1995). *The Dominica Story: A History of the Island*. University of Michigan. First Published 1975. https://archive.org/details/thedominicastory/page/n5/mode/2up
Honychurch, L. (2014). *Negre Mawon: The Fighting Maroons of Dominica*. Island Heritage Initiatives.
Iacono, V. L., & Brown, D. (2016). Beyond Binarism: Exploring a Model of a Living Cultural Heritage for Dance. *Dance Research, 34*(1) Summer, 84–105.
Junko, G. (2011). Tanedori of Taketomi Island: Intergenerational Transmission of Intangible Heritage. *International Journal of Intangible Heritage, 6*, 86–94.
Maddox, C. (2015). *Drum, Dance, and the Defense of Cultural Citizenship: Bélé's Rebirth in Contemporary Martinique*. PhD dissertation, University of Florida.
Malone, J. (1996). *Steppin' on the Blues: The Visible Rhythms of African American Dance*. University of Illinois Press.
Mitra, R. (2015). *Akram Khan Dancing New Interculturalism*. Palgrave Macmillan.
Morris, G. (2001). Bourdieu, the Body, and Graham's Post War Dance. *Dance Research, 19*(2), 52–82.
Noland, C. (2009). *Agency and Embodiment. Performing Gestures/Producing Culture*. Harvard University Press.
Osumare, H. (2012). *The Hiplife in Ghana: West African Indigenization of Hip-Hop* (12th ed.). Palgrave Macmillan.
Preston-Dunlop, V., & Sanchez-Colberg, A. (2010). *Dance and the Performative: A Choreological Perspective: Laban and Beyond*. Dance Books.
Szwed, J. F., & Marks, M. (1988). The Afro-American Transformation of European Set dances and Dance Suites. *Dance Research Journal, 20*(1, Summer), 29–36.
Taylor, D. (2016). *Performance*. Durham, North Carolina: Duke University Press.
UNESCO. (2003). Text of the Convention for the Safeguarding of the Intangible Cultural Heritage. Retrieved January 4, 2017, from https://ich.unesco.org/en/convention
UNESCO. (n.d.) *1982–2000: From Mondiacult to Our Creative Diversity*. Retrieved January 4, 2017, from https://ich.unesco.org/en/1982-2000-00309
Wason, J. (2010). Bélé and Quadrille: African and European Dimensions in the Traditional Dances of Dominica, West Indies. In S. Sloat (Ed.), *Making Caribbean Dance: Continuity and Creativity in Island Culture* (pp. 227–246). University of Florida Press.
Yartey, F. (2013). Dance Symbolism in Africa. In T. Manuh & E. Sutherland-Addy (Eds.), *Africa in Contemporary Perspective: A Textbook for Undergraduate Studies* (pp. 413–429). Sub-Saharan Publishers.
Younge, P. (2011). *Music and Dance Traditions of Ghana: History, Performance and Teaching*. McFarland and Company Limited.

CHAPTER 7

Entangled Threads: Creolization of Plants and Landscape

Carol Sorhaindo and Violet Cuffy

1 Introduction: Entanglement and Creolization

Whilst much debate on Creole culture focusses on elements such as language, lifestyle, dress, music and dance, this chapter extends further to explore a model of entangled botanical heritage. The concept of viewing history collectively as an intertwined global one, or 'Histoire Croisee' as Anastassiadis (2020) rationalizes, is becoming increasingly popular as a theoretical framework when re-establishing cultural connections. The term 'Botanical entanglement' in this instance is used as a metaphor to highlight these complexities. A metaphor is a means of expression common in many African and indigenous cultures, often drawing on natural references to create mental imagery, which aids understanding and learning (Ehondor, 2017).

Theories of separation and division go back to the birth of scientific racism and the taxonomic system of classifying humans according to

C. Sorhaindo (✉)
Independent Artist, Roseau, Dominica

V. Cuffy (Deceased)
University of Bedfordshire, Luton, UK

V. Cuffy, J. Carr (eds.), *Creole Cultures, Vol. 1*,
https://doi.org/10.1007/978-3-031-24275-5_7

appearance and behaviour. This system, instigated by Swedish naturalist Carolus Linnaeus in the early eighteenth century, is one which he also applied to plants (Fara, 2003). According to Gikandi (2013), creolization in a Caribbean context could therefore be viewed as an expression of modernism born out of the cultural entanglement of invaders and exploited peoples which is rooted in transatlantic trade and colonialism, systems grounded in theories of separation. In contrast, according to the psychotherapist Schwartz (2017), inseparability offers understanding and empathy, foundations for developing good human relationships.

Postcolonial studies highlight the importance of being open to more than one viewpoint which comes to light through the complex interweaving of both colonial and postcolonial histories (Mzali, 2011; Marschal, 2008). Das and Lowe (2018) emphasize that history, science, racism and colonial power are intrinsically connected. Presenting one side of colonial history, which excludes the knowledge of local flora gained from Africans and Indigenous peoples, perpetuates structural racism and distances audiences. As an alternative, Sealey (2021) describes the Creole Garden as a tiny plot of land crammed with a multitude of crops. The roots are so tightly intertwined they are difficult to disentangle. Glissant (1989, p. 26) believes that in order to move forward positively and as a survival strategy,

> We *must return to the point from which we started,….to the point of entanglement, from which we were forcefully turned away; that is where we must ultimately put to work the forces of Creolization….*

The botanical heritage of the island of Dominica in the West Indies, as investigated below, highlights these entangled complexities which are explored through my artistic practice.

2 Entangled Botanical Roots in a Dominica Context

Human Entanglements in the Land

The island of Dominica sits in the Windward chain in the Eastern Caribbean. The land is blessed with the natural resources of fertile soil, clean water and lush rainforests. Culture in Dominica is embodied through interaction with nature including a diversity of plants which are a primary source of support for the people, being used for food, trade, shelter, healing and creative industries. The national Creole motto 'Apres Bondie C'est La Terre', which means 'after God the earth', speaks of this connection to nature, with agriculture being one of the major economies.

Before colonization Dominica was called *Waitukubuli* by the indigenous Kalinago people who still live on the island today. They are noted throughout history as having a reverence for and knowledge of the land and plants around them. In a technological modern world, much of this traditional plant-based knowledge has disappeared. The Creole phase 'tete calbas', which translates as 'empty headed', refers to the erasing of cultural identity and traditional knowledge—a dilemma experienced on the island today.

Dominica has undergone many waves of migration throughout its history, each introducing new plants and cultures. The earliest inhabitants in Dominica were Amerindians said to have arrived around 5000 BC. According to Honychurch (2011), the exact origin of the last wave, the Kalinago people who live on the island to this day, is uncertain. His historical account indicates the Kalinago were the inhabitants in 1492 when Columbus first sighted Dominica and that they are descendants of the Taino in the Greater Antilles.

Invasion by European nations, Spanish, French and British led to the next major influx of migration. Soon thereafter the transatlantic slave trade, built on the practice of economic botany and fed by human exploitation, uprooted Africans and treated them as commodities shipped alongside plant materials, all crossing the Atlantic together. According to Peck and Bogansky (2013), allegedly more care and attention was given to the transplantation of plants than to that of human beings. Plant roots were carefully protected and packed for shipping in specially made barrels or containers called 'wardian cases', to ensure their healthy survival. Atwood (1791) in his accounts of Dominica in the eighteenth century mentions a few Italian and Genoese migrants selling groceries and tobacco around the island.

Plants, like the people in this intertwined 'Creole' landscape, have a mixture of origins. The historical entanglement of the plants within this 'Nature Isle' has a key role to play in this cultural dialogue. Yarde (2012) concludes that Dominica, due to its strong relationships with nature provides a context and framework for fully exploring notions of Creole culture. In addition, DeLoughrey et al. (2005) highlight the Caribbean as being one of the areas in the world greatest affected by the phenomenon of migration and most drastically altered in terms of both human and botanic migration and transplantation. The subject of cultural connection and rootedness is of utmost importance and the least recognized human need (Weil 2002). The following section highlights Dominican botanical heritage and entangled cultural connections which are the grounding of its Creole communities.

Plants and Creolization

We will never know exactly what plants the earliest settlers in Dominica grew, but the 'Caribbean Ties' research project hosted in Dominica 2019 names the following as Indigenous Caribbean food: maize, beans, sweet potatoes, peppers, soursops, pineapples, paw paws, manioc, calabash, cotton, arrowroot, sea grape, squash, annatto and tobacco (Honychurch, 1984; Hofman et al., 2019). Many of these are still cultivated in Dominica today. The use of traditional plant-based materials such as Vetivert and Laroument for craft production is still very much alive in the Kalinago territory. This tradition is at risk however as cheap mass-produced Chinese imports flood the island. Dominican historian Honychurch (2011) highlights that records indicate plants such as annatto, cassava and cotton were grown and used on the island by the Kalinago people before the first Europeans arrived. To this day many of the words for plants and places in Dominica are called by their indigenous names (Honychurch, 2011).

Africans came with their own skills and knowledge of tropical plants. There was a sharing of information with the Kalinago they met on the island, as well as with Europeans. Schiebinger (2017) speaks of a plantation medicine system which combined West African, Amerindian and European healing traditions. She gives account of enslaved Africans assisting trained European doctors who collected and recorded West Indian herbal cures. In the eighteenth century, Arrowroot was used in plantation hospitals as a nutritious and economical food for the enslaved. Arrowroot is still used as a staple food crop today. Africans also utilized some food growing wild on the island to sustain their resistance to the colonial system. The wild yam locally known as 'Wah wah' was an important source of food for the Maroons, enabling them to survive in the forests of Dominica after escaping the plantations. There are also historical accounts of yams being traded with Europeans for goods such as salt and guns (Patullo & Wiltshire, 2017; Honychurch, 2017; Atwood, 1791).

Our perception of place is informed by the familiar. However, Aspinall (1952) suggests that plants Caribbean people perceive as indigenous such as sugarcane, coffee, cocoa, banana, nutmeg, bamboo and oranges are botanical migrants. Crosby (1986) opines that 'Economic Imperialism' was at its peak before, during and even after the abolition of slavery. The impact of this period cannot be underestimated. Hodge and Taylor (1957) previously lamented the disappearance of the native flora and fauna, including man himself, along with traditional knowledge of plant uses. Cain and Hobson (1978) refer to this mass exploitation of landscape and people as the 'economic tap root'. Hofman et al. (2019) emphasize how new plants introduced from Europe, Asia and Africa such as sugar cane, plantain, guinea yam, rubber, pigeon pea, coconut, rice, lentil, coffee, breadfruit, cocoa and limes, transformed land, people and culture. The impact on Dominican land and culture today has both negative and positive connotations.

Although great efforts were made to sever the 'cultural roots' of Africans in a brutal plantation system, Quinlan (2003, p. 98) declares that practices such as 'bush medicine' and knowledge of plant uses are still deeply rooted in Dominican Creole culture today. She observes that Dominicans have faith in 'bush medicine' and herbal remedies as they have stood the test of time over many generations. Research in phytotherapy (Caribbean plants for common ailments) by Pascal (n.d.) documents many of these cures.

Another reason for this strong connection is that Africans on Dominican plantations were often allowed to cultivate provision grounds for their own use (Trouillot, 1989; Mantz, 2007). Recent ethnobotanical research has unearthed some of Africa's botanical legacies shifting the focus from plants Africans were forced to grow, to foods they planted for their own nourishment and survival, such as yam, millet, banana, groundnut, tamarind, guinea squash, hibiscus, sesame and okra (Carney & Rosomoff, 2011; Schiebinger, 2017). With modern technology used in the identification of plant residues in the soil, we learn more about the past. Recent excavations on the Morne Patates estate by Oas and Hauser (2017) reveal evidence of crops that included maize, barley, millet and coffee possibly planted on the provision grounds of the enslaved Africans. They explain these as a mix of African, American and European cereal crops. Sadly, today maize, barley and millet are no longer grown in Dominica

Well into the twentieth century, Europeans were on a hunt not only to establish fresh food supplies to feed the masses in their own countries but also to feed their fascination of the 'exotic', by showcasing plants in stately homes and botanic stations. Plants played a central role in Britain's colonial expansion. John Ellis (1775), acting colonial agent for Dominica in 1770, wrote extensively about tropical plants such as breadfruit and mangosteen which he observed in other parts of the world. According to Isaac (2018), Ellis noted that the breadfruit was an energy giving food for the hard-working Africans on the plantations.

Kew, London was founded in 1759 and is described by Mabey (2010) as the central nervous system of global botany. The Dominica Botanic Gardens located in Roseau, the capital of Dominica, was one of Kew's satellite stations, established in 1889 for economic and experimental purposes. The site is on a former sugar plantation within the Bath Estate which was later well known for lime cultivation (James, 2007). The West India Royal Commission report (1897) declared that the botanic station was regarded as one of the most successful in the West Indies, with a distribution of 165,000 economic plants in a six-year period. Patullo and Jno Baptiste (1998) refer to a stream of influential Dominican-based doctors and botanists such as Sir Henry Alfred Alford Nicholls and Dr John Imray. Documentations by Jones (1892) of the planting of fruits such as mangosteen and limes at St Aroment Estate by Dr Nicholls are held at Kew archives in London. The area is now a residential area with few traces of the original planting.

Botanical culture is fluid and ever changing as new plants and modern agricultural methods are introduced. In the 1980s, the Republic of China offered a programme of technical support to the Dominica Ministry of Agriculture. Patullo and Jno Baptiste (1998) refer to introduction of a Taiwanese 'super sweet corn' hybrid along with a new paw paw variety, cauliflower, broccoli, Chinese cabbage, long white radish, string beans and cherry tomatoes. These are now regular produce at the local markets. In recent years the migrant Haitian population have played an active part in the modern agriculture industry. Future research will be needed to examine the impact of further Creole botanical influences introduced by these new settlers.

In keeping with Dominica's tourism brand of 'Nature Isle', Henry (2001) describes tourists attracted to Dominica as being nature orientated. These tourists engage in immersive tours led by guides with a lived experience of the land, offering detailed traditional information about the rich local flora and fauna. Today, the Dominica Botanic Gardens represent not only a green space within a busy capital of Roseau but a valuable cultural resource of rare and exotic plants from all over the world. It still functions as an active botanic station providing plants and seedlings to farmers and gardeners on the island to this day.

Botanical research is even more poignant after the devastation of Dominica due to the passing of Hurricane Maria in September 2017. James (2018) bemoans that tree stocks across the island were drastically reduced, with 168 trees of economic and cultural value in the Botanic Gardens being destroyed. Dominica's agricultural sector was also largely eradicated, but island wide tree planting initiatives have since been spearheaded by the government (Tuitte, 2018). The agricultural division is on a restoration drive, urging the public to bring in seeds of fruit bearing trees such as cashews, cocoa, coffee and mangoes to the Botanic Gardens, a national attempt to replenish tree stocks.

Creolization of the botany permeates the island, with plants known by a mix of Kalinago, Creole, African and European names. By retaining traditional languages in the naming of plants, Dominica holds strong to its cultural legacy and retains a sense of liberty while recognizing the entangled roots of Dominican heritage.

3 Dominican Plants as Creole Entanglements

In this section I provide some detailed examples of plant entanglements that are of particular cultural interest.

Sugar Cane

Sugar cane (Saccharum officinarum) is a tall sturdy grass, with prominent knots, native of Southeast Asia. This crop grown for the production of molasses, sugar and rum for export is an important aspect of Creole heritage in Dominica being one of the major historical economic crops. Sugar production is associated with the generation of great wealth at the expense of human suffering and degradation. It also contributed to the physical and forceful removal of the indigenous Kalinago and displacement of African people from their homelands. The legacies of colonialism and sugar production are very much embedded in the psyche, culture and landscape of island Creole culture. Higman (2000) refers to this as the sugar revolution, sugar being the one single commodity to have such transformative power. Hauser (2021) highlights sugar cane as being linked to the rise of capitalism, related social and environmental change, fuelling the entanglement of people at a rate not seen before.

Until recently sugar cane was still planted for rum production, but with the passing of natural disasters such as tropical storm Erica in 2015 and hurricane Maria in 2017 the Belfast estate suffered severe damage. Nevertheless, sugar cane is still planted on a small scale for the production of cane juice and for eating in its raw fibrous state. James (2008) suggests different varieties are given Creole names according to appearance such as ***kann blanc*** (white cane), ***kann diven*** (wine cane) and ***kann wouje*** (red cane).

The sugar cane crop demands huge water and nutrient intakes, requiring widespread deforestation of virgin rainforests in order to prepare the land for cultivation and building of the mills (Atwood, 1791). Several mill ruins, 'taches', and rusting industrial machinery exist sparingly dotted around the national landscape, a constant reminder of this brutal history. Honychurch (1976) describes 'taches' as large copper bowls used for boiling the cane juice to produce molasses syrup, one of the stages of sugar production. Some of these mills have been renovated for use as cultural heritage centres and tourist sites, machinery used as decorative garden ornaments and plant containers.

Rum is the alcoholic drink made from the heated and distilled cane juice which was then barrelled for export. It is still very much associated with Caribbean life with 'rum shops' seen in every village on the island. These little bars often display an array of bottles filled with fruit and herbal rum infusions, such as spice, meze mawi, nannie and bois bande. Rum is commonly used as a disinfectant for cuts and bruises and a body rub to cure chills and achy muscles (Quinlan, 2003, p. 98). This enforces

Dominican's collective connection to the land and keeps natural healing traditions alive.

Farming tools such as the 'cutlass', a wooden handled device traditionally used to cut mature canes on the plantations, are a possession in most Dominican households. Today used for general gardening, weeding and cutting of the famous coconuts. The cane press crushes the sugar cane stalks to make 'visou', a Creole word for fresh cane juice (James, 2008). These are still made using local wood for small-scale production of natural, chemical free juices, which are bottled and sold by street vendors.

Cotton

Cotton, very rarely seen in Dominica today, was once significant in indigenous Kalinago history and went by the name of ikalotopue, maulu.

According to Hodge and Taylor (1957), two types of cotton were cultivated in Dominica: Cotton noir (Gossypium vitifolium) and cotton blanc (Gossypium barbadense). The latter known as West Indian Sea Island cotton or 'black seed' is a rare strain of the cotton plant. In some areas of Dominica this is called black cotton or 'Kouton nue' in Creole (Quinlan, 2003, p. 132). This small, bushy tree bears a stunning yellow flower which develops to a mature pod producing fluffy cotton bolls. Stephens (1976) argues that this high-quality cotton with long, silky fibres played an important role in economies of many West Indian islands, unmatched on the world markets.

Dodsworth (1904) gives an account of cotton growing near Kalinago dwellings, which was spun and woven into head and leg bands prior to colonization. Additionally ethnobotanical research by Hodge and Taylor (1957) discusses findings of Dr Changa, a surgeon on Columbus' fleet. Records describe cotton shrubs as large as peach trees, laden with cotton ready for spinning and fine quality cloth comparable to that of his country. Hammocks were made from cotton by indigenous Amerindians and were adopted and used by Europeans and Africans (Heath et al., 2017). Arguably cotton was one of the first items the indigenous people traded with Europeans in exchange for items such as beads, glass and textiles (Hofman et al. 2019). Early accounts by Taylor (1938) refer to the Kalinago as having vivid memories of their grandmothers picking, drying, preparing and spinning cotton fibre.

However, weaving stopped after the introduction of more efficient equivalents from European traders (Hodge & Taylor, 1957). This tradition appears now lost as part of Dominica's indigenous heritage.

Quinlan (2003, p. 132) gives account of the leaves of Gossypium barbadense being used as a tea in some areas of Dominica as a cure for a phenomenon elderly people call 'fright'. This is referred to by behavioural psychiatrists as a 'culture bound syndrome' specific to certain cultures, demonstrating symptoms similar to post-traumatic syndrome resulting from extreme emotional trauma.

Recent conversations in 2019 with elders in Dominica highlight the value of oral tradition and intangible heritage in Caribbean cultural research. Memories were rekindled of grandparents filling pillows and cushions with soft cotton bolls and making wicks of hand rolled cotton. They fondly describe as children, how they watched elders attaching the wick to a floating contraption called a 'viege' made with a cork and cross of 'cocoye sticks' (the hard central stem of the coconut palm frond). The 'viege' was then floated in a container of oil and lit. Evidence of locally made wicks can be found in testimonies to the British government. For instance, Taylor (1936) describes these as essential plantation items and one of the few cotton products specified to be made in the Caribbean for use in lamps for boiler houses for sugar production. Such recounts which link the past to the present reinforce the value of oral traditions and endorse intangible elements of botanical heritage thereby preserving them for the future.

Archaeologists Armstrong and Hauser (2017) refer to the finding of two spindle whorls, recovered within an archaeological site at Bois Cotlette in Dominica, associated with enslaved African labourers. Whorls are discs made of wood, metal or clay with a hole in the middle through which a stick (spindle) is inserted. The process of spinning involves a rotating movement of the spindle using gravity to create threads. Additionally, Heath et al. (2017) believe that enslaved and free blacks produced items such as hammocks, fishing line, netting and specialized cloth. This would have involved spinning as part of the thread making process.

Conversations with elders narrate the growing of cotton and locations where plants are still seen on the island. Today cotton is not grown commercially and the art of cotton spinning and weaving appears long lost. Cotton however is still symbolic in the form of the Dominican national Creole wear which contributes to collective cultural identity and island pride. The women's costume or 'wob dwiyet' comprises of a colourful chequered madras skirt and headpiece contrasted with white cotton broderie anglaise lace top and underskirt. On annual Creole Day, independence and cultural celebrations, Dominicans both at home and abroad are encouraged to dress in national Creole wear. Madras is also utilized in creative industries, home decor, tourism displays (Fig. 7.1).

Breadfruit

The story of the breadfruit (Artocarpus altilis) and its journey to the Caribbean is one which highlights complexities of biotic transplantation and cultural appropriation. After nearly three decades worth of lobbying from the West Indian planters, Captain Bligh successfully transported approximately 700 potted breadfruit saplings from Tahiti to St Vincent on his second voyage on HMS Bounty in 1792. From there they were taken to Jamaica and saplings were then sent to the other West Indian botanic stations (Paravisini, 2014). The plant was introduced to the West Indies as

Fig. 7.1 Madras and white cotton

a high energy food to feed enslaved Africans working on the plantations who initially resisted eating this new 'foreign food' imposed on them by Europeans (DeLoughrey, 2007; Fara, 2003).

The breadfruit is known locally as 'Yampen' a name derived as a fusion of West African and Central African words combined with the French word 'pain', for bread (Honychurch, 1984). These trees are a common sight in most Creole gardens on the island today. Breadfruit is a large, round, starchy fruit which can be prepared in many ways, boiled, fried, or pound to make a local delicacy known as 'tonton'. One of the much sought-after Creole delicacies, loved by locals and visitors alike is breadfruit roasted over an open fire accompanied with salt fish 'sancoche', a stew flavoured with local spices and fresh coconut milk. Today breadfruit is processed and commercially packaged on a small scale as gluten free flour and as a snack in the form of fried breadfruit chips. Drinks are made with the ripe fruit, consumed as juice, rum punch or cured wine; and elders have memory of a thick gelatinous soup eaten as an evening meal. Regardless, legacies of African resistance remain, with local stories of people who will not eat breadfruit due to its traumatic historical connections. However, short logs of the breadfruit tree are used for making the skirting on 'Bele' drums (James, 2008), 'Bele' being a traditional African-inspired cultural dance.

4 Migration Stories, Botanical Entanglement and Art Practice

In this section I reflect upon my artistic practice that engages with the subjective impact of migration and the terrapsychology of space and place that are relevant to the entangled Creole cultural phenomenon. Reflection on migration experiences between the United Kingdom and Dominica at various stages of my life combined with a questioning of how transatlantic trade impacts upon both land and people led to my interest in documenting insight about local plants and their entangled botanical roots. This led to my deeper engagement and understanding of the significance of plant knowledge and uses. Dominica's botanical history and the three plants detailed above—sugarcane, cotton and breadfruit—highlight Dominica's entangled biotic heritage. My investigation as an artist researcher currently living in Dominica provides a unique perspective on the value of creative approaches to research on Creole culture that I share below.

The Significance of Creole Culture in Terms of Space and Location

Each of us sees culture through the lens of our own experience. Having lived in both Dominica and the United Kingdom at different stages of life, I opine that Creole culture can be viewed differently depending on environment and location. Cultural embodiment is a holistic experience which includes:landscape and surrounding plants, weather, architecture and interaction with people who often share and can relate to common experiences. When one of these elements is missing culture is still enjoyed but it evokes different sensory and emotive experiences such as feelings of misplacement and unbelonging. Such feelings become even more poignant as generations of West Indians in Britain reflect on the 70th anniversary of the 'Empire Windrush', a mass migration from the West Indies which Beccles (2018) equates to the second Middle Passage.

I was born in England and migrated to Dominica with my family at a very young age. Playing with plants was a common past time for children in Dominica. As James (2011) confirms this includes botanical edible treats. Earliest childhood memories are of connections to plants in the

Dominican landscape, playing in fields of guava, lime and banana, eating freshly picked fruit such as mangoes and mangosteen and walking on sandy beaches lined with coconut, almond and sea grape trees. Childhood games were with the flowers and shakers made from the long seed pods of flamboyant trees.

The Botanical Gardens were a memorable space, an economic botanic station planted with specimens brought in from all over the world by British colonial curators (James, 2007). As children we searched in the grass for the black velvet hearts of the rare monkey tamarind tree (Dialiun indum) and cracked the shell to suck on the sour pulp inside. The cannon ball tree (Couropita guianensis) with its round rusty coloured fruit was also a marvel. This velvet tamarind was the only one I knew of on the island. Unfortunately, it was uprooted by hurricane Maria in 2017, and the cannon ball is now still in recovery from the storm.

As part of Dominica 'bush medicine' tradition, regular '*wash outs*' or bowel cleanses with doses of castor oil or senna leaves after annual mango season were a common childhood experience. Herbal teas such as semen contra, basilic, ginger and scents of freshly ground cocoa tea and coffee on an evening, especially on countryside visits were common practice. This was the natural way of growing up in Dominica.

Childhood playgrounds were once planted with sugar cane and cocoa with little knowledge or connection to the botanical history buried within. Education in Dominica in the 1970s was still very colonial in approach. My family's heritage is rooted in Dominican soil with members who were and still are farmers, agricultural consultants and keen gardeners.

In contrast, at the age of 13 I was uprooted once again when my parents migrated back to the United Kingdom. As a West Indian living in Britain, one has to go that extra mile to seek out foods, plants and cultural experiences in order to feel grounded and at home in what feels like 'foreign soil'. As part of the diaspora living in England, cultural references can be difficult to find. Imported bananas, dried coconut, yams and the occasional mango were bought from local Asian grocery stores. The closest connection to tropical foliage was a visit to a British stately home to admire 'exotic' botanical specimens such as ferns, palms, castor plants and colourful heliconia in covered greenhouses. Though comforting, their very extra-terrestrial environment made me feel disconnected, alienated and different. On trips to British West Indian carnivals, I excitedly followed the trail of Kennip (Dominican fruit) seeds and the sugar cane bagasse in a nostalgic hunt for the taste of Dominican cultural references.

Plants trigger enquiry, questioning roots, identity and the entangled nature of Creole culture. I have now relocated to Dominica, to reconnect to people who share common cultural experiences and immerse myself in nature by planting seeds, observing and documenting plant growth to connect historical dots. For me rootedness and connection to land is a fundamental human need as confirmed by Buzzwell and Chalquist (2009, p. 14).

> *We have a deep need for rootedness and connection with nature, particularly nature of our home places.*

The Aspects of Creole Heritage I Capture in My Art

Art is a form of cultural heritage and expression. Creole heritage is therefore captured through art and art is a part of my Creole heritage. My art practice advances the phenomena of entanglement and Creole heritage. In a land such as Dominica where nature is a key focus, my art practice, by virtue of its being underpinned by botanical research, reinforces Chalquist's (2020) theory of Terrapsychology. He emphasizes our deep human need for rootedness in nature and home places, stating a claim for more subjective experience and valued stories in land-based research. Ethnobotanical research by Hodge and Taylor (1957) highlights many plants growing in Dominica which were once utilized in creative industries. Investigation into sources of fibre and botanical pigment brings indigenous Kalinago and African craft practices to light. The documentation of botanical findings in different ways such as drawing, painting and planting not only reaffirms history but allows for discovery of exciting new materials, uses and techniques for art and craft applications. Some of the sampling techniques used draw on colonial archival documentation methods such as the creation of herbarium pages, botanical drawing and sampling of botanical dyes and fibres.

As an artist researcher living in the land associated with my practice allows for a fully immersive and holistic experience—the true 'Dominican way'—observing all the senses of sight, touch, taste, smell and spirit. Walking the land, visiting ruined mill sites, following the steps of the Maroons on nature trails and visiting the Kalinago Territory, allows for deeper questioning and understanding of the cultural heritage and plants encountered in the landscape.

The Relationship of My Current Work to a Sense of Heritage

Creole heritage is best explained through the lens of bricolage, an approach applied to my artistic research practice. McClean and Wiggings (2010) describe bricolage as a creative and complex interweaving of concepts and ideas. I argue that this approach offers a multi-layered view of Creole culture. Additionally, Mersch (2017) explains that research entangles the artist and their imagination thereby transforming thought, understanding and action.

I have used varied research methods to explore and document both tangible and intangible elements of botanical Creole heritage. Community interaction is a daily lived experience, constantly adding to wonder and enquiry of the plants and human interaction. Through sharing of stories, memories and experiences, intangible elements of culture are unearthed.

Tangible methods of documentation such as botanical fibre and dye sampling, planting, drawing and painting and journaling can be exhibited and shared to encourage dialogue. Theories of Entanglement inform creative choices of using textiles, plant pigments and botanical art in my creative practice. Examples of this work can be seen in Fig. 7.2.

Textiles and natural dyes were significant trade items exchanged for enslaved Africans (Peck & Bogansky, 2013). Plant dyes and weaving are still visible Kalinago, and African cultural traditions mainly seen in the form of basket weaving.

Embodiment in nature and physical engagement with plants creates exciting discoveries not possible when disconnected. One such example was the successful planting of a cotton seed sourced from the Kalinago territory in 2019. The original seed was planted where the entire growth cycle could be observed and documented, from initial seed through to fibrous cotton bolls in which new seeds were encased. The fibre extracted was taken through traditional preparatory processes of cleaning, spinning and weaving to create a small cloth sample. By the actual experience of planting, it was easy to identify cotton plants on various sites in travels around the island, confirming the stories recounted by community elders. This documentation is important as the diversity of trees and associated skills steeped in the cultural memory of the island are rapidly diminishing with modern development.

Creole culture can be collectively perceived as one cloth, like the tightly woven colourful madras fabric which makes up our cultural wear. Each thread having a separate root which can be pulled and examined. By

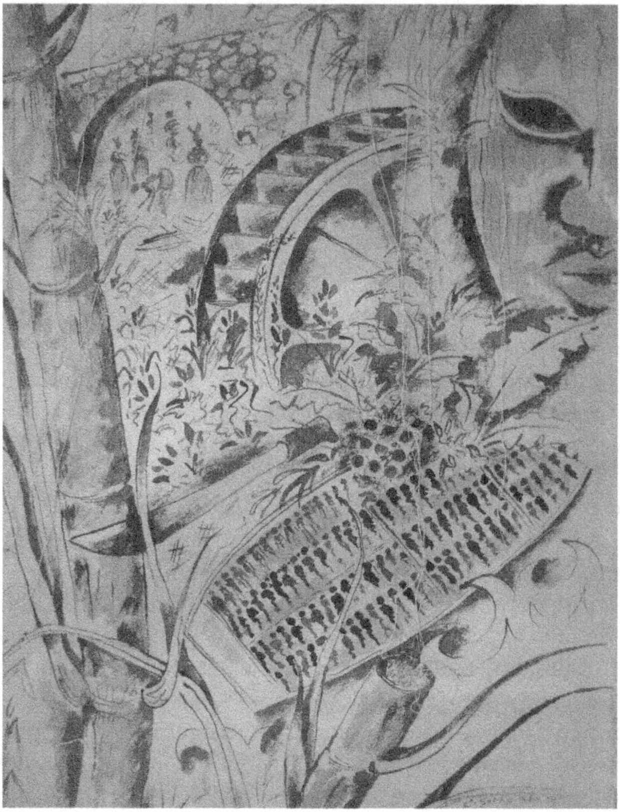

Fig. 7.2 Sugar cane artwork

reassembling pulled threads something new and exciting can be created. Loose and hanging threads, deconstruction techniques, weaving and stitch are often features of artwork combined with earth and plant pigments sourced from the land. This roots the work in nature.

Meyerowitz-Katz and Reddick (2016) suggest that both the use of materials and process function as valuable means of communication. For example, my presentation delivered at the Dominica Country Conference (Sorhaindo, 2019) was supported by a textile art display featuring 'entangled plants'. The textile artworks with natural dyes and hanging threads added a visual element which strengthened the presentation adding an alternative method of communication, thereby stimulating different senses and emotions. Conference participants who viewed the artwork were able to deeply connect to the concept of biotic exchange in the context of transatlantic trade. An image of Captain Bligh's shipment of breadfruit plants from Tahiti to the West Indies with breathing space between the carefully packed seedlings was juxtaposed with the more popular image depicting the horrors of transporting human cargo from Africa to the West Indies with no care and attention taken to protect the roots.

5 Conclusions

This chapter highlights how plants and our interaction with them over time are a significant factor of collective identity. Botanical heritage can be utilized as a valuable model for exploring entangled histories, especially in regard to Creole culture. Stenvoll-Wellsn (2021) asserts that botanical links can contribute towards formation of significant cultural foundations and strengthen familial and community ties. Mulira (2015) states that Creole culture is strengthened by the diversity of its roots and the ability to endure centuries of auspicious situations. We can never truly retain cultural authenticity or know what plants are indigenous. We can however learn from the information gained from the past and those who engage with plants in various ways. Steps can be made to better connect to the tangible and intangible attributes of our botanical heritage through increased sharing of subjective and multisensory experiences which encourage questioning, reflection and conversation. Art has the ability to make visible the contradictions obscured and the tumultuous aspects of reality (Bentz, 2020). Looking to the past is equally as important as exploring new possibilities. As humans we feel comfortable with what we are familiar with, what makes us feel rooted and safe. An artistic bricolage approach with plants at the core provides a means by which people can remain grounded in a significant element of their heritage.

References

Anastassiadis, T. (2020). Eastern Orthodoxy. An Histoire Croisée and Connected History Approach. *Bulletin de Correspondence Hellénique Modern* (2), Open Edition Journals. Retrieved June 01, 2022, from https://journals.openedition.org/bchmc/463

Armstrong, A. D., & Hauser, M. W. (2017). *Cotton Estates and Cotton Craft Production in the Colonial—Era Caribbean*. Routledge.

Aspinall, A. (1952). Comment and Opinion. *Nature, 169*, 1081.

Atwood, T. (1791). *History and Geography: The History of the Island of Dominica, Containing a Description of its Situation, Extent, Climate, Mountains, Rivers and Natural Productions*, &c. &c. ECCO Print, Eighteenth Century Online Print Edition.

Beccles, H. (2018), *The Culture Diary, British Trade in Black Labour: The Windrush Middle Passage*. The British Library, London, U.K. June 15. Retrieved June 01, 2022, from https://www.theculturediary.com/events/british-trade-black-labour-windrush-middle-passage

Bentz, J. (2020). Learning About Climate Change In, With and Through Art. *Climatic Change, 162*, 1595–1612.

Buzzwell, L., & Chalquist, C. (2009). *Eco-therapy: Healing with Nature in Mind.* Sierra Club Books.

Cain, P. J., & Hobson, J. A. (1978). Cobdenism and the Radical Theory of Economic Imperialism, 1898–1914. *The Economic History Review, 31*(4), 565–584.

Carney, J., & Rosomoff, R. N. (2011). *In the Shadow of Slavery: Africa's Botanical Legacy in the Atlantic World.* University of California Press.

Chalquist, C. (2020). *Terrapsychological Inquiry Restoring Our Relationship with Nature, Place and Planet.* Routledge.

Crosby, A. W. (1986). *Ecological Imperialism: The Biological Expansion of Europe, 900–1900* (1st ed.). Cambridge University Press.

Das, S., & Lowe, M. (2018). Nature Read in Black and White: Decolonial Approaches to Interpreting Natural History Collections. *Journal of Natural Science Collections, 6*, 4–14, NatSCA (Natural Science Collection Organisation).

DeLoughrey, E. M. (2007). Globalizing the Routes of Breadfruit and Other Bounties. *Journal of Colonialism and Colonial History, 8* (3, Winter), 1.

DeLoughrey, E. M., Gosson, R. K., & Handley, G. B. (2005). *Caribbean Literature and the Environment: Between Nature and Culture* (New World Studies). University of Virginia Press.

Dodsworth, F. (1904). *The Book of the West Indies.* George Routledge & Sons.

Ehondor, B. (2017). *The Concept of Proverbs as a Theoretical Category in Communication in Africa*. Pan Atlantic University.

Ellis, J. (1775). *A Description of the Mangostein and the Breadfruit: Directions to Voyagers, for Bringing Over These and Other Vegetable Productions.* The Author (Available on Microform at Welcome Library).

Fara, P. (2003). *Sex, Botany and Empire: The Story of Carl Linnaeus and Joseph Banks.* Icon Books ltd.

Gikandi, S. (2013). *Slavery and the Culture of Taste.* Princeton University Press.

Glissant, E. (1989). *Caribbean Discourse: Selected Essays.* Caraf Books, The University of Virginia.

Hauser, M. (2021). *Mapping Water in Dominica: Enslavement and Environment under Colonialism.* Washington University Press.

Heath, J. H., Breen, E. E., & Lee, L. L. (2017). *Material Worlds: Archaeology, Consumption, and the Road to Modernity.* Routledge.

Henry, S. (2001). *A Thick Environment: Notes on Dominica's World Music Festivals.* Shinc Productions.

Higman, B. W. (2000). The Sugar Revolution. *The Economic History Review, 53*(2), 213–236. Retrieved August 22, 2021. https://onlinelibrary.wiley.com/doi/10.1111/1468-0289.00158

Hodge, W. H., & Taylor, D. (1957). *The Ethnobotany of the Island Caribs of Dominica*, X11(2), 513–644, Firenze: Instituto Botánico dell' Universita.

Hofman, C., Hung, J. U., & Nava T. S. (2019). Caribbean Ties: Connected People, Then and Now. *Caribbean Ties Exhibition Magazine,* Macmillan Caribbean Press.

Honychurch, L. (1976), *The Dominica Story: A Story of the Island.* Macmillan Education

Honychurch, L. (1984). *The Dominica Story: A History of the Island.* Macmillan Caribbean Press.

Honychurch, L. (2011). *The Archaeology of Dominica.* Dominica.

Honychurch, L. (2017). *In the Forests of Freedom: The Fighting Maroons of Dominica.* Papillote Press.

Isaac, S. (2018). *Botany in the Age of Empire* (Catalogue Entry). Royal College of Surgeons.

James, A. (2007). *An Illustrated Guide to Dominica's Botanic Gardens.* Forestry, Wildlife and Parks Division.

James, A. (2008). *Plants of Dominica's South-East: Descriptions, Uses, Folklore, Trailsa and Eco-sites.* South-East Environment and Tourism Development Committee (SETDC).

James, A. (2011). *Playing with Plants in the Nature Isle.* Forestry, Wildlife and Parks Division.

James, A. (2018, March 2). How Hurricane Maria Ravaged Dominica's Botanic Gardens' Dominica. *The Sun Newspaper.*

Jones, J. (1892). *Notes on Antigua Pine Apples, Supplement to the Leeward Island Gazette.* Leewards Island Gazette.

Mabey, R. (2010). *Weeds: The Story of Outlaw Plants.* Profile Books.

Mantz, J. W. (2007). How a Huckster Becomes a Custodian of Market Morality: Traditions of Flexibility in Exchange in Dominica. *Identities, 14*(1–2), 19–38.

Marschal, L. S. (2008). *The Heritage of Post-colonial Societies* (Ashgate Research Companion to Heritage and Identity). Routledge.

McClean, A., & Wiggings, G. (2010). Bricolage Programming in the Creative Arts. 22nd Psychology Interest Group Madrid, December 22.
Mersch, D. (2017). Art, Knowledge and Reflexivity. *Artnodes, 20*, 33–38.
Meyerowitz-Katz, J., & Reddick, D. (2016). *Art Therapy in the Early Years: Therapeutic Interventions with Infants and Their Families*. Routledge.
Mulira, S. R. (2015). Edouard Glissant and the African Roots of Creolization. *Ufahamu: A Journal of African Studies, UCLA, 38*(2), 4.
Mzali, I. (2011). *Postcolonial Readings of Resistance and Negotiation in Selected Contemporary African Writing*. PhD thesis, Département d'études anglaises, Université de Montréal.
Oas, S. E., & Hauser, M. (2017). The Political Ecology of Plantations from the Ground Up. *Environmental Archaeology, 23*(1), 4–12.
Paravisini, L. (2014). The Breadfruit Tree Repeating Islands News and Commentary on Caribbean Culture, Literature, and the Arts. *Repeating Islands*. https://repeatingislands.com/2014/08/10/the-breadfruit-tree/
Pascal, Fr. (n.d.). Research in Phytotherapy: Caribbean Plants for Common Ailments (Private Compilation)
Patullo, P., & Baptiste, A. J. (1998). *The Gardens of Dominica*. Papillote Press.
Patullo, P., & Wiltshire, B. (2017). *Your Time is Done Now—Slavery, Resistance and Defeat: Maroon Trials (1813–1814)*. Papillote Press.
Peck, A., & Bogansky, A. E. (2013). *Interwoven Globe: The Worldwide Textile Trade, 1500–1800*. The Metropolitan Museum of Art.
Quinlan, M. B. (2003). *From the Bush: The Front Line of Health Care in The Caribbean Village, Case Studies in Cultural Anthropology*. Cengage Learning.
Schiebinger, L. (2017). *Secret Cures of Slaves: People, Plants, and Medicine in the Eighteenth-Century Atlantic World*. Stanford University Press.
Schwartz, M. (2017). *The Possibility Principle: How Quantum Physics Can Improve the Way You Think, Live, and Love*. Sounds True Inc.
Sealey, K. F. (2021). *Creolizing the Nation*. Northwestern University Press.
Sorhaindo, C. (2019). *Entangled Threads: Creolization of Plants & Lands*. Creole as Cultural Heritage, Framing, Strengthening and Advocating. University of the West Indies Open Campus, Dominica, August 15.
Stenvoll-Wellsn, D. (2021). Cereus: A Blooming Obsession: An Extraordinary Plant Through the Lens of Migration, Ritual and Memory. Linnean Society, The International Organization for Migration. Retrieved June 01, 2022, from https://www.linnean.org/news/2021/02/21/cereus-a-blooming-obsession
Stephens, S. G. (1976). The Origin of Sea Island Cotton. *Agricultural History, 50*(2), 391–399.
Taylor, D. (1936). Additional Notes on the Island Caribs of Dominica B.W.I. *American Anthropologist, 38*(3), 225–463.

Taylor, D. (1938). Anthropological Papers, No. 3, The Caribs of Dominica. Smithsonian Institution Bureau of American Ethnology: Bulletin 119, Washington.

Trouillot, M.-R. (1989). Discourses of Rule and the Acknowledgment of the Peasantry in Dominica, W. I., 1838–1928. *American Ethnologist, 16*(4), 704–718.

Tuitte, K. (2018, May 7). Months After the Devastation of Hurricane Maria Dominica Launches a Tree Planting Campaign But Is it Enough? *globalvoices.org*, Retrieved June 01, 2022, https://globalvoices.org/2018/07/05/months-after-the-devastation-of-hurricane-maria-dominica-launches-a-tree-planting-campaign-but-is-it-enough/

Weil, S. (2002). *The Need for Roots: Prelude to a Declaration of Duties towards Mankind*. Routledge.

West India Royal Commission. (1897). Bulletin of Miscellaneous Information (Royal Botanic Gardens, Kew), 1897(131). Springer, Berlin.

Yarde, T. N. (2012). *Perceptions of Nature in the Caribbean Island of Dominica*. PhD dissertation, University of Edinburgh.

CHAPTER 8

Tourism Development in Creole Spaces: A Saint Lucia Island Perspective

Chrisentia Combie and Violet Cuffy

1 Introduction

International tourism statistics record that globally, travel and tourism's direct contribution to Gross Domestic Product (GDP) was approximately US $2.9 trillion in 2019 (Lock, 2021). Governments all around the world prioritize the tourist industry, placing an emphasis on tourism products, the stakeholders involved in the delivery of these products and the economic linkages and international investment possibilities which they create. Recent attention has also been focussed on the challenges of climate change, global migration, pandemics, and other crises threatening the industry. The World Tourism Organization (UNWTO, 2014) highlights that in building more sustainable futures for Small Island Developing

C. Combie (✉)
Ministry of Education, Saint Lucia, Castries, Saint Lucia
e-mail: ccombie@scss.edu.lc

V. Cuffy (Deceased)
University of Bedfordshire, Luton, UK

V. Cuffy, J. Carr (eds.), *Creole Cultures, Vol. 1*,
https://doi.org/10.1007/978-3-031-24275-5_8

States (SIDS), tourism address these challenges by strengthening resilience through effective risk management, communication, and researched-based information.

The World Travel and Tourism Council (WTTC, 2017, p. 7) recorded in 2016, 46.7 million international overnight visitors to the Caribbean region who spent US$31.4 billion which supported a total of $56.4 billion in GDP and 2.4 million jobs. The domestic market generates more than 25% of the region's Travel & Tourism GDP. Overall travel and tourism contribute 15.2% of the Caribbean's GDP and 13.8% of employment. The physical attributes of countries are a significant selling point for tourists and investors (Torres, Skillicorn & Nelson, 2011; Padilla & McElroy, 2010). Consequently, Caribbean governments invest heavily in tourism, in exploring ways of increasing its competitiveness and protecting the region's sun, sea, and sand brand. Lopez (2021) analysed statistics provided by the UNWTO for a period of ten years (2010–2019) and concluded that for the Caribbean region, revenue created by tourism during that period increased steadily. By 2019, revenue in the Caribbean amounted to approximately $34.6 billion, a 5.8% increase from the previous year.

In this swiftly shifting era, the Caribbean as a region must focus on one of the most important problems facing the industry, tourism product diversification (Zappino, 2005, p. 26). Moreover, improvement and development of the sites, attractions, community tourism, events and festivals, and cultural product areas are essential for the region's competitiveness in the future. Fortunately, the Caribbean Tourism Organization (CTO) recognizes the need for a collective approach to managing and promoting the industry within the region. Accordingly, the combination of the 24 member states, together with several corporate entities collectively promote sustainable tourism development "in the most desirable year-round, warm, weather destinations" (Caribbean Tourism Organization, 2021). The Caribbean has adopted an integrative approach where countries market the region as a single destination comprising of island territories that each offer unique cultural experiences.

This chapter explores tourism development in the Saint Lucian Creole context. It reviews the development of cultural tourism in the Creole Space and draws on the collection of qualitative data to delve into St. Lucians' perspectives of their Creole cultural identity, the marketability of culture as part of tourism development, how tourism development impacts upon Creole culture and the role of policy makers such developments.

2 Literature Review: Cultural Tourism in the Creole Space

The concept of cultural tourism is a broad one. Mousavi et al. (2016) conclude that cultural tourism involves the consumption of a wide range of cultural manifestations such as heritage, art, and folklore. Cultural tourism can be generally seen as a socio-cultural relationship between people that is promoted, moderated, and mediated by a range of various actors including planners, politicians, marketing professionals, and travel agencies. Additionally, cultural tourism is a move towards sustainable tourism which increases backward and forward economic linkages and creates direct and indirect revenue for the country (Jules, 2005). Heritage tourism, for example, underscores the effectiveness of the promotion of natural and cultural heritage in which links to culture and tradition must add value (Renard, 2001). The St. Lucia Heritage tourism Programme founded in 1999 continued its drive for cultural safeguarding whilst marketing St. Lucia as a tourist destination through effective use of websites (Brown, 2021). Tourism in a Creole space however, as discussed below, involves engagement of tourists in emergent cultures which stem from European colonialization.

Tourism Culture, Policy, and Marketability

The relationship between culture and tourism development is important to Governments and International agencies. This sentiment is illustrated by the current United Nations World Tourism Organization (2021) Chair who aptly opined that tourism is a driving force for the safeguarding of "natural and cultural heritage" (Pololikasvili, 2020). Also, the Ethnic, Culture and Social Responsibility Department of the UNWTO is geared towards accessible tourism for all which emphasizes the protection of culture of a people. Significantly, of particular concern is Intangible Cultural Heritage (ICH). Arguably, Lenzerini (2011) espouses that the loss of ICH—languages, knowledge, know-how, customs, and ideas—leads to the progressive impoverishment of human society, thus signally its invaluable resource for nation states. Skounti (2009) describes ICH as fluid and ever-changing, presenting specific challenges for safeguarding due to the complex influences involved. Regardless, UNESCO successfully engaged over a hundred states in creating a "List of Masterpieces of Intangible Cultural Heritage" to support recognition of the significance of cultural practices and ensuring their continuation (Hafstein 2015).

Richards (2003) describes cultural tourism as a "good form" of tourism that stimulates the economy and help conserve culture. His work explores cultural tourism as part of cultural consumption presenting an interesting framework for the island context. Further, a UNWTO Report on Tourism and Cultural Synergies (2018) indicates that 89% of national tourism administrations confirmed that cultural tourism was part of their tourism policy. The report places substantial value on cultural tourism but cautions that if not properly managed it may have adverse effects on communities.

Whilst the development of tourism may enhance perception and economy of a country, negative impacts on culture may result in questioning the viability of the industry. Economic viability in terms of overall financial contribution may come into conflict with socio-cultural viability. Situations such as the destruction of artefacts and "looting and theft of prehistoric artefacts are unfortunate consequences of heritage tourism" (Di Lernia, 2005, p. 447). There is however the contrasting view that sustainable tourism development can curb these issues by ensuring the authenticity of culture is kept while marketing the experience to tourists (Abbasi & Mohammed, 2013).

Caribbean literature over the years has emphasized the need for the relationship between tourism and culture to be explored and maximized to its full potential. Nurse (2002, p. 127) underscores the region's inadequacy in researching the "synergy between tourism and the cultural industries." As Jayawardena (2002) and Boxill and Severin (2004) point out, there are numerous challenges to locals within the Caribbean space as ownership of resources does not lie with locals. Jordan (2012, p. 2) indicates that "at the core" of the relationship between tourism and culture is the "extent to which the culture of a destination can be developed and packaged into a cultural tourism product while maintaining its authenticity." Torres, Skillicorn and Nelson (2011) earlier describe this dualism—nature and culture—as the ultimate tourist package. Irwin-Hunt (2020) describes the Caribbean as the world's most tourism dependent region and proposes that in light of the challenges presented to the industry today, stakeholders must rethink the tourist product. As such she proffers that historical, adventure, and eco-tourism must all be developed. Interestingly, O' Farrell (2021) highlights that plans for recovery from challenges experienced in tourism development explore "horizontal integration" which promotes tourism in amalgamation with other sectors such as environment and culture.

Following on from the above insights, it is useful to explore frameworks for tourism development which consider the culture of the destination. McElroy (2003) suggests that developing states would require three major policy directions: the restoration of environmental damage, management of visitor arrivals, and the extension of time spent in the region by encouraging alternatives to mass tourism such as heritage tourism. Arguably, mass tourism requires more air access and infrastructure, a continuous challenge for SIDS to overcome. In response, the policies of developing countries lean towards frameworks which support a strong relationship between nature and cultural tourism.

Interestingly, the evaluation of tourists' interest levels regarding aspects of culture provides feedback on tourism product viability. For example, the omnivorous-univorous framework (Barbieri & Mahoney, 2010) examines tourists' interests and behaviours. Omnivorous tourists have higher tastes and univorous tourists, who tend to be of lower economic strata, have fewer specific tastes in examining culture. An understanding of tourists' interests in cultural tourism will result in creation of better suited marketing strategies.

It is evident that the relationship between tourism and culture presents a myriad of issues for consideration for small island developing states (SIDS). As such, careful thought and planning must be implemented to ensure successful tourism development which in turn limits negative impacts.

Tourism Development and the Impact on Locals

That tourism development impacts upon locals in various forms can be observed in cases around the globe. Cole (2008, p. 32) reminds us that "tourism is not only seen as a generator of foreign exchange but also a means to promote pride in a country's heritage." As locals identify with and become versed in their cultural traditions they present, package, and promote them as tourism products. This phenomenon is embraced by destination management organizations (DMOs) and other relevant authorities; for instance, the National Tourism Policy of Botswana strategy focuses on encouraging "stronger emphasis on communities, participation and local culture in tourism development and products" (Lenao & Saarinen, 2015, p. 204).

Heritage tourism has the potential to generate socio-cultural and economic benefits, including the reduction of poverty for people living in and around them. Further, cultural tourism preserves local culture while providing significant economic benefits to locals.However, Robinson (1999) warns that cultural tourism can result in cultural conflicts, as the invasion of foreign cultures may not always be positive. For example, Canizares et al. (2014) laments that in Cape Verde, artists may benefit from tourist development but unfortunately locals wishing to purchase land are negatively affected by increased prices. According to Abbasi and Mohammed (2013) a sustainable tourism framework, which considers involvement of locals in safeguarding and marketing culture, is essential in order to address this dilemma.

In this regard, Liu and Wall (2006) suggest that tourism planning should cater for all residents as much as for tourists. They posit that too often inadequate attention is given to locals to energize growth. Poignantly, they stress that cultural concerns and determinants of human resource development are also pivotal considerations alongside tourism development. Even earlier, Johnson et al. (1994) had proffered a Human Resource Development Framework for tourism for developing countries. In their view, first, the public sector must cultivate a vision for tourism; second, a committee is put in place to establish the specific focus on the vision; and third, the human resource base is empowered with relevant skills and knowledge. Clearly, in the context of this work, central to the process are the persons involved in marketing and those responsible for facilitating the sharing of culture within Creole spaces.

The Creole Space, Culture, and Identity

Examining the concept of a Creole space considers the language and culture which identifies a people of a specific geographic location. Caribbean islands, including Saint Lucia, Dominica, Barbados, and Aruba are renowned for their Creole cultural heritage way of life, with historic and racial heritage demarking rich traditions of Creole spaces. As Holm (2004) reminds us, rising from a plantation slave economy are the *Kwéyòl* languages; and importantly, "to speak a language is to appropriate its world and culture" (Fanon 2008). Following on from Cruse's (2015) perspective, that the linguist must first guide the geographer, interestingly, Creole spaces are conceptualized by *Kwéyòl* languages which spring from the experience of European, African, and Indigenous cultures within the region.

Research on Creoles has increased over the years receiving a level autonomy in the academic world (Bettina & Leglise, 2007, p. 18). The debates have surrounded the definition of concepts such as a Creole, the origin, structure, syntax, lexicon, the *Kwéyòl* speech communities, Creole spaces and, the maintenance and revitalization of Creoles (Degraff 2005). Thus, defining Creole spaces is a dynamic and complex phenomenon. The space is multidimensional, factoring the relationships among geographies, sociolinguistic concerns, and individual identities within the perceived conceptual area.

Academic discussion of space has evolved over the years across disciplines. Auer and Schmidt (2010) present a comprehensive review of the concept, mapping out the evolution of the research done in the field. The early work of Rogers (1983) examined diffusion across space, communicative networks, distance time, and social structure. Students of language and space began to draw on humanistic and discursive geography. More recently, Auer and Schmidt (2010) conclude that Creole space is first and foremost a sociolinguistic space. They present the efforts of Ferguson in Haiti 1959, Decamp in Jamaica 1971, and Rickford in Guyana 1987 in delineating the concept of a Creole continuum. A Creole continuum refers to diglossic situations in which two varieties of a language are used by speakers in varying situations leading to the creation of a social space rather than solely a geographical space. This generates on one hand, the "high" status of the dominant imposed language while on the other hand the "low" status of the local thus producing a dilemma over language use, variety, and choice.

Auer and Schmidt (2010, p. 446) further review Carrington's definition (1999, p. 98) highlighting that a Creole space has four characteristics namely:

(i) Creole space is multidimensional;
(ii) the individuals who inhabit Creole spaces have multisystemic repertoires;
(iii) the density of networks of communication will determine the stability and consequently the identifiability of systems within this space;
(iv) the space coheres because networks of communication overlap.

Accordingly, an understanding of the Creole space within which ICH is effectively explored, gives stakeholders the relevant contextual industry support, marketing strategies, and resource allocation to facilitate cultural tourism development. In this scenario the question of identity becomes a contention between what is "common" and what is "proper."

Lenzerini's (2011) evaluation of the 1989 UNESCO General Conference's international legal instrument on ICH offers further insight for exploring the above phenomenon. He opines that one of the most important steps in creating such an instrument is "self-identification" which is transmitted through generations, facilitating group identification. Dwivedi (2005) suggests Caribbean creolization (metaphor for the process of emergence of a Creole culture) emerges from multiple/plural identities arising simultaneously in the region. Such identity is specific to situation and context. Dwivedi (2005, p. 12) further clarifies that "creolization of a language is easy to understand" but creolization of identity is not. "The Creole languages adopted the content words, phonologically strong syllables, simple word-order with a loss of ordering possibilities from the European languages, and employed relexification or intertwining, and convergence." The Creole culture therefore comprises an amalgamation of the languages and identities which influence the creation of a new identity within the space. It is this phenomenon that the chapter seeks to continue to explore within Saint Lucians Creole cultural identity and tourism development context.

3 Cultural Tourism in Saint Lucia

Saint Lucia is a small island (238.2 m^2) in the Caribbean. Today, tourism is the main stay of the economy contributing 9,597 jobs in 2014 (Hutchinson, 2015, p. 4). Additionally, the World Travel and Tourism Council in 2015 reported that travel and tourism supported 16,500 jobs (21.5% of total employment) directly, and 36,000 jobs (46.3% of total employment) indirectly. Today, the western part of the island in which this research was set records 23% hotels, and 24% of sites and attractions of the island's registered establishments and one out of the three marinas (Ministry of Tourism (MOT), n.d.). The MOT acknowledges that there may be several properties and products which are not registered but utilized by tourists (Fig. 8.1).

St. Lucia's journey of exploring culture and tourism development in the late sixties led to relevant changes including new policy creation (Jules, 2005). The Governments' National Plan in 1979 focused on eight specific objectives including the development and protection of attractions and

Fig. 8.1 Map of St. Lucia (Google, n.d.)

free movement for tourist (Ministry of Planning, Personnel Establishment & Training, 1979). In the 1980s, Joseph Eudovique, an African trained wood carver and sculpture pioneered the business and training of persons to explore the folkways as tourism products. As a result, the folks and arts sector saw an upward trend supported by government assistance programmes. Policy implementation evolved over the years and explored several policy initiatives in cultural tourism development as illustrated below:

(i). National Policy of Saint Lucia (1999, p. 28; Section C, Number 10) Culture and Tourism policy initiatives will ensure the development of tourism:

- to reduce the negative impacts of tourism on cultural identity;
- to develop programmes geared towards orienting on cultural heritage and contemporary cultural identity;
- to provide more space available for the orientation and for touristic activities.

(ii). St. Lucia's Tourism Policy (2003), focuses on: Objective 6, to "project a positive and unique identity of Saint Lucia in tourism generating markets through developing a marketing strategy that moves beyond physical beauty to incorporate cultural assets." This experienced-based approach will result in increased attention on areas such as cultural and heritage tourism.

(iii). The National Cultural Policy (Cultural Development Foundation CDF, 2021) focuses on Objective 7 "to ensure the full integration of culture into national planning and development." The policy also highlights that there should be research the economic value of cultural activities.

While the relationship between culture and tourism has been addressed in various cultural and tourism policies, evidence of a specific cultural tourism policy for Saint Lucia has not been found. The existing policies, however, create a context for future formation of such policy.

Central to the tourist product portfolio is Saint Lucia's unique history of battles between the French and English over sovereignty of the island. Likened to Helen of Troy, the beautiful Saint Lucia is considered as the "Helen of the West"; the battles for her make for a fascinating tale which would pique the interest of tourists (Saint Lucia Tourism Authority, 2021). Consequently, Saint Lucia's history reveals an interesting linguistic *Kwéyòl* culture with a strong French influence. However, eventual victory of the British over the French in 1803 resulted in the gradual movement towards English as the dominant language. As suggested by Simmons-Mc Donald (2006), formal English language was accompanied by the creation of a non-standard English vernacular. *Kwéyòl*, classified as a French-lexified creole, is one important derivate of this diverse and turbulent history. As such, *Kwéyòl* is a significant aspect of Saint Lucia's Creole culture. As St. Hilaire (2000, p. 32) points out, "in St. Lucia, *Kwéyòl* is the cultural property of descendants of enslaved Africans." It is through language that many other traditions, rituals, and arts forms are maintained and transmitted. Therefore, the survival of the *Kwéyòl* language is inherent to the continued existence of all other aspects of the Creole culture. Undoubtedly, this is an area which needs to be further developed as the island seeks to advance its place in the cultural tourist market.

Meanwhile, over the last decades, local research has evaluated the impact of tourism and focused mainly on: the physical environment and the socio-economic climate (Barker, 2003; Nicholas & Thapa, 2010; Issac, 2013; Emmanuel-Flood, 2017; Sutton, 2019); heritage tourism initiatives (Renard, 2001); sustainability (Jules, 2005); and more recently public policy on the *Kwéyòl* language and traditional knowledge (Charles, 2011). In contrast, this chapter seeks to add to the discussion by exploring the impact of tourism on culture:

1. To what extent do locals identify with Saint Lucia's Creole Culture?
2. What is the role of the local authorities in using Saint Lucian culture as a tool for tourist development?
3. What do locals think is the impact of tourist development on Creole culture in Saint Lucia?
4. How marketable do locals think Saint Lucia's Creole culture is as a tourist product?

This case study focuses on conceptualizations of locals from the western part of the island, Soufriere, an area known for its numerous hotels and tourist attractions. The research employs qualitative data which provides information on perceptions and behaviour (Xu & Park, 2017) (Fig. 8.2).

The sample population included 60 randomly selected locals. Five managers of the largest hotel chains in the western area were specifically chosen for interview due to their seniority and expert knowledge. The problem-centred expert interview, as proposed by Doringer (2021), was employed as it relies on persons who are involved in decision-making and who are involved in development and implementation. The questionnaire used to collect qualitative data from the locals was deemed the best option for its quick response time, affordable distribution, and specific question

Fig. 8.2 Map of Soufriere

style (Rahman, 2016). Data was collected over a period of three weeks via Google forms due to the COVID-19 pandemic and to secure wider reach. Hotel managers and respondents were all anonymized.

4 Identity Within Creole Spaces

In establishing the significance and context of this research it was important to ascertain St Lucians' perceptions of their affinity with the Creole culture as described by Lenzerini (2011) as Self- identification. Most of the respondents associated with Saint Lucia's Creole culture although to varying degrees. All respondents, from ages 18 to 65, remarkably from diverse occupations including farming, teaching, banking, service work, construction, journalism, art, architecture, and entrepreneurship claim to be speakers of *Kwéyòl*. Whilst all respondents speak Creole with varying levels of competence, they did not claim to be very knowledgeable about different aspects of Saint Lucia culture.

The above phenomenon draws attention the status of Creole culture in Saint Lucia. *Kwéyòl* has evolved over the last 100 years due to what Simmons-Mc Donald (2006) refers to as "English linguistic imperialism." With the drive to ensure that English was the language of choice and simultaneously the rise of the traditional non-standard English vernacular, *Kwéyòl* was under threat. Consequently, the Creole culture became vulnerable to influences from the metropolis and other Caribbean islands (Simmons-Mc Donald, 2006). In this regard, it is commendable that Creole identity resonated among nationals. Furthering this view, Chow (2009, p. 9) opines that the transformational and dynamic nature of the Creole identity points to the reclamation of the identity. Dwivedi (2005) emphasizes how identification with the Creole culture is integral to establishing and promoting that culture as a tourist product. It is locals who engage tourists as self-employed, as independent entities, or as workers and policy makers in Creole spaces. Hence, it is essential that local peoples are active stakeholders and meaningfully involved in planning and decision-making processes in cultural tourism development.

5 The Role of Local Stakeholder

Discussions revealed that concern over the approach towards the promotion of cultural tourism was significant. The perception was that tourism was predominantly geared towards American and European culture which negatively impacted upon the Creole culture. St. Hiliare (2013) supported this perception indicating that US culture has substantial influence on Saint Lucian culture. Also, a point of concern was that cultural activities were not promoted perennially. Currently, the focus is on *Jounen Kwéyòl* (Creole Day), and most of the promotion is done for Creole Heritage Month (October) and Carnival. Meanwhile, other cultural activities such as the flower festivals are ignored.

Interestingly at two of the hotels where weekly classes in *Kwéyòl* are offered, tourists are immersed in the culture throughout the year. In another case, an award-winning resort, specializing in heritage tourism, offers plantation history, tours about local flora and fauna, cultural performances, and traditional cocoa-processing techniques to their guests.

The study reveals that there is a perceived failure of institutions to properly define, document, and transmit Creole culture to the younger generation. Consequently, cultural transmission is left solely to the family. Moreover, *Kwéyòl* is not taught in schools. There is a widely held view of Creoles as debauched and little value attached to the language. According to Simmons-Mc Donald (2006, p. 65) "the institutions in St. Lucia have not allowed *Kwéyòl* to be a powerful voice in the shaping of the St. Lucian cultural imagination." Not surprisingly, Frank (2009) argues that at the heart of the many political, religious, and economic factors influencing language choice in Saint Lucia, perception of the language is critical. Regardless, the Curriculum and Materials Development Unit (CAMDU, 2021) of the Department of Education is currently pursuing the development of a National Language Policy in collaboration with regional and international agencies. The 2018 draft policy is actively going through implementation steps.

Another concern was that government does not adequately invest in the safeguarding of the history, culture, and traditions and have implemented no antiquity laws to preserve artefacts. Importantly, Simmons-Mc Donald (2006) recognizes the work of the Folk Research Centre (FRC), the National Archives of St. Lucia, and the National Trust in their attempts to preserve and transmit culture. However, Charles (2011) suggests institutions have been handicapped, probably through little fault of their own, in the preservation and transmission of Creole culture. He laments the underfunding of institutions, and the low priority given to programmes that safeguard Intangible Cultural Heritage which have been left to "hobbyist" and non-government agencies like the FRC. Commendably, the Saint Lucian government has recently promised to reinstate the subvention to the National Trust and support Official Language status for *Kwéyòl* ("Government to Support National Trust", 2021).

Nevertheless, local authorities have an immense responsibility to engage in effective cultural tourism planning. Consideration must be given to the level of exploration of cultural tourism within frameworks which examine supply and demand (Hutchinson, 2015), the nature of experiences which tourists travel for (Barbieri & Mahoney, 2010) and the level of knowledge and skill which the human resource in the destinations are equipped with (Johnson et al., 1994). Proper management of culture will curb the possibility of destruction (Scher, 2011) ensuring that cultural preservation and involvement in tourism is properly managed by authorities (Lenao & Saarinen, 2015; Cole, 2008). Notwithstanding, establishing a strong identity and drive for Saint Lucian Creole culture is pivotal to defining the cultural tourism product.

6 Impact of Tourism Development on Creole Culture

Economic activity does not occur in a vacuum and involves development of a space with physical and socio-economic implications. As such inevitably it has both positive and negative impacts. Table 8.1 proposes such impacts for tourism development within Creole spaces.

Of note, safeguarding Creole heritage, cultural promotion, creating new employment opportunities, and enhanced legislation are mirrored in discussion on the positive social, economic, and political impacts of culture as a tourist product (Torres, Skillicorn & Nelson, 2011; Padilla & Mc Elroy, 2010). Despite several positive impacts there are concerns that tourism may result in the disappearance of traditions. For instance, Robinson (1999) earlier warned of cultural conflict arising due to tourism

Table 8.1 Cultural tourism development in Creole spaces

Positive impacts	*Negative impacts*
Employment opportunities for performing artistes and persons in the creative industries	Tourism will take priority over traditional occupations such as farming
Development of innovative business opportunities for diversification in marketing Creole culture	Loss of traditions in favour of lifestyle of tourists
Maintenance of cultural practices as the tourist experience the Creole culture	Locally hand-crafted products are replaced with foreign commercial products
Identification and maintenance of historical sites and artefacts	Loss of *Kwéyòl* language
Greater interest in the writing of *Kwéyòl* and publications	Negative influences on traditional values
Creation of environment for authorities to engage in legislative action regarding conservation	

development, while later, Canizares et al. (2014) revealed fears around local traditions vanishing. In this case, as illustrated in Table 8.1, Saint Lucians have expressed unease over the integration of the culture of the tourists and with their own cultural identifiers.

7 Marketability of Saint Lucian Creole Culture

Without question, cultural tourism in Saint Lucia could be a viable economic investment strategy if implemented effectively. Of more relevance, this study seems to suggest that the Saint Lucian Creole culture could be augmented as part of the tourism product. The active role and involvement of the local government officials, policy makers, and key stakeholders are central to moving the cultural tourism agenda forward. In the case of Saint Lucia, some ongoing challenges noted around the Creole culture are: there is little or no use of the *Kwéyòl* language in advertisements and in the operations involving the industry; Creole activities are not promoted as part of the tourist package throughout the year; instead major promotions are mainly of physical or natural sites. Currently, the majority of locals believe that the physical environment is the main marketing tool for tourism.

Other marketing tools observed are ratings or accreditations that the destination receives, particularly as a honeymoon destination and for its hotel accommodations. Further, culture was not identified as a main marketing tool.

The aspects of Saint Lucian culture currently promoted are predominantly tangible and easily visible. Currently offered to tourists are Creole foods, artefacts, and sites and to a lesser extent the intangible aspects such as traditions and history. Deliberate engagement with folk lore, language, and other more didactic and involved aspects of culture are less featured. Undoubtedly, proactive hotel involvement is essential in promoting the overall cultural destination product. Credit must be given to the establishments with initiatives already in place such as décor, furniture, cultural print and handcrafted material, Creole designed uniforms, and Creole art and culture. Overall, managers posited that there is much untapped potential of Saint Lucian Creole culture "lying in wait" as a marketing tool for tourism development.

Moreover, the use of *Kwéyòl* language is mostly absent as an oral communication tool or as signage at establishments. Arguably, the responsibility of marketing culture as a tourist product falls with policy makers and tourism professionals as well as that of hotel establishments. Cole (2008) presents extensive research to support involvement of government, guides, and cultural groups in a successful strategy for advancing cultural tourism. Similarly, Skounti's (2009) perspective on ICH proposes policy implementation which ensures safeguarding of culture whilst enhancing development. Following on these concepts we now advance a framework proposed for practicality and relevance to the Creole tourism space in the Caribbean region.

8 The Four Cs Framework for Creole Cultural Tourism Space (CCTS) Development

Aligned with the ethos of UNWTO (2018), the perception within Creole spaces is generally that cultural tourism is a viable industry but should be effectively managed. The findings of this study support the need for governments to invest in a cultural tourism industry which is profitable and serves to enhance the nation's Creole identity, particularly for Caribbean based Creole self- identifying destinations. Importantly, this requires balance between profitability and safeguarding of the rich heritage and traditions, along with in-depth stakeholder involvement at all levels of development.

In that regard, we proffer the Four C's framework as a structured conceptual approach for exploring and furtherance of Creole Cultural tourism Space (CCTS) within the context of SIDS as presented and illustrated below (Fig. 8.3):

Conceptualization: As argued by Liu and Wall (2006) cultural tourism should cater to the experience of both tourist and locals. In that regard, the initial Phase I focuses on goal setting, headed by a select expert steering committee. A clear mission and vision are established and clarity is gained around pivotal positioning questions.

- What is the nature of the Creole culture with which locals identify?
- Why are we doing this?
- What do we hope to achieve?
- What product and brand do we develop?
- What resources are required?
- Who are the key stakeholders?
- What governing structures are required?

Fig. 8.3 The four Cs framework for Creole Cultural Tourism Space (CCTS) development

- What operational systems will be regarded?
- Who are the competitors?
- What challenges might we face and need to overcome?

These will bring centre stage pertinent areas of significance for debate and discussion in phase II.

Creation: Phase II involves designing/redesigning of a Creole cultural tourism policy and documentation with operational bylaws. This phase allows for stakeholder engagement and re-engagement for policy review with steering committee. Working groups are organized to facilitate in-depth stakeholder consultation with representatives of various sub-sectors such as tourism development, cultural development, the environment, and finance among others. Other suggested participants include cultural groups and icons within the Creole space, community leaders, and interested professional and practitioners.

As presented by Skounti (2009) stakeholders will engage in identifying ICH Masterpieces as well as aspects of tangible culture. Organizational responsibility for managing and preserving key aspects of the Creole cultural tourism product is established. Partnerships with other countries within the regional and international Creole space are initiated.

Consolidation: Implementation of an agreed action plan within CCTS occurs. Following on Hutchinson (2015), creating a marketing strategy, designing advertisements, and establishing cultural tourism packages are all part of this phase III. A human resource development plan is designed and implemented. Quality assessment and assurance processed for entrepreneurs and other frontline industry players undertaken. Sector wide training programmes implemented.

Continuance: Implementation of a sustainable development strategy for advancing of the CCTS. This involves product evaluation for efficacy, policy appropriateness for future development, branding, international marketing, and niche campaign positioning. Importantly, evaluation must also ascertain the level of interest by tourist and locals (Barbieri & Mahoney, 2010). Hence, there is a need for continuous product monitoring and improvement. There should also be reassurance that the CCTS development drive aims at ensuring cultural safeguarding. Therefore, research and development, employing customer exist surveys to collect valuable feedback is a critical pillar in the safeguarding process.

These four phases of advancing the CCTS should not occur in isolation nor be treated with rigidity. Instead, the processes are recursive. Creole culture is dynamic and evolutionary. Therefore, the aspects of culture offered and promoted for tourism must be constantly reviewed (Bettina & Leglise, 2007) as stakeholder dynamics undergo change, and the sector evolves. Thus, the conceptualization, creation, and consolidation process require continuity. At the creation phase, there may be need to revisit the conceptualization and determine whether goals remain attainable or whether the consolidation plan continues to be effective and feasible, resulting in further sensitization or input.

9 Conclusion

Within the Caribbean visitor economy, identification with Creole culture means embracing a strategy for cultural tourism. Moreover, with the onslaught of numerous global challenges, particularly the rising negative impacts of climate change, expanding the marketing strategy beyond the physical environment—"sun, sand, sea" brand—to include dimensions of Creole culture is strongly advocated. Embracing UNESCO ICH status initiatives has several potential benefits: (i) wider international markets; (ii) tourism product employment opportunities particularly for the artforms; (iii) identification and maintenance of the cultural space; (iv) greater transmission of culture to younger generations; (v) greater interest in the promotion of *Kwéyòl;* (vi) the development and enforcement of legislature to promote and maintain the rich heritage. Regardless, tourism development may be detrimental to the Creole culture. The invasion of the Creole space by tourists can result in the mass movement away from traditional occupations such as farming and the craft industry and the adoption of foreign culture at the expense of *Kwéyòl.*

These findings lead to the creation of the Four Cs Framework for Creole Cultural Tourism Space (CCTS) development. The recursive stages of Conceptualization, Creation, Consolidation, and Continuance engage stakeholders in establishing the systems and processes aimed at building, and sustaining a potentially dynamic Creole Tourism Development Product (CTDP).

Future research could further explore possible strategic regional approaches with other sister Creole-speaking countries and comparatively analyse with similar cultural tourism developmental product elsewhere.

Acknowledgements Thanks to Dr Morgan Dalphinis for the introduction to the project. Zial, Sanjay, and Nikel for technical support. To Jane and Eyan for your support. To our families for the love, especially Mikey, Daya, and Shine.

References

Abbasi, D. S., & Mohammed, B. (2013). Local Perception of Tourism Development: A Conceptual Framework for Sustainable Cultural Tourism. *Journal of Management and Sustainability.*, *3*(2), 31.

Auer, P., & Schmidt, J. E. (2010). *Language and Space: An International Handbook of Linguistic Variation. Theories and Methods.* W. de Gruyter.

Barbieri, C., & Mahoney, E. (2010). Cultural Tourism Behaviour and Preferences Among the Live Performing Arts Audience: An Application of the Univorous-Omnivorous Framework. *International Journal of Tourism Research, 12*(5), 481–496.

Barker, N. (2003) *Ecological and Socio-economic Impacts of Dive and Snorkel Tourism in St. Lucia, West Indies.* Dissertation. United Kingdom: The University of York, ProQuest Dissertation Publishing.

Bettina, M., & Leglise, I. (2007). Language and colonialism: Applied Linguistics in the Context of Creole Communities. In M. Hellinger & A. Pauwels (Eds.), *Handbook of Applied Linguistics: Language and Communication* (Vol. 9, pp. 297–338). Mouton De Gruyter.

Boxill, I., & Severin, F. O. (2004). An Exploratory Study of Tourism Development and is Impact on the Caribs of Dominica. *International Journal of Hospitality & Tourism Administration., 5*(1), 1–27.

Brown, V. (2021). *Responsible Tourism in St. Lucia.* https://www.responsible-travel.com/holidays/saint-lucia/travel-guide/responsible-tourism-in-st-lucia

Canizares, S. M. S., Tabales, J., & Garcia, F. J. F. (2014). Local residents' Attitudes Towards the Impact of Tourist Development in Cape Verde. *Tourism & Management Studies, 10*(2), 87–96.

Caribbean Tourism Organization. (2021). https://www.onecaribbean.org/

Carrington, L. (1999). The Status of Creole in the Caribbean. *Caribbean Quarterly, 45,* 41–51.

Charles, E. (2011). Traditional Knowledge the Kweyol Language and Public Policy in a Small Nation State. WACC. https://waccglobal.org/traditional-knowledge-the-kweyol-language-and-public-policy-in-a-small-nation-state/

Chow, R. S. E. (2009). *Post-colonial hauntologies: Creole identity in Jean Rhys, Patrick Chamosieu and David Dabydeen.* Dissertation. ProQuest Dissertations & Theses Global.

Cole, S. (2008). Tourism and Cultural Change. In M. Robinson & A. Phipps (Eds.), *Tourism Culture and Development; Hopes, Dreams and Realities in East Indonesia.* Channel View Publications.

Cruse, R. (2015). Diffusion and Spatial Dynamics of Creole Languages in the Caribbean. *L'Espace Geographique (English Edition), 44*(1), 1–17.

Cultural Development Foundation (2021). National Cultural Policy, Saint Lucia: Cultural Development Foundation. Available at: https://www.cdfstlucia.org/who-we-are/national-cultural-policy/

Curriculum and Materials Development Unit. (2021). *St. Lucia National Language Policy.*

Degraff, M. (2005). Linguists Most Dangerous Myth: The Fallacy of Creole Exceptionalism. *Language in society, 34,* 533–591.

Di Lernia, S. (2005). Incoming Tourism, Outgoing Culture: Tourism Development and Cultural Heritage in Libyan Sahara. *The Journal of North African Studies., 10*(3–4), 441–457. https://doi.org/10.1080/13629380500350285

Doringer, S. (2021). The Problem-centred Expert Interview; Combining Qualitative Interviewing Approaches for Investigating Implicit Expert Knowledge. *International Journal of Social Research Methodology., 24*(3), 265–278. https://doi.org/10.1080/13645579.2020.1766777

Dwivedi, A. V. (2005). Language, Identity and Gender; A Study of Creole in the Caribbean. *Linguistic and Literature Studies., 3*(1), 11–17.

Emmanuel-Flood, J. (2017). Striking a Balance with the Future (Special Report). *International Trade Forum, 1* (2), 20.

Fanon, F. (2008). *Black Skin, White Masks.* Grove Press, New ed. Harvard University.

Frank, D. (2009). *Political, Religious and Economic Factors Affecting Language Choice in St. Lucia.* De Gruyter Mouton, 1993 (102): 39–56

Google. (n.d.). *Map of Saint Lucia.* https://www.google.com/maps/@13.9238853,-61.1555533,10.56z

Government of Saint Lucia. (1999). *Saint Lucia National Cultural Policy.*

Government of St. Lucia National Plan. (1979). Ministry of Planning, Personnel Establishment & Training.

Government to Support national Trust, Examine Possibility of Making *Kwéyòl* an official Language. (2021, August 4). *The Voice.*

Hafstein, V. T. (2015). Intangible Heritage as Diagnosis: Safeguarding as Treatment. *Journal of Folklore Research, 52*(2–3), 281–298.

Holm, J. (2004). *An Introduction to Pidgins and Creoles.* Cambridge University Press.

Hutchinson, M. (2015). *The Determinants of Tourism Demand to Saint Lucia.* Ministry of Finance, Research and Policy Unit.

Irwin-Hunt, A. (2020). Caribbean Tourism Adjusts to Pandemic Disruption. *fDi Intelligence.*

Issac, M (2013). The Implications of Sea Level Rise for Tourism in St. Lucia. Dissertation. *Geography- Tourism Planning and Policy.* University of Waterloo, Ontario.

Jayawardena, C. (2002). Future Challenges for Tourism in the Caribbean. *Social and Economic Studies, 51*(1), 1–23.

Johnson, J. D., Snepenger, D. J., & Akins, S. (1994). Resi-dents' Perceptions of Tourism Development. *Annals of Tourism Research, 21*(3), 629–642.

Jordan, L. A. (2012). Tourism, culture and the creative Industries; Exploring Linkages. *Journal of Eastern Caribbean Studies, 37*(3&4), 1–5.

Jules, S. (2005). *A Sustainability of Assessment and Trade and Liberalization in Tourism Services.* Heller School Programmes in Sustainable Development. Brandis University.

Lenao, M., & Saarinen, J. (2015). Integrated Rural Tourism as a Tool for Community Tourism Development: Exploring Culture and Heritage Projects in the North- East District of Botswana. *South African Geographical Journal, 97*(2), 203–216.

Lenzerini, F. (2011). Intangible Cultural Heritage: The Living Culture of Peoples. *The European Journal of International Law., 22*(1), 101–120.

Liu, A., & Wall, G. (2006). Planning Tourism Employment: A Developing Country Perspective. *Tourism Management, 27*, 159–170.

Lock S. (2021). Global Tourism Industry—Statistics & Facts. *Travel Tourism & Hospitality*. Statista Research Department.

Lopez, A. (2021). International Tourism Revenue in the Caribbean 2010–2019. https://www.statista.com/statistics/814155/caribbean-totalcontribution-travel-tourism-gdp-country/

McElroy, M. (2003). The New Knowledge Management. Complexity, Learning, and Sustainable innovation. Boston, MA: KMCI Press, Butterworth-Heinemann.

Ministry of Tourism Saint Lucia. (n.d.). Saint Lucia, Unpublished Data. https://tourism.govt.lc/

Mousavi, S. S., Doratli, N., Mousavi, S. M., & Morandiahari, F. (2016). Defining Cultural Tourism. In *International Conference on Civil Architecture and Sustainable Development*. London

Nicholas, L., & Thapa, B. (2010). Visitor perspectives on sustainable tourism development in the Pitons Management Area World Heritage Site, St. Lucia. *Environment, Development and Sustainability, 12*(5), 839–857.

Nurse, K. (2002). Bringing culture into tourism: Festival tourism and Reggae Sunsplash in Jamaica. *Social and Economic Studies, 15*(1), 127–143.

O'Farrell, S. (2021, June 30). Tourism- Dependence and Its Discontents. *fDi Intelligence: Financial Times Ltd*.

Padilla, A., & McElroy, J. L. (2010). The Three C's of Caribbean Tourism: Contexts, Characteristics and Consequences. *ARA Journal of Tourism Research, 2*(2), 78–90.

Pololikasvili, Z. (2020) Tourism and Rural Development, UNTWO World Tourism Day 2020: UNTWO. Available at https://www.unwto.org/world-tourism-day-2020

Rahman, S. (2016). 'The Advantages and Disadvantages of Using Qualitative and Quantitative Approaches and Methods in Language "Testing and Assessment" Research: a Literature Review', *Journal of Education and Learning*, 6(1), pp. 102–112.

Renard, Y. (2001). Practical Strategies for Pro-poor Tourism: A Case Study of St. Lucia Heritage Tourism Programme. Working Paper PPT No. & CRT 11Edo01.

Richards, G. (2003). *Cultural Tourism: Global and Local Perspectives*. The Haworth Press.

Robinson, M. (1999). Cultural Conflicts in Tourism: Inevitability and Equality. In M. Robinson and P. Boniface (Eds.), *Tourism and Cultural Conflicts* (pp. 1–32). CABI Publishing. Saint Lucia Tourism Authority (2021). https://www.stlucia.org/en/

Rogers E. (1983). Diffusion of Innovations, Third edition. New York Free Press.

Saint Lucia Tourism Authority (n.d). Saint Lucia. Available at https://www.stlucia.org/en/

Scher, P. W. (2011). Heritage Tourism in the Caribbean: The politics of Culture after Neoliberalism. *Journal of the Society of Latin American Studies: Bulletin of American Studies, 30*(1), 7–20.

Simmons-Mc Donald, H. (2006). Cultural Preservation and Language Reclamation: The St. Lucian Paradox. *Caribbean Quarterly, 52*(4), 57–73.

Skounti, A. (2009). *The Authentic Illusion: Humanity's Intangible Cultural Heritage, the Moroccan Experience.* Routledge.

St. Hilaire, A. (2000). *It's Our Culture; Global Process, Community Development and Language Survival in Louisiana and St. Lucia, Part 1.* Dissertation. John Hopkins University. Baltimore; Maryland.

St. Hiliare, A. (2013). Creolizing globalization: Pan-cultural Identities and Languages in St. Lucia. *Caribbean Studies, 41*(1), 3–25.

Sutton, M. (2019). *Climate Change Vulnerability of St. Lucia Tourism.* Dissertation. University of Waterloo, Ontario.

Torres, R. M., Skillicorn, P. and Nelson, V. (2011) 'Community Corporate Joint Ventures: An Alternative Model for Pro-Poor Tourism Development', *Tourism Planning & Development, 8*(3), pp. 297–316. Available at: https://doi.org/10.1080/21568316.2011.591158.

United Nations World Tourism Organization. (2014). *Small Island Developing States.* Madrid, Spain. https://www.unwto.org/sustainable-development/small-islands-developing-states

United Nations World Tourism Organization. (2021). *Cultural Tourism and Covid 19.*

UNTWO (2018). Tourism and Cultural Synergies, UNTWO e-library. Available at https://www.e-unwto.org/doi/book/10.18111/9789284418978

World Travel and Tourism Council. (2017). Caribbean Report; Resilience and Recovery 2018.

Xu, W. W., & Park, H. W. (2017). Versatile Networks in Combining Qualitative & Quantitative Data. *Quality &Quantity, 51*, 959–961.

Zappino, V. (2005). *Caribbean Tourism and Development: An Overview.* Discussion Paper No. 65, European Centre for Development Policy Management.

CHAPTER 9

Advancing a Creole Centre of Excellence Framework

Violet Cuffy

1 Introduction

Centres of Excellence (CoEs) have existed since the 1980s, but the concept lacks a commonly accepted definition, with most of the literature focused on structure and practices (Terbullino & Gabriel, 2021). The key purpose of such centres is for the creation of collaborative structures within which excellent research and knowledge development occurs and thrives. The advantage of the CoEs lies in the expertise of the team and the level of specialisation in a distinct field and/or discipline.

At a conceptual level the establishment of COE's begs the questions, what then is excellence? What are its key dimensions? How is it identified and measured in general and, of more significance to this work, in the context of Intangible Cultural Heritage (ICH) Creole space? Further, how can these institutions be better placed to enhance knowledge development, efficient university-industry collaboration and stakeholder engagement, but more importantly achieve meaningful impact through innovative research centres?

V. Cuffy (Deceased) (✉)
University of Bedfordshire, Luton, UK

V. Cuffy, J. Carr (eds.), *Creole Cultures, Vol. 1*,
https://doi.org/10.1007/978-3-031-24275-5_9

In terms of the focus of this chapter, the CoE perspective of relevance is synonymous to concepts such as development of the necessary scientific and technological environment for advancing the state-of-the-art in research (Leventis et al., 2018) from the standpoint of higher education institutions. CoEs take on a variety of foci and structure, from a team of academic researchers within one university, partnerships across universities, to a consortium with practitioners and industry enterprises.

In this chapter we explore these abovementioned phenomena with a view of advancing a workable Creole Centre of Excellence Framework applicable to the fundamental characteristics of countries within the international Creole space. In our discussions particular consideration is given to countries that currently have representation on the recently established International Creole Research Network (TICERN) a direct output of the 2018–2021 Arts and Humanities Research Council funded grant (RefAH/R004498/1) discussed more fully in a later section 'Contextual Setting: TICERN'.

2 Defining Centre of Excellence (CoEs)

Of note, the term 'excellence' is defined by Thürer et al. (2018) as a combination of operational excellence (efficiency) and service excellence (effectiveness). Interestingly, Hellström (2011) aligns excellence to the political and the scientific community due to its (i) evaluative dimensions, (ii) focus on common themes that most researchers can relate to and (iii) it is often tangible enough for external interests to partake and discuss its implication.

Arguably, excellence has different meaning in varying context, but our focus here is in the area of centres of excellence led by academic researchers within the higher education system. For further background and context, some of the most commonly used definitions from literature of CoEs are presented in Table 9.1.

In addition to the conceptualisation of CoEs, several models have been advanced to help frame discussions around systems and processes of excellence within organisations. The most commonly used models as identified in the literature are the Deming Prize, the Baldrige performance excellence programme and the European foundation for Quality Management Excellence Model, upon which many other programmes are based (Thürer et al., 2018).

Table 9.1 Definitions of Centre of Excellence (CoE)

Authors	*Definition*
Birkinshaw and Hood (1998)	An area of expertise for which the subsidiary is recognised by the corporation, and which other parts of the corporation draw on.
Moore and Birkinshaw (1998, p. 81)	A centre of excellence as a small group of individuals recognised for their leading-edge, strategically valuable knowledge, and mandated to leverage and/or make that knowledge available throughout the global firm.
Forsgren et al. (2000, p. 69)	Units, frequently subsidiaries, that have gained a more strategic role than others, implying that they have a wider responsibility concerning the competence development of the MNC.
Frost et al. (2002, p. 998)	A set of capabilities possessed by a particular organisational unit that has been explicitly recognised by the firm as an important source of value creation, with the intention that these capabilities be leveraged by and/or disseminated to other parts of the firm.
Forsgren et al. (2000, p. 47)	A concentration of excellence in the MNC and a source of excellence for the whole or a larger part of the MNC in its efforts to gain excellency generally.
Ensign et al. (2000, p. 134)	A set of activities that are recognised by the corporation for their superior capabilities, with the intention that those capabilities shall be leveraged and/or disseminated to other parts of the corporation.
Prescott C. Ensign (2002)	An organisational unit that embodies a set of capabilities that has been explicitly recognised by the firm as an important source of value creation, with the intention that these capabilities be leveraged by and/or disseminated to other parts of the firm.
Björkman (2001)	They have some kind of district competence that give them a competitive advantage and centre with competencies of use for other corporate units.
OECD (2014)	Focused on promoting high-quality scientific research, facilitating basic research through funding, promoting the internationalisation of national research, raising the profile of the host institution through the establishment of a CoE, formulating influential research groups and collaborations, and attracting experts and highly skilled researchers.
Fekadu et al. (2021)	Are defined within the area of specialty based on specific organisational vision and mission and have specialty expertise that other institutions in the same field or domain lack.

Adapted from Reger (2004, p. 55)

On the one hand, industry-based excellent models are strongly related to quality (Hermel & Ramis-Pujol, 2003) and business excellence is quite often synonymous with Total Quality Management (TQM) (Oakland & Tanner, 2008; Dahlgaard-Park, 2011; Dahlgaard et al., 2013). One criticism raised in past studies is that most excellence models have been frequently closely linked to award systems, with a heavy focus on prizes (Hermel & Ramis-Pujol, 2003), raising further questions on the absence of critical academic review and vigour in these processes of accreditation. On the other hand, the Baldrige performance excellence programme focuses on the core values of: 'An integrated approach to organisational performance management that really resolves in (1) delivery of ever improving value to customers and stakeholders, contributing to ongoing organisational success; (2) improvement of organisation's overall effectiveness and capabilities; and (3) learning for the organisation and for people in the workforce'.

In the field of business TQM has been a widely used strategy mainly centred on the following nine dimensions: (i) total employee involvement, (ii) continuous improvement, (iii) continuous training, (iv) teamwork, (v) empowerment, (vi) top management commitment and support, (vii) democratic management style, (viii) customer satisfaction and (ix) culture change (Voon, 2011). From an industry perspective these are useful criteria for evaluating service quality and service culture within organisations and is widely adopted across a number of sectors.

In one study, Kinyondo and Huggins (2020) explore the efficacy of Centres of Excellence as training centres for goldminers in Tanzania. The focus was on issues of financial sustainability, technical capacity and institutional connections of the CoEs, demand for the CoE service and whether the service would stimulate artisanal and small-scale mining formalisation. The interest was centred on the usefulness and impact of the initiative to lead to development into medium-sized organisations. However, the study found that in the context of small-scale companies, establishment of CoEs did not necessary translate into formalisation of organisational structures.

For Small Islands Developing States (SIDS) achieving such high level of excellence requires concerted effort and much deliberation of relevant stakeholders around developmental priority issues, and more often than not basic survival demands at national and regional levels take precedence.

Although recognised for its contributions to the wellbeing of a peope, ICH tends to be further down the pecking line on policy agendas. As such what would it mean for lesser developed countries not only to reach and/or achieve excellence but then also to maintain such high criteria in an era of so many global shifts and crisis? To explore these ideas more fully we review the work of Fekadu et al. (2021) on processes of excellence in the following section.

3 The Three Interactive Processes of Excellence

Focus now turns to Fekadu et al.'s (2021) conceptualisation of three interactive processes of excellence deemed essential to drive a CoE to become an agent of change at a national, regional and eventually global level. For its relevance to this body of work we highlight this framework and present it here for exploration within the present discussion on the efficacy of CoEs within the lesser developed world as a possible response to the myriad challenges faced for knowledge development and innovation around ICH. These three fundamental interactive processes are presented and discussed in Fig. 9.1.

As illustrated above Fekadu et al. (2021) postulate that the three pillars of participatory leadership, knowledge management and interdisciplinary collaboration are essential elements required for CoEs to be truly effective. Arguably, these processes serve to elevate a centre from a centre of

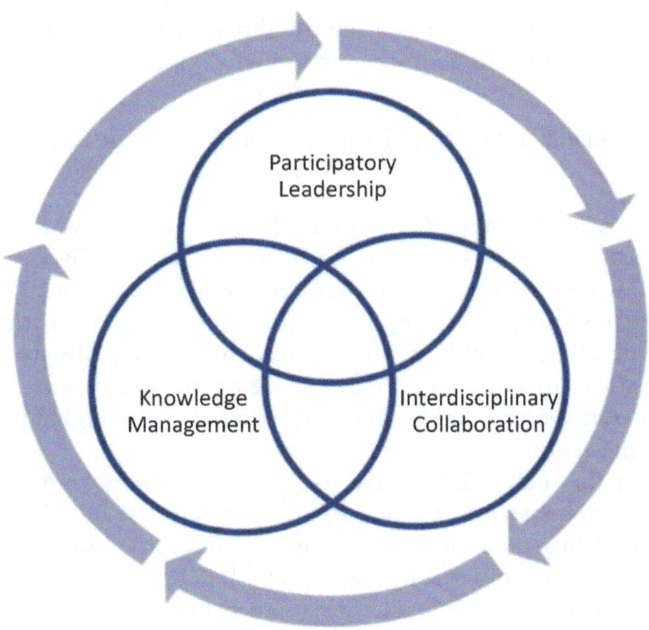

Fig. 9.1 The three interactive processes of excellence. (Adapted from Fekadu et al. 2021)

competency (a centre that is capable of doing things) to a Centre of Excellence (a centre capable of delivering the best outcomes or results following the most efficient procedures) (Fekadu et al., 2021, p. 4). The position hypothesised through this framework is that to be impactful and achieve excellence, it is essential that leadership is demonstrated in the following core dimensions: group participation in leadership decisions, clear and coordinated objectives, visionary leadership and well-managed hiring and selection practices. In addition, equally important is knowledge management, which is an effective system of bidirectional flow, obtaining information and input as well as disseminating knowledge, with prioritisation of commitment to both eliciting and disseminating information, knowledge and input from internal and external stakeholders alike. For Fekadu et al. (2021), the third critical element of interdisciplinary collaboration demands inclusion of diverse disciplines, backgrounds, cultures and perspectives, coming together to solve a common problem or pursue common goals.

In the area of higher education, with an emphasis on knowledge creation, research and innovation a slightly different focus is advanced from within industry as explored in the section which follows.

4 Structure and Purpose of Academic Centres of Excellence

Within the academic arena CoEs are traditionally located within a university or led by a university-industry collaborative team of diverse organisations. Below we present select practice case studies of prominent HE CoEs for the purpose of illumination of best practice models. In that regard, in the more developed worlds, within the academic arena CoEs are traditionally located within a university or as university-led consortium comprising a number of universities and industry specialist firms as highlighted in the examples in section.

Funding for such collaborative work tends to be government policy directed and supported by strategic funding system and agenda channelled through well-managed and structured organisations. One such leading body based in the United Kingdom is 'The UK Research and Innovation (UKRI)' with a national mandate discussed below.

First, we present a synopsis of a typical funding structure of university-led CoEs in the United Kingdom, *The UK Research and Innovation (UKRI)*.

The UK Research and Innovation (UKRI)

UK Research and Innovation (UKRI) was established by the Higher Education and Research Act 2017 and was launched in April 2018. The purpose of UKRI is to create a strong, agile and joined up funder of research and innovation for the UK. UKRI brings together the seven Research Councils, Innovate UK and Research England (formally the Higher Education Funding Council for England (HEFCE)). UKRI and its constituent Councils published their first Delivery Plans in June 2019.

UKRI delivers the majority of public funding for research and innovation in the UK. It will play a central role in realising the UK Government's ambition of 2.4% of gross domestic product (GDP) investment in research and development (R&D) by 2027. This explainer summarises UKRI's structure, governance and operation to support discussion over how this funding is distributed.

The Government has committed to increase levels of R&D investment in the UK to at least 2.4% of GDP by 2027. Research and innovation in the UK must flourish to achieve this.

The United Kingdom Research Institute Funds Interdisciplinary Research Collaborations (IRCs) are centres of internationally acknowledged scientific and technological excellence, with sufficient critical mass to make a real impact in areas of key future industrial relevance to the UK. The collaborations are funded through large, long-term grants, typically around £10 million over six years. IRCs generally involve several universities together with industrial partners.

Source: UK Research and Innovation (n.d.), The Royal Academy of Engineering

Second, the Australian model of the *Australian Research Council ARC Centres of Excellence* presents a template for best practice within the HE sector.

Australian Research Council ARC Centres of Excellence

ARC Centres of Excellence have prestigious foci of expertise through which high-quality researchers maintain and develop Australia's international standing in research areas of national priority.

Through the ARC Centres of Excellence, significant collaborations occur between universities, publicly funded research organisations, other research bodies, governments and businesses in Australia and overseas, all to support outstanding research.

The objectives for the ARC Centres of Excellence are to:

- undertake highly innovative and potentially transformational research that aims to achieve international standing in the fields of research envisaged and leads to a significant advancement of capabilities and knowledge;
- link existing Australian research strengths and builds critical mass with new capacity for interdisciplinary, collaborative approaches to address the most challenging and significant research problems;
- develop relationships and build new networks with major national and international centres and research programmes to help strengthen research, achieve global competitiveness and gain recognition for Australian research;
- build Australia's human capacity in a range of research areas by attracting and retaining, from within Australia and abroad, researchers of high international standing as well as the most promising research students;
- provide high-quality postgraduate and postdoctoral training environments for the next generation of researchers;
- offer Australian researchers opportunities to work on large-scale problems over long periods of time;
- establish Centres that have an impact on the wider community through interaction with, and beneficial outcomes for, higher education institutions, governments, industry and the private and non-profit sectors.

Source: ARC Centres Excellence, Australian Government, Australian Research Council (2015)

Third, the *Networks of Centres of Excellence of Canada* presents a different perspective based on and developed around a network of organisational structure.

Networks of Centres of Excellence of Canada

Finding solutions to major social, economic or health issues calls for a collaborative approach and a wide range of research expertise. Since its creation in 1989, the Networks of Centres of Excellence (NCE) programme has successfully brought together the best minds in many disciplines and sectors to solve these critical issues for Canadians.

The programme supports large-scale academically led research networks that harness the creativity and inventiveness of Canadian health, natural and social scientists and engineers. Partners from industry, government and not-for-profit organisations contribute additional expertise and contribute nearly $90 million per year of cash and in-kind support. International acclaim has led other countries, including Australia, South Africa and some within the European Union, to incorporate the NCE model into their programmes.

NCEs focus on issues that are critical to Canadians, and to the world by:

- Mobilising multi-disciplinary research capacity from across Canada.
- Engaging partners from multiple academic institutions and various public and private sector organisations.
- Training the next generation of highly qualified people—more than 36,000 to date.
- Working with end users to accelerate the creation and application of new knowledge.
- Increasing collaboration between researchers in Canada and abroad Quick facts.
- The NCE was created in 1989 as a joint initiative of the Natural Sciences and Engineering Research Council, the Social Sciences and Humanities Research Council, the Canadian Institutes of Health Research, Industry Canada and Health Canada.
- In addition to the traditional NCE networks, the programme includes the NCE Knowledge Mobilization (NCE-KM) and the Canada-India Research Centre of Excellence (CIRCE) initiatives.
- In 2013–2014, network activities involved the participation of more than 1900 public and private sector organisations in Canada and abroad.

Source: Networks of Centres of Excellence of Canada (2019). Government of Canada, an initiative of CIHR, NSERC and SSHRC

The three examples offered above from well-developed research structures are among some of the best practice templates useful for further exploration as frameworks for advancing CoEs within the Creole space.

5 Defining the Creole Space

Creole countries share a common history of the social ills of the slave trade, an oppressive colonial past and post-colonial mixed heritage. Most of these countries are part of the lesser developed world and more often than not are SIDS with limited resources for nation building and by extension safeguarding intangible culture heritage. Table 9.2 provides a list of the main French Creole-speaking countries.

Table 9.2 Creole-speaking countries

Country	*Surface area (km²)*	*Population*	*Centre of administration*	*Languages spoken*
Commonwealth of Dominica	751	100,000	Roseau	English, Antillean Creole
French Guiana	91,000	157,277	Cayenne	French, French Guiana Creole, various Amerindian languages, Hmong, Chinese, Haitian Creole, various Businenge languages (English-based creoles)
Grenada	344	100,000	Saint-George	English, Antillean Creole (residual)
Guadeloupe	1709	422,496	Basse-Terre	French, Antillean Creole
Haiti	27,750	7,000,000	Port-au-Prince	Haitian Creole, French
Louisiana	235,675	4,000,000	Baton Rouge	English, Louisiana Creole (residual), Cajun
Martinique	1100	381,441	Fort-de France	French, Antillean Creole
Mauritius	2040	1,100,000	Part-Louis	English, French, Mauritian Creole, Bhojpuri, Hindi, Urdu, and some other Indian languages, Chinese
Réunion	2511	707,758	Saint-Denis	French, Réunion Creole
St. Lucia	616	150,000	Castries	English, Antillean Creole
St. Thomas	83	56,000	Charlotte Amalie	English, Antillean Creole (residual)
Seychelles	410	70,000	Victoria	English, French, Seychelles Creole
Trinidad	5128	1,300,000	Port-of-Spain	English, Antillean Creole (residual)

Source: Developed from Creoles.free.fr (n.d.)

Due to their small size, institutional structures are marred by challenges of scale. As such local national research organisations tend to be too small to have international impact as individual institutions; hence, capacity to achieve major developments is a significant dilemma.

Further, specialism and expertise tend to reside in and are embodied by elders who lack the means and know-how to formalise their knowledge into accessible formats for widespread use. Moreover, institutional focus and national priority are largely placed on performance and living traditions rather than on knowledge creation.

Accordingly, it is not surprising that desk research on well-established centres of knowledge development in the Creole space revealed a significant void of CoEs operating at the very high level of international collaborative expert institutions producing a steady body of state-of-the-art research. At the time of this publication there was no known or established institution meeting the criteria of CoEs as earlier defined in this chapter either from the industry, policy or academic perspective within the Creole Space.

Of note are three organised bodies presented below in individual countries with potential for further growth and institutional strengthening in that regard:

- Seychellois Creole Language and Culture Research Institute, Seychelles
- St Lucia Folk Research Centre, St Lucia
- Konmité pou Etid Kwéyòl (Committee for the Study of Creole), Commonwealth of Dominica

6 Current Creole Research Institutions and Organisations

As alluded in previous discussions, coordinating university-industry partnerships in less developed countries are not without its challenges due to less well-established structures. Following on Thürer et al. (2018), we may therefore contend that the capacity of SIDS to deliver operational and operational excellence in the area of ICH knowledge creation and innovative state-of-the-art research is constantly undermined by other pressing priorities. In that regard, on the one hand CoEs are largely non-existent, while on the other hand existing alternative institutions of relevance, such as St Lucia's Folk Centre and Dominica's KEK, have much less formalised and benchmarked structures. For the purpose of illumination of this dynamics in the context of SIDS and other lesser developed countries, three of the more organised research centres within the Creole space are highlighted as follows.

Seychelles: In the African region, the Seychelles are set in the Western Indian Ocean and comprise about 115 islands scattered across 1,400,000 sq. km. of ocean (The Seychelles Islands, 2021). The neighbouring countries are Kenya, around 1600 kilometres to the west, and Madagascar, approximately 1100 kilometres south. With a population of 96,762 (2018), occupying 452 square kilometres, the Seychelles include 40 inner rocky and mountainous islands and another group of outer low-lying and coralline islands. The islands are located between latitudes 4° and 11° S and longitudes 46° and 56° E; the capital, Victoria, is situated on Mahé (Commonwealth Secretariat, 2021). The languages spoken are English and French Patois Kwéyòl/Seychellois Creole.

Seychellois Creole Language and Culture Research Institute

As is the case in most countries, it is the university that should play an important role in the construction of the country's national identity, social and psychological stability. CLCRI's main objective was to create an academic forum for the advancement of the creole language, culture and the Creole society as a whole. This is to be done by collaborating with other organisations in our region and in other parts of the world.

Vision

To be the knowledge hub of Creole languages and cultures in the Indian Ocean.

Mission

The mission of the Creole Language and Culture Research Institute is to create an academic forum for the advancement of the Seychellois Creole language, culture and society within the context of and in collaboration with Indian Ocean and other Creole societies in the world through research and dissemination, the creation of databases, publications and engaging in and promoting academic activities such as debates, criticism and intellectual creativity.

(*continued*)

(continued)

Values

Adherence to professional and moral ethics in the performance of the institute's activities. Working as a team and in collaboration with others to achieve common goals.

Upholding the University's good reputation through adherence to high standards of performance. Bringing innovation to modes of practice in research, dissemination and use of socio-cultural data to stimulate new respect and enthusiasm in the youth particularly, intellectuals and others, for the Creole culture, language and society.

Structure

Currently the Institute falls under the Faculty of Arts and Social Development at the University of Seychelles. It has a Director, a Senior Research Officer and an advisory committee chaired by the Director and ten other members.

Funding

The Institute functions with research grants, donations and assistance from the University of Seychelles for some of its activities.

Source: Creole Language and Culture Research Institute (2021). University of Seychelles

Saint Lucia: The island is located in the Caribbean and is the second largest of the Windward group in the Lesser Antilles. The closest islands are Martinique in the north, and Saint Vincent in the south-west. The island is 616 square kilometres, is 27 miles (43 km) long and has a maximum width of 14 miles (23 km). The island has a population of 182,000 (2018) (Commonwealth Secretariat, 2021).

The island gained independence in 1979. Its capital is Castries and the languages spoken are English and French Patois Kwéyòl.

St Lucia Folk Research Centre

Folk Research Centre, also known as FRC, Plas Wíchès Foklò, was founded in 1973 and is devoted to local history and culture.

It is a repository for cultural heritage—a vehicle for research, study and recording, aimed to promulgate the rich heritage of the island, including the local music of Saint Lucia. It houses archives, heads research groups, hosts exhibitions and organises cultural events such as the Creole Film Festival and the Creole Music Festival.

Source: Commonwealth Walkway (2021). Folk Research Centre, St. Lucia, The Commonwealth Walkway Trust, England and Wales

The Commonwealth of Dominica is a small island of 750 square kilometres, part of the Caribbean archipelago and the Lesser Antilles within the eastern Caribbean Sea and situated at latitude 15° 20' N and longitude 61° 22' W (Government of Dominica, 2021). It is located between the French islands of Guadeloupe and Marie-Galante to the north and Martinique to the south. The population at the last census (2018) was 72,000. The country gained political independence in 1978 and has since been a member of the Commonwealth. The island is 29 miles (47 km) long and has a maximum breadth of 16 miles (26 km). The capital and chief port is Roseau. Dominica's great natural beauty, especially its spectacular mountainous topography, has impressed generations of nature lovers (Commonwealth Secretariat, 2021).

The main languages spoken are English and French Patois Kwéyòl.

Konmité pou Etid Kwéyòl

KEK, the abbreviated form for 'Konmité pou Etid Kwéyòl' (Committee for the Study of Creole), has among its objectives to foster a deeper awareness and respect for our Mother Tongue—Kwéyòl. KEK was established in 1981.

(*continued*)

(continued)

KEK's early activities included literacy classes and the celebration of Jounen Kwéyòl (Creole Day). The first Kwéyòl day was held in October 1981 and has been held ever since. Simenn Kwéyòl (Creole Week) has been held since 1986. This week starts on Jounen Eritaj (Heritage Day), that is, the Sunday preceding Jounen Kwéyòl which is celebrated on the last Friday in October.

KEK has published several books on various oral traditions such as proverbs and riddles (timtim) and a Kwéyòl-English dictionary.

Source: Division of Culture (2021). Government of the Commonwealth of Dominica, Kommite pou etid Kwéyòl (KEK)

These three countries and related organisations presented above are representative of the subtleties within the Creole space. They are typical of the basis of the underpinning background on which the key arguments for advancement of more elaborate and formalised collaborative specially tailored CoEs appropriate to the existing dynamics within the Creole space is advanced. More particularly they are integral to the work of The International Creole Research Network (TICERN), with the long-term goal of pursuing the agenda and framework for CoEs within the Creole space.

7 Setting: TICERN

The International Creole Research Network was established in partial fulfilment of the project outcome of an Arts and Humanities Research Council project funded via a Research Networking Grant REfAH/R004498/1. Over the life of the project several collaborative initiatives were held with a number of international partners from the Creole-speaking world.

Among events held include Creole Fest 2018 at the University of Bedfordshire as part of the National Social Science festival celebrations in the United Kingdom. The research seminar forming an integral part of the festival focused on the theme 'Building Bridges Across Borders: An ESRC & AHRC Social Science Festival'. In addition, an international three-day conference was held in the Commonwealth of Dominica in collaboration with the University of the West Indies, Dominica campus, with the theme 'Framing, Strengthening and Collaborating'. This current volume is an additional output of the collaboration.

As a result of the successful accomplishments of four-year project, there was a strong desire among participants from different Creole countries to continue working collaboratively to advance knowledge development, research and innovation within the Creole space at the level of higher education institutions. In that regard, TICERN was established early 2021. The network seeks to further its work in the area of joint pursuits under the umbrella of this international organisation (TICERN) to make stronger representation on issues and challenges faced as a collective within the Creole space.

One such representation was initiated in the summer of 2021 in the form of a UNESCO Policy consultation, in preparation of the UNESCO World Higher Education Conference (WHEC2021):

> Reinventing the Role & Place of Higher Learning for a Sustainable Future (14/07/2021). In addition to pursuit of the abovementioned agenda, the consultation led to much broader follow-on debate and working paper positions to drive its mandate and underpin terms of operations as explored below. These in part serve to guide some of the areas of work for adoption by TICERN.

8 Case Study: TICERN Analysis of the Creole Space

Resulting from much debate and focus group discussions, TICERN members arrived at a set of positions on the possible agenda for collaborative work to impact change within HE and through collaborative efforts with industry and policy stakeholders.

Discussion Point: How Can HE Initiatives Through CoEs Better Serve Creole and Indigenous Communities? What Are the Relevant Context Drivers of Safeguarding Intangible Cultural Heritage of Relevance for TICERN?

Higher education needs to be reformed to include the knowledge, skills and understanding to bring Creole and indigenous traditions into the modern world, thus leaving no one behind and progressing Kwéyòl knowledge, skills and understanding, as solutions to modern and future problems.

Historically in Creole and indigenous societies education was seen as continuous and inclusive. Proverbs were used to continuously embed the precepts of traditions and the 'truths' already learned by our elders, example,

> 'Zandoli sav ki pye bwa I ka monte'—Lizard knows the nature of the tree that it is climbing.

All adults were involved in guiding the young, irrespective of whether they were family members or not.

Specialists at particular activities for instance, war, teaching, boat building, medicines, singing and storytelling, incantations and spells were recognised and called upon by individuals and/or by the whole society.

Our concept of higher education was, therefore, both for collective benefit and communally shared. Historically, HE was also deemed as a place for specialist and elitist education for particular individuals and families.

Now, in the modern times, a number of specialisms, useful to the common good, have been eroded, such as herbal medicine and its use in the modern context. The psychotherapeutic role of medicinal specialists, example, the garde—'seer(s)' and barbers, similarly needs to be developed for the modern context.

The role and standing of teachers, particularly in Creole history, language and culture, using Information Technology and other digital culture, needs to be progressed. Singers and storytellers need to be informed of and develop skills in traditional Kwéyòl forms namely, kóntes—'song stories' as well as their social responsibilities of telling truth to power.

Discussion Point: What Are the Main Challenges, Gaps or Deficiencies Observed? What Limitations Exist and Could Be Addressed by TICERN?

There is a major void in teaching Kwéyòl in schools and at the level of Higher education.

There is the need to promote specialist Kwéyòl courses or modules, which promote the Creole knowledge, skills and understanding.

The promotion of IT and digital formats to facilitate documentation, storage and dissemination of key traditions needs to be addressed.

TICERN should support ongoing research by Creole and indigenous peoples themselves which underpin, validate and innovate the developments in education and the safeguarding of ICH.

Consequently, higher education should formulate Certificate programmes, Education Degree and PGCE's in and on Kwéyòl teaching in schools and in further, adult and higher education. In addition, courses in Creole education and teacher training courses should be offered. Further, specialist courses and modules in Creole knowledge, skills and understanding should be provided in higher education example, on literature, psychology, agriculture, medicine and all existing specialisms as they relate to Creole societies and cultures.

Through research and innovation existing Creole content should be digitalised in a range of formats such as Kwéyòl songs, kóntes, writing and conversations. Software programs, including apps should be developed which help disseminate this digitalised content.

Discussion Point: How Might TICERN Influence Positive Productive Change? What Operational and Service Excellence Role May TICERN Seek to Deliver?

Major changes in social and political attitudes need to occur among power bearing stakeholders who gained from and are still benefiting from the exploitation of Creole and indigenous peoples. To facilitate such changes in attitudes, more awareness and publicity must be given to Creole origins and history. Debates and questions around the financial benefits to colonial powers through the decimation of Taino, Kalinago and other first (Indigenous) peoples, the enslavement of Africans and the use of Asian indentured labour are quite pertinent. More awareness and publicity need to be given to modern day exploitation, for example, the further loss of Taino lands within existing Caricom states and the role of current Caribbean elites in contracts resulting in the transfer of Creole land ownership due to dependency on foreign investment and hoteliers.

While some of original practices and traditional knowledge particularly in term of indigenous and Kwéyòl language is available through the teaching of history, a new education strategy is needed in order to change attitudes so that Creole and indigenous societies can be properly understood.

Without such education and a public awareness strategy, many Kwéyòl speakers continue to see themselves, their languages and cultures as inherently inferior and remain reluctant to participate in personal upliftment. They believe, either consciously or unconsciously, that the only path is assimilation into the societies and cultures of the colonies or other powerful more developed countries.

Publicity and promotion of successes in Creole development and advances over the decades are vital to propel its advancement. For example, the use of Kwéyòl as part of Dominican national marketing, within the tourist industry of creole countries, and bible translations in both English and French Kwéyòl languages, as well as the transfer of Creole medicines to modern medicinal forms in Cuba, introduction of pilot Kwéyòl programmes in schools, speaking Kwéyòl in the House of parliament in Mauritius, cultural folk centres in St Lucia and Dominica and the research centre at the University of Seychelles, advancing of Kwéyòl texts and dictionary in Dominica, among others.

Benefits of Establishing CoEs Within the Creole Space

Based on the evidence of the research findings on the work of individual Creole-speaking countries, their institutions, processes, challenges and structural limitations around the Creole culture, language and traditions we proffer the establishment of Creole Cultural Centres of Excellence a possible solution for the efficient fulfilment of the safeguarding of Intangible Creole Heritage.

As such, we argue that a Creole Cultural CoE under the auspices of TICERN would address the following:

- barriers to entry for research collaboration with individual countries;
- reducing negative impact of gatekeepers;
- enhance community participation;
- facilitate wider key stakeholder engagement;
- knowledge/concept sharing;
- stronger commitment to initiatives;
- provision of expert technical capability;
- greater incentive for local participation;
- increased motivation and ownership of relevant stakeholders within consortium.

In that regard we advance the following framework for enabling advance research, innovation and development via an HE led and funded collaborative Creole Cultural Centres of Excellence (CCCoE).

9 Framework for Creole Cultural Centres of Excellence (CCCoE)

Following the work of Fekadu et al. (2021), the following framework advances four key processes that underpin the structure, organisation and delivery of systematic processes for establishment and the operations of a Creole Cultural Centres of Excellence (CCCoE) (Fig. 9.2).

The conceptual operational structure of excellence processes delivered by TICERN is proffered within the following four domains:

Research Leadership: A fundamental element of the 'culture of excellence' within the CCCoE is the ability to produce state-of-the-art research

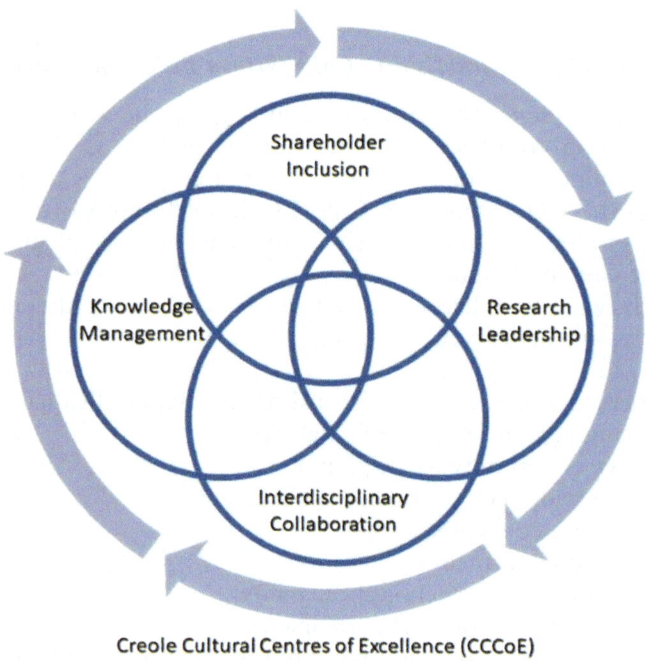

Fig. 9.2 The four interactive processes of Creole Cultural Centres of Excellence

utilising innovative technologies and systems to advance the work of the network collaboratively.

Stakeholder Inclusion: An effective CCCoE requires stakeholder inclusion from the conceptualisation of project ideas, decision making around priority areas for research, project agendas and structural arrangements for implementation processes and localised involvement and participation at the ground level, taking care to include practitioners as well as policy makers within the relevant arenas locally, nationally, regionally and internationally. Following on Fekadu et al. (2021) for efficacy, creating the internal energy and harmony that drives the organisation forward is key.

Interdisciplinary Collaboration: Of critical importance is interdisciplinary collaboration from a diverse cross section of fields and skill sets ensuring that specialised capabilities are fundamental characteristic of team building within the CCCoE network. As with the Fekadu et al. (2021) interactive processes of excellence both intra-organisational and extra-organisational interdisciplinary collaboration is pivotal to success.

Knowledge Management: The quality of scientific output is a key pillar within the CCCoE research excellence framework. As with most CoEs models the flow of knowledge both within and without the collaborative network in eliciting and dissemination information, knowledge in a bidirectional systematic approach with all relevant stakeholders is crucial.

10 Conclusion

Creole-speaking countries over the years have been marred by a dark history which have left them challenged in a number of developmental areas. Regardless, they have been equally oddly blessed with a diverse and rich mixed cultural heritage enabling them to reshape their nationhood through independence from colonial powers. In so doing, embracing the Creole cultural heritage has had significant benefits in the area of cultural tourism, citizenship and pride of country. As alluded by Pietrobruno (2009), intangible heritage deem worthy of safeguarding is regarded as traditional culture that reflects the identity of a particular nation or group. It is this element of a history, birthed in the dark days of slavery, which has led to the phenomenal intangible Creole cultural heritage which has been the focus of this chapter.

Pietrobruno (2009) highlights the importance of cultural research in providing a comprehensive understanding of intangible culture in both its lived and digital contexts, knowledge that challenges the process of categorisation proposed by the Convention for Safeguarding of the Intangible Cultural Heritage (2003) by the United Nations Educational Scientific and Cultural Organisation (UNESCO).

The chapter has explored ways in which the concept of CoEs can be exploited to move the development of this rich cultural heritage forward, while safeguarding its key traditions for future generations, embracing its continuous evolving forms and advancing knowledge development and systems of practises within a formalised, collaborative international research network structure, which is university lead and funded under the auspices of CCCoE as proposed by TICERN.

This conceptual framework is an offshoot of the Arts and Humanities Research Council project funded via a Research Networking Grant REfAH/R004498/1, previously outlined and forms basis of the agenda of the newly establish TICERN. It is therefore recommended that further work be done in the area of in-depth research analysis and future collaborations among the next works partners and founding members to refine this concept proffered in this chapter.

References

ARC Centres Excellence. (2015). Australian Government, Australian Research Council. https://www.arc.gov.au/grants/linkage-program/arc-centres-excellence

Birkinshaw, J., & Hood, N. (1998). Multinational Subsidiary Development: Capability Evolution and Charter Change in Foreign-owned Subsidiary Companies. *Academy of Management Review, 23*(4), 773–795.

Björkman, I. (2001). JIBS Book Review, Holm, U.,& Pedersen, T. (1999). The Emergence and Impact of MNC Centres of Excellence: A Subsidiary Perspective. Macmillan Press, London, March.

Commonwealth Walkway. (2021). Folk Research Centre, St. Lucia, The Commonwealth Walkway Trust, England & Wales. https://www.commonwealthwalkway.com/place/folk-research-centre/

Creole Language and Culture Research Institute. (2021). University of Seychelles. https://unisey.ac.sc/clcri/

Creoles.free.fr. (n.d.). Creole Speking Countries and Their Populations. http://creoles.free.fr/Cours/anglais/Creole.pdf

Dahlgaard, J. J., Chen, C.-K., Jang, J.-Y., Banegas, I. A., Yuan, Z. E., & Dahlgaard-Park, S. M. (2013). Business Excellence Models: Limitations, Reflections and Further Development. *Total Quality Management & Business Excellence, 24*(5–6), 519–538.

Dahlgaard-Park, S. M. (2011). The Quality Movement: Where Are You Going? *Total Quality Management & Business Excellence, 22*(5), 493–516.

Division of Culture. (2021). Government of the Commonwealth of Dominica, Kommite pou etid Kwéyòl (KEK). http://www.divisionofculture.gov.dm/cultural-institutions-and-groups/11-kommite-pou-etid-Kwéyòl-kek-and-the-folk-research-centre

Dominica. (2021). Commonwealth Secretariat 2021. https://thecommonwealth.org/our-member-countries/dominica

Ensign, P. C., Birkinshaw, J. M., & Frost, T. S. (2000). R&D Centres of Excellence in Canada. In U. Holm & T. Pedersen (Eds.), *The Emergence and Impact of MNC Centres of Excellence: A Subsidiary Perspective* (pp. 131–153). Macmillan Press.

Fekadu, A., Oppenheim, C., Manyazewal, T., Nislow, C., Woldeamanuel, Y., Hailu, A., Belete, A., Wondimagegn, D., Hanlon, C., Gebremariam, T., Collins, A., Larson, C. J., Gebreyes, W., Aklilu, E., Muula, A. S., Mugus, S., Caffrey, C. R., Giday, M., Yimer, G., Davey, G., Medhin, G., & Makonnen, E. (2021). Understanding the Key Processes of Excellence as a Prerequisite to Establishing Academic Centres of Excellence in Africa. *BMC Medical Education, 21*, 36.

Forsgren, M., Johanson, J., & Sharma, D. D. (2000). Development of MNC Centres of Excellence. In T. Pedersen & U. Holm (Eds.), *The Emergence and Impact of MNC Centres of Excellence: A Subsidiary Perspective* (pp. 45–67). Palgrave Macmillan.

Frost, T. S., Birkinshaw, J. M., & Prescott, C. E. (2002). Centers of Excellence in Multinational Corporations. *Strategic Management Journal, 23*, 997–1018. Wiley InterScience. www.interscience.wiley.com. https://doi.org/10.1002/smj.273

Government of Dominica. (2021). Country Profile, Dominica. https://dominica.gov.dm/about-dominica/country-profile

Hellström, T. (2011). Homing in on Excellence: Dimensions of Appraisal in Center of Excellence Program Evaluations. *Evaluation, 17*(2), 117–131. https://doi.org/10.1177/1356389011400891

Hermel, P., & Ramis-Pujol, J. (2003). An Evolution of Excellence: Some Main Trends. *The TQM Magazine, 15*(4), 230–243.

Kinyondo, A., & Huggins, C. (2020). Centres of Excellence for Artisanal and Small-scale Gold Mining in Tanzania: Functions are Wrong at Timer Entrepreneurship and Formalisation. *The Executive Industries and Society, 7*, 758–766.

Leventis, G., Kyriakidis, P., Agapiou, A., & Lysandrou, V. (2018). Designing a Science and Technology Centre of Excellence for Archaeology and Cultural Heritage in the Eastern Mediterranean, June 2018, Conference: 3rd CAA-GR Conference "Spreading Excellence in Computer Applications for Archaeology and Cultural Heritage".

Moore, K., & Birkinshaw, J. (1998). Managing Knowledge in Global Service Firms: Centres of Excellence. *Academy of Management Executive, 12*(4), 81–92.

Networks of Centres of Excellence of Canada. (2019). Government of Canada, An initiative of CIHR, NSERC and SSHRC. https://www.nce-rce.gc.ca/Programs-Programmes/NCE-RCE/Index_eng.asp

Oakland, J. S., & Tanner, S. J. (2008). The relationship between Business Excellence and Performance—An empirical study using Kanji's Leadership Excellence Model. *Total Quality Management & Business Excellence, 19*(7–8), 733–749.

OECD. (2014). *Promoting Research Excellence: A New Approach to Funding.* OECED Publishing.

Pietrobruno, S. (2009). Cultural Research and Intangible Heritage. *Journal of Current Culture Research, Culture Unbound, 1*, 227–247.

Prescott, C. E. (2002). Centers of Excellence in Multinational Corporations. *Strategic Management Journal, 23*, 997–1018.

Reger, G. (2004). Coordinating Globally Dispersed Research Centres of Excellence—The Case of Philips Electronics. *Journal of International Management, 10*(1), 51–76.

Terbullino, C., & Gabriel, P. (2021). Barriers to University-Industry Linkages and International Partnerships: The Cases of Centres of Excellence in Chile and Peru, Thesis (Ph.D.), University of Sussex, ISNI: 0000-0005-0292-6728

The Seychelles Islands. (2021). https://www.seychelles.com/app-planyourvisit-categories?selectedcat=DESTINFO&cla=ISLANDS&bannerCat=islands

Thürer, M., Tomašević, I., Stevenson, M., Fredendall, L. D., & Protzman, C. W. (2018). On the Meaning and Use of Excellence in the Operations Literature: A Systematic Review. *Total Quality Management & Business Excellence, 2*, 1–28. https://doi.org/10.1080/14783363.2018.1434770

UK Research and Innovation. (n.d.). The Royal Academy of Engineering. https://raeng.org.uk/media/npifmlaz/ukri.pdf

Voon, B. H. (2011). Measuring Culture and Service Excellence: The Development Validation Journey. In *The 2nd International Research Symposium in Service Management, Yogyakarta, Indonesia, July 26–30.*

CHAPTER 10

Conclusions: Looking Ahead to the *After Acts*

Violet Cuffy and Jane Carr

The development of this volume ran alongside events that were unimaginable when the project was first envisaged to explore the concept of safeguarding Intangible Creole Cultural Heritage. A number of problematic challenges were encountered that severely delayed the commencement of the initial phase and more seriously threatened the viability of the project. First, hurricane Maria brought severe devastation to the north-eastern Caribbean, in particular to the island of the Commonwealth of Dominica, a major partner and the contextual setting of the 2018–2021 Arts and Humanities Research Council funded grant: RefAH/R004498/1 Creole collaborative project. Regardless, the resilient Creole spirit prevailed and work progressed despite several challenges.

V. Cuffy (Deceased)
University of Bedfordshire, Luton, UK

J. Carr (✉)
University of Bedfordshire, Luton, UK

Bird College, Sidcup, UK
e-mail: Jane.Carr@beds.ac.uk

V. Cuffy, J. Carr (eds.), *Creole Cultures, Vol. 1*,
https://doi.org/10.1007/978-3-031-24275-5_10

The two main events of relevance were academic conferences which sought to bring together a diverse range of stakeholders including researchers, policymakers and practitioners from the Creole space involved in work on or concerned with issues around with safeguarding a common Intangible Cultural Heritage. The first event was hosted at the University of Bedfordshire on the theme 'Building Bridges Across Borders: An ESRC & AHRC Social Science Festival' (9–10 November 2018). While the second, under the theme 'Creole as Cultural Heritage: Framing, Strengthening & Advocating' at the University of West Indies campus in Dominica (15–16 August 2019). These two events brought together persons concerned with advancing the debate, research and the livelihood of Creole communities around the globe. It is the work of these two forums as well as the input of other contributors that formed the basis of this volume.

Notwithstanding such achievements, the recent global pandemic inevitably added complexities to peoples, their cultures and lifestyle everywhere. Further, global shifts of climate change, widespread migration, economic downturn and political unrest continue to test the survival of indigenous populations worldwide. These challenges, particularly climate change, previously purely framed as an environmental issue from the very beginning of United Nations Framework Convention on Climate Change (UNFCCC) negotiations, are now more conceived as a matter of a fundamental issue of human rights and global justice (Gach, 2019; Mottley, 2021). According to Mottley, the current trajectory 'is immoral and it is unjust' (Mottley, 2021).

Such circumstances have served to emphasise both what is lost when people cannot come together to participate in cultural activities and the vulnerabilities of elements of rich heritage and the wider society through which culture is shared. How to safeguard intangible cultural heritage, so that the lifeworld of a particular community continues in spite of the disruption nature brings, has become an increasingly urgent question. In contrast to those cultures built around an imagined fixed national identity, Creole cultures, being born out of change, may perhaps be better able to respond organically to shifts in the world in which they are situated. Here the recognition of African-based academics Aristedes Narh Hargoe, Terry Ofosu and Nii Tete Yartey (in Chap. 6) of the resilience of diasporic intangible cultural heritage in connecting Creole populations with their ancestral roots provides some optimism.

As an example, the artist Carole Sorhaindo (in Chap. 7) acknowledges the entangled nature of Creole culture that informs her creative practice. In contrast to many western-orientated traditions, Creole cultural practices provide for improvisation and responsiveness to a changing context. This is evident in the Bélé practitioner Delia Cuffy-Weeks' account (Chap. 6) of how the songs comment on current affairs and how dancers may incorporate new moves but within a shared framework governed by the interaction between dancer and drummer. UNESCO's emphasis on safeguarding rather than attempting to preserve (UNESCO, 2003) intangible cultural heritage is significant in that it allows for practices to retain their vitality and relevance. Changes may be hotly contested but, as we have argued, the debates engendered can themselves be understood as part of a living tradition.

As argued by Mottley (2021) the pandemic has also reminded us of the inequalities that affect everyday lives. The chapters in this book are a testament to those injustices that have been the background to the formation of Creole cultures. As Rhyesa Joseph reminds us in Chap. 5, those peoples who celebrate their hard-won independence from former colonial powers continue to work to resist the remaining vestiges of imperial power. They are now increasingly faced with the challenges of a globalised economy. Here Joseph refers us to traditional practices such as 'koudmen' practised in Saint Lucia which may counteract global capitalism's reach by offering the 'economy of reciprocity' rather one based on profit at all costs. Referring to the work of the group Creoles cultures/Kiltir Kreol/Cultures creoles, Alexis Weedon in Chap. 2 points to how their sense of Kreolitude resists branding to offer an alternative set of values on which to build a global cultural network.

Careful management of tourism and economic growth is needed if Creole cultural activities are to resist becoming superficial representations of tradition that feed the demand for globalised variants of 'local colour' for the tourist industry. National government support for festivals, such as Dominica's National Day, and Independence celebrations that acknowledge the importance of sustaining local cultural heritage are vital if cultural practices are to retain significance to the daily lives of the inhabitants of Small Island States. Yet, as Didier Michel and Daniella Police-Michel (Chap. 4) and Chrisentia Combie (in Chap. 8) and Violet Cuffy (in Chap. 9) reveal, there is a need for education that values Creole heritage.

Otherwise, those representing their Creole culture to tourists may not always themselves be aware of the histories and values that inform their practices.

Nevertheless, the rich Creole cultures explored in these pages suggest how strong Creole communities have been created out of adversity. The resourcefulness, flexibility and ingenuity that are the hall marks of Creole cultures are features that will be much needed as all communities face a future of changes on a global scale—whether in relation to climate, health, economic conditions or (more likely) the interrelated impact of them all. It is a sign of hope that young people are finding new ways to draw on their Creole heritage to engage with a global contemporary cultural scene on their own terms. For example, as Penda Choppy observes (in Chap. 3), rap artists in the Seychelles draw on traditional proverbs and Cuffy discusses evolution of the national wear in the introduction.

To encourage the safeguarding of intangible, Creole cultural heritage is vitally important, although, as we argued in the introduction, we would prefer to refer to embodied Creole heritage. Following the ethical principles outlined by UNESCO should help ensure that communities play a key role in decisions as to what aspects of culture are safeguarded and the means through which this takes place. However, the formal processes through which this is implemented may not always mesh with the formal requirements of UNESCO inscription. Alexis Weedon (in Chap. 2) acknowledges how the demands for evidence require organisational capacities that may not always be attainable.

UNESCO's focus on ICH has certainly raised awareness of the value of cultural practices and the need to establish the means to support them. While a Creole perspective adds recognition of the interconnections between the material and immaterial, the tangible objects and the practices in which they are used, and in relation not only to people who act but the spirit that acts upon them. Elsewhere such relationships are often the subject of debate, even conflict between different cultural agencies. Moreover, Weedon emphasises how a Creole cultural platform that transcends national boundaries would counteract any lingering colonialist structures embedded in the UNESCO strategy.

In this regard, as discussed by Cuffy in Chap. 9, we look ahead towards creating ways through which Creole communities will continue to share processes and systems of ensuring that their songs, stories, dances, music, food, costume and decoration foster new generations of Creoles who take pride in their identities. Following the tragic loss of Cuffy herself just as this volume was being produced, these are the 'after acts' that will be the most important legacy of this project. They are inextricably linked to the promotion of Creole languages that will be the subject of the following volume.

References

Gach, E. (2019). Normative Shifts in the Global Conception of Climate Change: The Growth of Climate Justice. *Social Sciences, 8*, 24. https://doi.org/10.3390/socsci8010024

Mottley, M. (2021). Prime Minister of Barbados at the Opening of the #COP26 World Leaders Summit. https://www.youtube.com/watch?v=PN6THYZ4ngM

UNESCO. (2003). Text of the Convention for the Safeguarding of the Intangible Cultural Heritage. Retrieved January 4, 2017, from https://ich.unesco.org/en/convention

Index

A
Africa, 139
Africans, 105, 107, 116, 118, 124, 126–129, 131–134, 136, 137
Agricultural, 128, 129, 135
Agriculture, 125, 128
Amerindian, 125, 126, 131
Annatto, 126
Archive culture, 3
Archives, 2, 3, 5, 16
Arrowroot, 126
Art, 42, 43, 46, 54, 136–139
Artist, 134
Artistic, 134
Asia, 127
Asian, 135

B
The Baldrige performance, 172
Banana, 127, 135
Behavioural psychiatrists, 131
Bélé, 106–111, 113–118, 134
Belfast estate, 130
Biotic, 134, 139
Boiler houses, 132
Bois Cotlette, 132
Botanical, 126
  dyes, 136
  heritage, 123, 124, 132, 139
  migrants, 127
Botanical Gardens, 128, 129, 135
Botanic station, 127–129, 135
Botanists, 128
Botany, 128, 129
Breadfruit, 127, 128, 132–134, 139
Bricolage, 137, 139
British government, 132
Broderie anglaise, 132
Bush medicine, 127, 135

C
Capitalism, 129
Captain Bligh, 132
Carolus Linnaeus, 124

V. Cuffy, J. Carr (eds.), *Creole Cultures, Vol. 1*,
https://doi.org/10.1007/978-3-031-24275-5

Cassava, 126
Castor oil, 135
Castor plants, 135
Centres of Excellence (CoEs), 169
Choreological analysis, 105, 118
Cloth, 131, 132, 137
Cocoa, 127, 129, 135
Coconut, 127, 130, 133, 135
Coffee, 127, 129, 135
Colonial, 124, 128, 135, 136
Colonialism, 124, 129
Colonization, 131
Columbus, 131
Community, 137, 139
Cooperativism, 91, 94
Cotton, 126, 130–132, 134, 137
Creative industries, 136
Creole, 24, 28, 30, 33–35, 62–74, 76, 77, 117, 118, 123, 130, 132, 133, 179, 183–187, 189
  continuum, 151
  cultural space, 2
  culture, 41, 42, 48, 129, 134–137, 139
  heritage, 105, 108, 111, 129, 137
  space, 2, 145–164, 169, 170, 178–180, 183–188
Creole Centre of Excellence Framework, 170
Creole Cultural Centres of Excellence (CCCoE), 187–190
Creole Garden, 124
Creolization, 124, 129
Cultural, 134, 135
  bound syndrome, 131
  heritage, 130, 136
  heritage spaces, 2
  identity, 125, 132
  memory, 137
  tourism, 147–150, 152, 154, 157–164
  wear, 137
Cutlass, 130

D
Dance, 134
Decolonisation, 99, 100
Diaspora, 135
Dòkpwê, 94, 95
Dominic, 107, 108
Dominica, 105–108, 111–114, 118, 126
Drums, 134
Dyes, 137, 138

E
Economic botany, 125
Economic Imperialism, 127
Ellis, John, 128
Embodied, 104, 117, 118
Embodied practices, 2, 3
Embodiment, 134, 137
Empire Windrush, 134
Entanglement, 124, 125, 129, 136, 137
Ethnobotanical, 127, 131, 136
Europeans, 105, 106, 118, 125–127, 129, 131, 133
Excellence, 169

F
Fibres, 131, 136, 137
Flamboyant, 135
Folklore, 41, 42, 44, 48, 49, 53
Fright, 131

G
Globalization, 49, 57
Governance, 98–100
Guava, 135

H
Haitian, 128
Hammocks, 131, 132

Healing, 126, 130
Herbal, 130, 135
  cures, 126
  remedies, 127
Heritage, 126
  tourism, 147, 148
Histoire Croisee, 123
Holistic, 134, 136
Hurricane, 129, 130, 135
Hybrid, 128

I
Identity, 8
Imray, John, 128
Indian botanic stations, 132
Indians, 134
Indigenous, 88, 98–100, 123–126, 129–131, 136, 139
Intangible, 132, 137, 139
  heritage, 131
Intangible Cultural Heritage (ICH), 1, 3, 5, 19, 21, 22, 26, 29, 30, 61, 68, 104, 147, 158, 169
Interactive processes, 173
International Creole Research Network (TICERN), 170

K
Kalinago, 125, 126, 129–131, 136, 137
Kew, 128
Konte, 11
Koudmen, 83–85, 87–100
Kwéyòl, 88, 182, 183, 185–187

L
Lamps, 132
Landscape, 125, 127, 129, 130, 134–136
Limes, 127, 128, 135

M
Madras, 132, 137
Mango, 129, 135
Mangosteen, 128, 135
Manioc, 126
Maroons, 126, 136
Middle Passage, 134
Migration, 125, 126, 134
Mills, 130, 136
Molasses, 129, 130
Maroon, 106, 109

N
Nicholls, Sir Henry Alfred Alford, 128
Nutmeg, 127

O
Omnivorous tourists, 149
Oral traditions, 131, 132
Orature, 41–45, 48, 50, 51, 56, 57

P
Phytotherapy, 127
Pigeon pea, 127
Plantations, 126–128, 132, 133
Postcolonial, 27, 30, 31, 35, 57, 62, 69, 71, 124
Postcolonialism, 23
Post-traumatic syndrome, 131
Provision grounds, 127

R
Racism, 124
Rejuve, 50, 53, 55, 56
Republic of China, 128
Republic of Mauritius, 65
Resistance, 133
Resistance to the colonial system, 126
Resources, 5

Rooted, 135
Rootedness, 126, 136
Roots, 124–129, 134, 138, 139
Rubber, 127
Ruins, 130
Rum, 129, 130
  punch, 133

S
Safeguarding, 1–5, 8, 19, 24, 25, 28, 104
St Aroment Estate, 128
Saint Lucia, 83, 85, 96, 152, 154, 160
Salt fish, 133
Sancoche, 133
Scientific racism, 123
Sea Island cotton, 131
Sega, 68, 69, 71, 77
Self-identification, 156
Self-help, 83, 87
Seychelles, 42, 44–50, 52–54, 56
Small Islands Developing States (SIDS), 172
Spices, 133
Spindle, 132
Spinning, 131, 132, 137
Storytelling, 11
Sugar, 128–130, 132
Sugarcane, 127, 129, 130, 134, 135
System, 123

T
Taches, 130
Taiwanese, 128
Tangible, 137, 139
Taxonomic, 123
Terrapsychology, 134, 136
Textiles, 131, 137
The International Creole Research Network (TICERN), 183, 190
Tobacco, 125, 126
Tourism, 128
Tourist, 130
Transatlantic slave trade, 125
Transatlantic trade, 124, 134, 139
Transplantation, 125, 126, 132
Trauma, 131
Traumatic, 133
Trees, 135

U
United Kingdom (UK), 134, 135
United Nations Educational, Scientific and Cultural Organization (UNESCO), 19–22, 24–30, 32, 34, 35
Univorous tourists, 149

V
Value, 2, 8

W
Wah wah, 126
Waitukubuli, 125
Wardian cases, 125
Wash outs, 135
Weaving, 131, 132, 137, 138
West, 132, 134
West African, 126, 133
West Indian, 131, 135
West India Royal Commission, 128
West Indies, 128, 132, 134, 139
Whorls, 132
Wicks, 131, 132
Wob dwiyet, 11, 132

Y
Yam, 126, 127, 135

SPRINGER NATURE

GPSR Compliance

The European Union's (EU) General Product Safety Regulation (GPSR) is a set of rules that requires consumer products to be safe and our obligations to ensure this.

If you have any concerns about our products, you can contact us on ProductSafety@springernature.com

In case Publisher is established outside the EU, the EU authorized representative is:

Springer Nature Customer Service Center GmbH
Europaplatz 3
69115 Heidelberg, Germany

The manufacturer's authorised representative in the EU is Springer Nature Customer Service Centre GmbH, Europaplatz 3, 69115 Heidelberg, Germany. If you have any concerns regarding our products, please contact ProductSafety@springernature.com

Printed and bound by CPI Group (UK) Ltd, Croydon, CR0 4YY
28/09/2026
02224074-0004